P9-APW-833

RESEARCH IN LAW AND ECONOMICS

Supplement 1 • 1980

THE ECONOMICS OF NONPROPRIETARY ORGANIZATIONS

LIBERTY FUND, INC. SEMINAR ON THE ECONOMICS OF NONPROPRIETARY ORGANIZATIONS
April 28 to May 1, 1977

List of Participants and Affiliations at the Time of the Conference

Armen A. Alchian
University of California, Los Angeles

Thomas E. Borcherding
Simon Fraser University

James M. Buchanan
Center for Study of Public Choice
Virginia Polytechnic Institute
and State University

Steven N. Cheung
University of Washington

Kenneth W. Clarkson
Law and Economics Center
University of Miami

David G. Davies
Duke University

Louis De Alessi
Law and Economics Center
University of Miami

Evsey D. Domar
Massachusetts Institute of Technology

Ross D. Eckert
University of Southern California

H. E. Frech, III
Harvard University

Erik G. Furubotn
Texas A & M University

C. M. Lindsay
University of California, Los Angeles

Henry G. Manne
Law and Economics Center
University of Miami

Donald L. Martin
Law and Economics Center
University of Miami

Roland N. McKean
University of Virginia

John McManus
University of Toronto

William Meckling
Graduate School of Management
University of Rochester

John H. Moore
University of Virginia

Alfred Nicols
Graduate School of Business
University of California, Los Angeles

Donald J. O'Hara
University of Rochester

Walter Y. Oi
University of Rochester

John J. Osborn
School of Law
Yale University

Mark V. Pauly
Northwestern University

Stephen Pejovich
University of Dallas

Earl A. Thompson
University of California, Los Angeles

Burton A. Weisbrod
Yale University

Andrew B. Whinston
Purdue University

Richard O. Zerbe, Jr.
Graduate School of Business
University of Washington

RESEARCH IN LAW AND ECONOMICS

A Research Annual

THE ECONOMICS OF NONPROPRIETARY ORGANIZATIONS

Editors: KENNETH W. CLARKSON
Law and Economics Center
University of Miami

DONALD L. MARTIN
Law and Economics Center
University of Miami

SUPPLEMENT 1 • 1980

 JAI PRESS INC.
Greenwich, Connecticut

ISBN NUMBER: 0-89232-132-6
Manufactured in the United States of America

CONTENTS

CHARITABLE ORGANIZATIONS

GOVERNMENTAL ORGANIZATIONS

PREFACE

It is a pleasure to offer this supplemental volume of *Research in Law and Economics*, devoted to the economics of nonproprietary organizations. The distinguished economists whose articles and comments are contained here present a lively, valuable, and far-reaching discussion of a general topic whose importance increases daily. The importance of the matters discussed here is now apparent. But this has not always been the case. In this regard it is well to note our debt to Armen Alchian whose basic approach to economics is felt in one way or another throughout this volume. I would like to express appreciation to Kenneth Clarkson and Donald Martin for their organization of the conference, and their help in editing this volume. Joan Manzer and I have spent long hours in editing the manuscripts and I would like to acknowledge her help.

Richard O. Zerbe, Jr.
Series Editor

INTRODUCTION

Kenneth W. Clarkson, UNIVERSITY OF MIAMI

Donald L. Martin, UNIVERSITY OF MIAMI

A nonproprietary organization is defined as an institution whose owners and employees do not hold private property rights in residual income generated from its operation nor in the capital value that is reflected in the transfer price of its assets. The nonproprietary form of
organizing economic activity has been a steadily increasing part of the
American economy.[1] In the early years of this century, about 5 percent
of all employed persons were hired by government units. About 16
percent were so employed by 1970. As a fraction of GNP, total government expenditures have risen fourfold from about 8 percent in 1900 to
approximately 32 percent by 1970. The role of nonproprietary organizations has also expanded in the private sector. For example, the Internal
Revenue Service reports that private tax-exempt organizations increased
from 200,000 in 1965 to well over 650,000 by 1972.[2]

Economics of Nonproprietary Organizations
Research in Law and Economics, Supplement 1, pages ix-xiii
Copyright © 1980 by JAI Press Inc.
All rights of reproduction in any form reserved.
ISBN: 0-89232-132-6

As the nonproprietary sector of the economy has become more important, ignorance of the forces that govern behavior within these institutions has become even more evident. Unfortunately, no generally validated theory of the nonproprietary firm exists. Analysts have nonetheless made some progress in explaining and predicting behavior in such organizations by applying some relatively simple principles of economics.

Neoclassical microeconomic theory implicitly assumes private property or proprietary ownership. This auxiliary assumption permits wealth maximization as the firm's objective function in conventional economic theory. Entrepreneurs with proprietary interests in the firm find it more costly to ignore wealth-increasing opportunities available to the firm than if proprietary rights were absent. Once the proprietary assumption is relaxed, wealth maximization as an organizational objective or viability criterion is weakened. This proposition is currently the major principle used in analysis of nonproprietary institutions.

Why is the nonproprietary form of organization chosen in a wide variety of instances? What is (or are?) the objective or viability functions of organizations without private property? Can such organizations be expected to exhibit behavior that is similar to or different from the neoclassical firm? Complete answers to these questions still escape those who have sought them. The contributions in this volume, we believe, represent an important step toward expanding our knowledge in this area.

A common thread that runs through many of the papers, either implicitly or explicitly, is the standard analytic procedure which assumes that decision-makers in both proprietary and nonproprietary institutions can be characterized as maximizers under constrained choice. Some of the papers suggest, and to some extent formalize, a link between the form of ownership and the constraint, which implies different maximizing behavior. See, for example, the papers by Clarkson, Frech, Martin, McKean, and Thompson.

The papers of Martin and Thompson focus on the choice of organizational form. This proved to be an important issue in the ensuing general discussion at the conference. Although never satisfactorily resolved, the discussion nevertheless shed light on the determinants of that choice. Except for Weisbrod, the contributors discussed differences in incentives facing owners and managers of proprietary and nonproprietary organizations. Weisbrod and Cheung, on the other hand, focused on problems in identifying and testing implications about nonproprietary organizations.

The comments on the papers and the general discussion were exceptionally frank. Criticism focused on ambiguities in the formulation of what each participant realized was a complex problem. Perhaps the two most significant points aired in the general discussion were the impact of private rights on capital values and the motivation for using the nonproprietary organization. Although no author could escape unscathed, all the contributions helped to further knowledge of the nonproprietary sector by extending received economic theory.

Obviously the nonproprietary rubric covers a wide variety of economic activity. Since the purpose of the conference was to aid work toward a generalized model of the nonproprietary firm, it did not seem appropriate to solicit research that would represent the hundreds of different types of economic activities that are organized in this sector. However, since several of the contributors analyzed specific activities within the nonproprietary sector, a large variety of economic activities is represented in the papers. The papers in this volume are arranged by four major topics: managerial constraints, mutual organizations, charitable organizations, and governmental organizations.

The first section consists of the papers by Clarkson and Cheung on managerial constraints. Clarkson searches for the key factors that contribute to differences among firms independent of their organizational structure. His analysis links several distinguishing characteristics of nonproprietary organizations to the incentive structure of decision-makers within such "firms," and several implications concerning their actions are derived. A number of important constraints, including the role of external monitoring, are also analyzed in the paper. Finally, differences in input use attributable to the nonproprietary organizational form are discussed in detail.

Cheung focuses on the importance of distinguishing between constraints that are attributable to the nonproprietary organizational form and those that can be linked to other factors, such as differences in transaction and monitoring costs. In particular, Cheung's paper investigates differences in costs of monitoring the sale and use of theater tickets, as examples of transaction cost effects. Both price and quantity adjustments are discussed. The analysis clearly reveals that implications previously attributable to nonproprietary status require further qualifications for their validity, lest they be associated with proprietary status.

The papers in the second section, by Frech and Martin, investigate the mutual form of organization in two very different institutions. Frech is concerned with the differences in output and total costs for processing health insurance claims that arise from differences between government agencies, private for-profit firms, and mutual organizations that perform processing functions. After discussing some of the existing literature, Frech presents empirical tests of these differences between organizational forms. He finds that, in terms of speed of handling claims and total cost, stock companies do better than mutual organizations which, in turn outperform their governmental counterparts.

Martin observes that the organizational structure of the trade union gives it a nonproprietary character. He postulates well-defined objective functions for union members as individuals and incorporates the nonproprietary structure of their organization into the formal constraints of utility maximization. Union bargaining goals are then analyzed in terms of wage demands, strikes, membership size, and pricing under proprietary and nonproprietary assumptions. The model sheds considerable light upon union activities.

The third section contains papers by Thompson and by Weisbrod on charitable organizations. These presentations are especially interesting because of their relative importance in the nonproprietary sector and the peculiarities of their financing activities. Thompson formulates a hypothesis designed to explain why charity is usually collected and dispersed through the nonproprietary sector. He then offers an explanation for the role of government in charity.

Weisbrod's paper raises a number of important questions for understanding the growth of museums, charities, and other nonprofit organizations. His analysis assumes that the form and source of revenues for the output of an organization will significantly contribute to our understanding of the behavior of agents within it. Using an organization's sources of revenues, Weisbrod develops an index to measure the significance of nonprofit-oriented firms across industries, which proves to be a provocative attempt at delineating the nonproprietary sector. The paper also examines some factors that are conjectured to have contributed to the growth of the nonprofit organization.

The final section contains papers by Lindsay and by McKean who explore some aspects of governmental organizations. Governments, like nonproprietary organizations, lack the capitalized value feature of proprietary institutions. However, they obtain revenues for the most part under constraints different from those associated with charitable organizations. Lindsay explores the basic, existing explanations of public organizations. He argues that the traditional divisions between governmental and nongovernmental activities are superficial and that the critical factors separating or operating on the constraints within governmental organizations have heretofore not been fully identified or analyzed. In particular, Lindsay examines the role of coercion and its differential effects in governmental organizations.

The last paper in the volume turns to a discussion of the production and use of knowledge in nonproprietary and, especially, government organizations. McKean investigates the overall constraints of operating in nonproprietary organizations and how those constraints influence the type of information produced and how it is used.

Each of the major sections in the volume is followed by the delivered comments, and then by informal replies by the authors and by extracts from the discussion by the other participants. The volume concludes with a review and comment on the more troublesome and significant points raised in the seminar.

The volume includes a list of selected references on the economics of nonproprietary organizations. A perusal of these references will reveal scholarly papers predating this conference by almost twenty years. Much of this earlier work was either inspired or written by scholars such as Armen Alchian, Kenneth Arrow, Roland McKean, and William Meckling who, while at the Rand Corporation, began to probe into the nature and consequences of alternative ownership arrangements. Subsequently, an impressive number of individuals have continued to expand various aspects of that inquiry. We submit this volume as part of that effort.

As nonproprietary organizations have sponsored the research, employed its authors, and conducted the conference leading to this volume, we feel it is appropriate to extend our gratitude to the Liberty Fund, Inc., sponsor of the conference, and to the Law and Economics Center at the University of Miami, which conducted it. We also wish to extend our special thanks to those individuals who aided generously during the final stages of manuscript preparation: Andrew Caverly, Randy Chartash, Linda Craig, Rosalie Gregory, Kathy McHugh, Ronald Perkowski, and Debbee Watkins.

FOOTNOTES

1. For various reasons that will be revealed below, the term nonprofit is less satisfactory and may even be misleading. For example, many "nonprofit" enterprises consistently generate a positive net income. This tends to confuse and focus attention on the existence of positive profits rather than on the behavior of decision-makers in the organizations that generate them. Moreover, nonprofit status is usually associated with a tax definition rather than organizational form.

2. However, not all tax-exempt firms are nonproprietary.

MANAGERIAL
CONSTRAINTS

MANAGERIAL BEHAVIOR IN NONPROPRIETARY ORGANIZATIONS

Kenneth W. Clarkson, UNIVERSITY OF MIAMI

Although the neoclassical theory of producer behavior has been subject to extensive criticism for several decades, the debate so far has failed to yield a general theory of producer behavior in economic organizations. This debate has been the result of both a dissatisfaction with the wealth-maximization axiom of the conventional theory of the firm, and a failure of ad hoc hypotheses to explain actions in public and other non-proprietary enterprises. Recent theoretical developments, however, have identified some key relationships between the nature of organizations and the activities which occur within them. This paper is concerned with the contributions and limitations of these developments to a more general theory of producer behavior in both profit-seeking and nonprofit organizations.

Economics of Nonproprietary Organizations
Research in Law and Economics, Supplement 1, pages 3-26
Copyright © 1980 by JAI Press Inc.
ISBN: 0-89232-132-6

Most of the theorems of producer behavior can be derived from variations in one or more of the general assumptions concerning (a) the level of technology and the endowment of resources,[1] (b) individual tastes,[2] and (c) managerial incentives which can be derived from the structure of rights to the use of resources.[3] Variations in the assumptions regarding technology and resources available to society yield a variety of generally agreed upon propositions. Many of the hypotheses concerning the structure of industry, for example, are derived by postulating differences in the laws of physical production (rate and volume of production, divisibility of factors, and so on), relative scarcity of resources, characteristics of the good (public versus private), and transaction costs (information, mobility). Sometimes the variations in assumptions are not specified exactly in these terms, but their essence can be reduced to some combination of the above factors. Thus, implications resting upon the number of firms ultimately can be traced to implicit assumptions about information, mobility, and other transaction costs, physical production laws, and relative scarcity of resources.

Variations in the assumptions concerning individual tastes and managerial incentives, however, fail to yield a similar level of agreement. This disagreement has, in part, resulted from observed deviations from the implications of the wealth-maximization model in proprietary institutions and from the lack of an adequate model of these organizations. The table presents a summary of many of the existing competing theories of managerial behavior which are associated with differing tastes and/or incentives. This table organizes these theories into univariate models where the marginal rates of transformation between the alternative sources of utility result in a "corner" solution and into multivariate models where the marginal rates of transformation result in some mix of the alternative sources of utility. In some cases, the relevant exchange between alternative sources of utility is directly linked to the nature of constraints found in the organization, as described in Alchian and Kessel (10):

> What is important is not a matter of differences in tastes between monopolists and competitive firms, but differences in the terms of trade of pecuniary for nonpecuniary income. And given this difference in the relevant price or exchange ratios, the difference in the mix purchased should not be surprising. (p. 163)

Yet, most analyses of the relationship between organization constraints and managerial incentives fail to successfully distinguish the interactions among tastes, capabilities, and rights to use resources in explaining producer behavior.

Section I of this paper investigates the relationship between resource rights and effective organization constraints in proprietary organizations. The analysis then turns to utility maximization by proprietary

Classification of the Major Existing Theories of the Firm

Classification of Theory	Theory
Univariate Criterion Models Single period:	(1) Profit maximization (2) Sales or assets maximization (subject to a profit constraint) (3) Organizational slack maximization
Multiple period:	(1) Wealth maximization (2) Rate of growth of sales or output (3) Present value of sales maximization (4) Target rate of return
Multivariate Utility Models Trade-offs between:	(1) Profits and leisure (2) Profits and congeniality in the firm (3) Profits for managers and owners (4) Profits and control (5) Profits and security (6) Profits and social responsibility (7) Profits and product perfection (8) Profits and congeniality outside as well as inside the firm (9) Profits and managerial discretion (10) Profits, output, and emoluments (11) Profits and other nonpecuniary rewards (12) Profits and certain asset portfolios (13) Profits and professional excellence (14) Profits, status, power, and prestige

Sources: Alchian and Kessel (10), Kaplan, Dirlan, and Lanzilotti (85), Levy (99), Machlup (105), and Needham (123), pp. 1–15.

decision-makers and the factors that contribute to variations in organizational constraints. Next, the identification of effective constraints in nonproprietary organizations and the resulting difference in behavior are presented. Problems in deriving differences in behavior among proprietary and nonproprietary enterprises are examined in Section III. Section IV is concerned with input use and total costs in proprietary and nonproprietary organizations. Finally, the use of maximands versus constraints for predicting managerial behavior is explored.

I. RESOURCE RIGHTS AND EFFECTIVE ORGANIZATIONAL CONSTRAINTS

Effective constraints facing individuals in economic organizations originate from two basic sources: differences in resources and the structure of rights to the use of these scarce resources. Resource characteristics are extremely important in shaping final production and exchange outcomes, and in determining the nature of the organization. The gains from specialization and cooperation in economic organizations, for example, have been shown to result partly from reductions in costs of specifying and monitoring market exchanges [Coase (46)] and partly from the technological advantages of "team" production [Alchian and Demsetz (9)]. Furthermore, the structure of financial capital has been associated with certain market transaction costs [Jensen and Meckling (83)]. Since resource characteristics are difficult to alter, they will be assumed to be exogenous.

While the rights to use resources may be equally as binding as the constraints arising from resource characteristics, they *can* be altered by members of society. Rights to use resources are determined by the sets of legal, social, and political rules, and other regulations and procedures. In the United States, the sets of rights to use resources are determined by formal written documents, such as the U.S. Constitution, constitutions of the fifty states, as well as tax, contract, securities, and other laws at various levels of government [Mofsky (119)], judicial interpretations of these documents, noncontractual arrangements [Macaulay (103)], and informal rules of conduct [Charnovitz (35)]. Furthermore, the resource rights governing exchange or production decisions are not always identical in organizations providing similar outputs. In particular, the rights to use resources in profit-seeking institutions differ from those in nonprofit enterprises.

A. Effective Constraints in Proprietary Enterprises

The effective constraints in proprietary enterprises implicitly assume that the organization's owners seek to maximize wealth. Apart from the problems associated with monitoring economic performance, the task of successfully maximizing organizational wealth is not an easy one. In addition to the commonly recognized problems in the selection of the optimal mix of customer outputs (a vector, Q_1, of k outputs that are generally bought by individuals outside the firm), the decision-maker must identify the optimal mix of employee-purchased outputs (a vector, Q_2, of n outputs that are "sold" to employees or other owners of resource inputs in exchange for lower remuneration).[4] The latter includes fringe benefits, such as life or health insurance and pensions, as well as goods with a high degree of the public good characteristic, such as personnel policies, pleasant working conditions, and congeniality of other workers. The resources (a vector, X, of t inputs supplied by resource owners) used in the organization often contribute to both customer and employee-purchased outputs, and they generally offer inseparable bundles of input services. Thus, the relationship between hired resources and final outputs is not direct since resources provide a number of input services which yield final outputs.[5] If individual resources, x_i, can be purchased by owners for r_i, then the constraints that maximize the wealth of the organization, π^0, are:[6]

$$\max_{\{x_i\}} \pi^0 = P_1 Q_1 - (RX - P_2 Q_2) \tag{1}$$

subject to: $G_1(Q_1) = f_1(X)$ and $G_2(Q_2) = f_2(X)$
where P_1 = prices (a vector) of consumer outputs (Q_1);
  P_2 = implicit prices (a vector) of employee-purchased outputs (Q_2);
  R = prices (a vector) of resources (X).

This formulation of the wealth-maximization rule implies that proprietary organizations face effective prices for the organization's outputs which differ from the prices or costs in the conventional model of the profit-seeking firm. For both customer outputs (where q_i is contained in Q_1 or $q_i \in Q_1$) and employee-purchased outputs (where q_i is contained in Q_2 or $q_i \in Q_2$), the effective price for outputs directly consumed from the organization is:[7]

$$p_i - \frac{\partial \pi^0}{\partial q_i} = + R \frac{\partial X}{\partial q_i} - P_1 \frac{\partial Q_1^y}{\partial X} \frac{\partial X}{\partial q_i} + P_2 \frac{\partial Q_2^y}{\partial X} \frac{\partial X}{\partial q_i} \tag{2}$$

where Q_2^y = customer output vector with $q_i = 0$ when $q_i \in Q_1$;
  Q_2^y = employee output vector with $q_i = 0$ when $q_i \in Q_2$.

This is because the change in the wealth of the organization due to the consumption or use of any particular output $(\partial \pi^0 / \partial q_i)$ consists of the cost of the resources used to produce q_i plus the increased revenues from other customer and employee-purchased outputs that are jointly expanded as resources are hired to produce q_i. In the conventional theory of the firm, the decision-maker's price of consuming the firm's outputs consists solely of the cost of the inputs $(R \, \partial X / \partial q_i)$, neglecting the second and third terms in Eq. (2). Since resources are used to produce any good, the price of customer or employee-purchased outputs, $p_i - \partial \pi^0 / \partial q_i$, will generally be greater than zero. This result may not hold, however, for all levels of employee-purchased outputs with a high degree of the public good characteristic. Thus, the effective price for certain working conditions, such as pleasant surroundings, may consist of only $\partial \pi^0 / \partial q_i$.

B. Utility Maximization by Proprietary Producers

Perhaps because we know little about when to expect or how to measure differences in tastes, economic theorems generally are not built on specific conditions about differences in preferences. Yet differing preferences do represent a fundamental condition in the pure theory of exchange. Since production can be viewed as the exchange of intermediate goods and services, it is somewhat puzzling that the conventional theory of producer behavior does not rest upon the utility-maximization postulate.

In the generalized theory of producer behavior presented in this paper, decision-makers are hypothesized to derive utility from a variety of goods and services ($q_1^m, \ldots q_k^m, q_{k+1}^m, \ldots q_{k+n}^m, q_{k+n+1}^m, \ldots q_{k+n+s}^m$). For present purposes, these sources of utility can be classified into three groups: customer-purchased outputs (Q_1); employee-purchased outputs (Q_2), both previously defined; and outputs (a vector, Q_3, of s outputs that are produced by outside organizations) provided by other firms.[8]

Initially the formulation also hypothesizes that the central decision-maker or manager receives the residual payments from the organization (π^m), where $\pi^m = H(\pi^o)$,[9] and from outside sources (W^m). Consequently, the managerial choice-theoretic structure of alternative goods, q_i, becomes:

$$\max_{\{q_i\}} Z = U^m (Q_1^m, Q_2^m, Q_3^m) = U^m (q_1^m \ldots q_{k+n+s}^m) \qquad (3)$$

subject to: $\pi^m + W^m - P_1 Q_1^m - P_2 Q_2^m - P_3 Q_3^m = 0$

where U^m = manager's utility;
   Q_1^m = customer outputs (Q_1) produced by the organization and bought by the manager;
   Q_2^m = employee outputs (Q_2) "sold" to the manager;
   Q_3^m = customer outputs (Q_3) produced by other organizations and sold to the manager;
   P_3 = market prices of other organizations' customer outputs;
   W^m = manager's outside wealth.

Utility maximization requires that $dZ/dq_i = 0$ for all i, yielding the conditions that:[10]

$$\frac{\frac{\partial U^m}{\partial q_i^m}}{P_i - \frac{\partial \pi^m}{\partial q_i}} = \frac{\frac{\partial U^m}{\partial q_j^m}}{P_j - \frac{\partial \pi^m}{\partial q_j}} \qquad (4)$$

The major differences between Eq. (4) and the neoclassical equilibrium conditions are the inclusion of customer- (Q_1) and employee-purchased (Q_2) outputs and the modification of the effective price to include the consequences of the manager's consumption choices on his compensation. Before implications can be derived, however, a more precise relationship between these differences must be specified.

The effective managerial price ($p_i - \partial\pi^m/\partial q_i$) in Eq. (4) of any source of utility is the difference between the customer (P_1 or P_3) or employee (P_2) price of that good or service and the change in the manager's "budget constraint," $\partial\pi^m/\partial q_i$ (where $\partial\pi^m/\partial q_i = 0$ when $q_i \in Q_3$ for goods and services produced by other firms), as a result of changes in managerial consumption or Q_1 of Q_2 outputs. Changes in the budget constraint may be related directly (as in the case of specified managerial discounts for the organization's customer outputs) or indirectly (through the managerial compensation package) to changes in the enterprise's performance. As noted earlier, if the output can be jointly consumed by all resource owners (for example, more pleasant surroundings), the effective managerial price for certain levels of Q_2 may consist only of $\partial\pi^m/\partial q_i$. One must also recognize that the effective price may vary for different levels of output chosen. The price of a public good, for example, may be close to zero for some levels of output, increasing rapidly as the owners impose additional constraints on managerial decision-makers.

The division of a firm's outputs into customer and employee classes also affects the implications of the neoclassical utility maximization hypothesis. Most of the resources (X) used in an organization contribute to both Q_1 and Q_2 outputs, as input services that are directly related to the firm's production of customer outputs and as services that simultaneously affect employees' working conditions, independently of their contribution to the firm's production of Q_1. For example, an individual may offer a certain number of hours as a typist *and* as a congenial worker. In many cases, the services offered by a resource cannot be provided separately. When inputs generally provide joint services to both customer and employee-purchased outputs, managerial purchase of any single Q_1 or Q_2 output will generally increase one or more additional Q_1 or Q_2 outputs because of the inseparability of resource input services. Thus, the change in utility in Eq. (4) from increased managerial consumption of customer or employee outputs is:[11]

$$\frac{\partial U^m}{\partial q_i^m} = \frac{\partial U^m}{\partial Q_1}\frac{\partial Q_1}{\partial X}\frac{\partial X}{\partial q_i^m} + \frac{\partial U^m}{\partial Q_2}\frac{\partial Q_2}{\partial X}\frac{\partial X}{\partial q_i^m} \qquad (5)$$

where $\{q_i^m \in Q_1 \text{ or } Q_2\}$.

In this revised model of managerial decision making, differences in the outcomes associated with organizations producing similar outputs arise from (a) the use of nonidentical resources,[12] (b) alternative combinations of pecuniary and nonpecuniary (employee-purchased outputs) benefits,[13] (c) diverse managerial preferences for customer outputs, employee-purchased outputs, and risk,[14] and (d) differential costs of information and transactions.[15]

This model also contributes to an understanding of behavior in alternative market structures once it is realized that an organization may face price-taking or competitive conditions for customer outputs but operates under price-searching conditions for one or more of its employee-purchased outputs. Consequently, differences in employee-purchased outputs among firms reflect alternative demand conditions in addition to the traditional tax, volume or group purchase, risk (to avoid moral hazard outcomes), employee preference, and transaction costs explanations. The model in this paper also implies that certain "fringe benefits" will be more uniform among firms than other employee-purchased outputs. One would expect, for example, less variation among insurance policies, which can be purchased under relatively competitive conditions, than among working conditions or personnel policies which are offered under price-searching conditions. Furthermore, since many of the employee-purchased outputs cannot be "resold," price discrimination is possible. Consequently, it is possible that firms, which are traditionally labeled as competitive in the customer output market, such as wheat farmers, are engaging in price discrimination for employee-purchased outputs.[16]

Since all firms are likely to be price searchers for at least some employee-purchased outputs (for example, those associated with the physical surroundings of the enterprise), inefficiencies due to monopoly (price-searching conditions) are understated.

C. Variations in Proprietary Organizational Constraints

For various reasons that go beyond the scope of this paper, proprietary institutions are not organized in the same manner.[17] In some cases differences in organizational structure and constraints can be linked to particular tax savings by decision-makers in the institution. Other differences reflect the desire to obtain significantly higher returns on financial capital by accepting residual net revenues after fixed contractual obligations and income taxes in the form of stocks. Since many of the owners of these financial resources (stockholders) are not directly involved with the organization, special constraints are placed on decision-makers in addition to written reports and oral procedures. Such constraints may take the form of outright prohibition of certain activities, such as sale of major assets without the approval of owners of financial capital who are usually represented by a board of trustees.

While the terms of the contractual arrangements associated with equity position give the board extensive discretionary power over all operations of the organization, the costs of personally coordinating activities of all the joint-input resource owners are usually so high that the manager is delegated rights to make many decisions involving explicit and implicit contracts within the organization. Because these managers, like other individuals, are utility maximizers who usually will not have tastes exactly identical to the stockholder's objective of maximizing wealth, monitoring the manager becomes especially important. When such conditions exist, owners have found that making the manager's compensation a function of the wealth of the organization's operations provides a superior form of monitoring the manager's activities [Alchian and Demsetz (9)]. Of course, managers are also "monitored" by the competition of other individuals who are able to replace them [Manne (106)]. But these potential managers will also be able to deviate from the highest wealth position for the organization when owner monitoring costs are high. Managers who are given a portion of the increased wealth of the organization also have greater incentive to institute internal monitoring regulations and procedures that are more accurate and complete, but require increased managerial effort, than managers whose compensation does not involve organizational wealth. This can be seen by specifying alternative managerial compensation schemes from the general form:

$$\bar{\pi}^m = \alpha \pi^0 \tag{6}$$

where $\bar{\pi}^m$ = manager's constrained share (α) of the change in organization's wealth.

From Eqs. (2) and (6), the effective managerial price, p_i^m, for q_i in Eq. (4) is:

$$p_i^m = p_i - \alpha \left(p_i - R \frac{\partial X}{\partial q_i} + P_1 \frac{\partial Q_1^y}{\partial x} \frac{\partial X}{\partial q_i} + P_2 \frac{\partial Q_2^y}{\partial x} \frac{\partial x}{\partial q_i} \right). \tag{7}$$

Utility-maximizing managers whose compensation is determined by a high α face a lower effective price of increasing q_i when $\partial \pi^0 / \partial q_i$ is greater than zero than managers with equal total compensation determined by a low α (and higher salary independent of the enterprise's stockholder wealth). Furthermore, if the outputs can be jointly consumed or if the costs of monitoring managerial consumption of outputs are high enough, p_i may be zero for some levels. In such cases, the effective managerial price is $\alpha (\partial \pi^0 / \partial q_i)$, and a higher α will imply increased prices of choosing q_i's since $\partial \pi^0 / \partial q_i$ may be less than zero when q_i is a good in the manager's utility function. Consequently, firms that tie managerial compensation to changes in overall profitability of the enterprise produce greater managerial incentives to seek higher organizational wealth positions. This implies that firms whose managers have weaker links between personal compensation and stockholder wealth will exhibit greater deviations from the highest potential wealth position. Such managers will have greater incentive to alter their distribution of work activities toward tasks which are more convenient or more pleasant [Clarkson (41, 42)]. A higher α in Eq. (6), however, would automatically increase the effective price to the manager of such activities. Recent evidence indicates that in firms with dominant stockholders where transaction costs of monitoring managers are a small percentage of individual equity positions), managerial compensation is more directly tied to overall profitability, and these firms outperform organizations that do not link managerial compensation to profitability [McEachern (112)].

II. EFFECTIVE CONSTRAINTS IN NONPROPRIETARY ENTERPRISES

Nonproprietary organizations exhibit a different set of effective constraints. For the purpose of this paper, a nonproprietary enterprise is defined as an organization whose "owners" or trustees cannot fully appropriate the costs and rewards associated with the activities of the organization. Weakened appropriability may take the form of (a) restrictions on the rate of return, as in regulation, (b) limitations on the accumulation or sale of the rights to ownership, as in mutual or governmental enterprises, (c) reductions in the exclusivity of claims to income or wealth, as in nonprofit organizations, or (d) restrictions on any other rights to use, exchange, or capture benefits from the organization, as in price controls. Each of these attenuations yields identifiable changes in the resource rights associated with the organization. Unless explicitly constrained by higher authorities, these changes in resource rights yield predictable changes in the set of options available to decision-makers in nonproprietary organizations when compared to those in proprietary enterprises.

The possible modifications of the overall constraints in Eq. (1) for producing managerial incentives consistent with the objectives of nonproprietary organizations are too numerous to examine here. However, considerable insight concerning the behavior of nonproprietary institutions can be obtained by examining certain modifications of the wealth-maximization constraints. Trustees or other owners of nonproprietary organizations will voluntarily choose such modifications whenever they wish to pursue objectives other than wealth maximization. The pursuit of such objectives plus the weakened right to use or capture the capitalized net flow of potential organizational wealth represents a change in effective managerial constraints.

Consider, for example, the general constraints facing the manager of a nonproprietary organization which is legally prohibited from earning positive profits. If nonproprietary trustees seek the lowest cost or most efficient means of pursuing the organization's objectives, if these objectives are specified as output or price constraints, and if the manager is paid a fixed salary, the effective constraint of the decision-makers is:

$$\pi^0(n) = P_1Q_1 + P_2Q_2 - RX - S - \lambda (\bar{P}_1Q_1 + \bar{P}_2Q_2 - RX) - \Delta\{G^r$$
$$(\bar{Q}_1, \bar{Q}_2)\} = 0 \tag{8}$$

subject to: $G(Q_1, Q_2) = f(X)$

where $\bar{P}_1$ = trustee assigned prices of customer outputs;

$\bar{P}_2$ = trustee assigned prices of employee-purchased outputs;

S = manager's salary;

$G^r(\bar{Q}_1, \bar{Q}_2)$ = restrictions on customer or employee-purchased outputs.

When the constraint $\bar{P}_1Q_1 + \bar{P}_2Q_2 - RX$ is binding (equal to zero), and Δ is zero, Eq. (8) requires more precise identification of the organization's objectives to obtain a determinate (unique) solution. Suppose, for example, that trustees of a nonproprietary enterprise establish prices of customer outputs below market clearing levels.[18] In this case, the price constraint in Eq. (8) becomes $\phi \equiv \bar{P}_1Q_1 + P_2Q_2 - RX$ or:

$$\pi_\phi^0(n) = P_1Q_1 + P_2Q_2 - RX - S - \lambda (\bar{P}_1Q_1 + P_2Q_2 - RX) = 0$$
$$\text{where } \bar{P}_1 < P_1. \tag{9}$$

From Eq. (2), it can be shown that the effective price of customer outputs to nonproprietary organization is:

$$\frac{d\pi_\phi^0(n)}{dq_i} = (1 - \lambda)\frac{d\pi^0}{dq_i} - \lambda \left\{ (\bar{P}_1 - P_1)\frac{\partial Q_1^i}{\partial X}\frac{\partial X}{\partial q_i} \right\} \tag{10}$$

$$\{q_i \in Q_1\}$$

and the effective price of employee-purchased outputs to decision-makers who bear full costs by salary reductions is:

$$\frac{d\pi_\psi^0(n)}{dq_i} = (1 - \lambda)\frac{d\pi^0}{dq_i} - \lambda \left\{ (\bar{P}_1 - P_1)\frac{\partial Q_1}{\partial X}\frac{\partial X}{\partial q_i} \right\} \tag{11}$$

$$\{q_i \in Q_2\}.$$

The first term in both Eqs. (10) and (11), $(1 - \lambda) d\pi^0/dq_i$, represents the direct cost to the organization of the use or consumption of outputs that could have been sold to customers or employees. The second term of the effective organization price represents the indirect benefits from providing additional customer outputs produced jointly with q_i. An inspection of Eqs. (10) and (11) also reveals that, in nonproprietary organizations characterized by choice theoretic structures like Eq. (9), the effective price to managers, if they pay for organization price, for both customer and employee-purchased outputs is lower than it would be in proprietary enterprises.

A. Differences in Producer Behavior

The weakened appropriability to use or capture rewards from fulfilling organizational objectives implies that nonproprietary enterprises are subject to basic constraints that differ from those in proprietary enterprises with greater appropriability. Trustees of nonproprietary organizations will establish different rules, regulations, and monitoring procedures to guide resource owners toward and reduce deviations from the outcomes desired by the trustees. Furthermore, since owners or trustees generally delegate many production decisions to managers, trustees of nonproprietary organizations will impose special constraints to prevent further deviations from desired outcomes when managerial preferences do not precisely match those of the trustees. Since this trustee-manager "preference-match" rarely occurs, the imposition of special constraints on managers will be the rule rather than the exception.

In this context, differences in producer behavior result from explicit differences in the constraints determined by the trustees or owners and by other external sources. In general, however, differences in constraints, such as those in Eq. (9), will be difficult to detect without an extensive investigation of the organization and its ownership characteristics. Nonproprietary enterprises, like their proprietary counterparts, will focus monitoring regulations and procedures on activities where deviations from desired behavior are easily detected and monitored by regulations or procedures. Because the wealth-maximization rule is not applicable, more activities with high detection or other monitoring costs will effectively be unconstrained (at certain levels) by the lack of indirect monitoring such as residual claim assignments. Differences in these effective constraints, for example, are revealed in the rules and regulations governing work effort by employees. Time spent on the job is highly, but not perfectly, correlated with the flow of input services from resources. In the absence of net profitability criteria, trustees attempt to monitor the flow of input services by placing controls on the actual amount of time spent on the job [Alchian and Demsetz (9)]. But the distribution of work effort is more costly to monitor and the absence of net profitability criteria implies that managers of nonproprietary enterprises will choose relatively more pleasant tasks. Available evidence supports these propositions. Proprietary institutions use significantly more supervisory staff during undesirable working periods such as night shifts and devote more time to direct supervision of employees

[Clarkson (41, 42)]. Nonproprietary managers will also ignore valuable market information on uses of resources more often than proprietary managers. Rather than make costly calculations (to the manager) on the relative payments to resources, these administrators choose simple (low cost) rules of thumb such as automatic salary increases that are easy to use but often result in higher costs to the institution [Kershaw and McKean (88)]. Sometimes the rules imposed by nonproprietary trustees allow managers to ignore the costs of acquiring, using, or holding resources. The opportunity costs of real property in the U.S. government, for example, are not usually included (explicitly or implicitly) in the effective managerial constraints of the agency using the land. Consequently, the U.S. government's real property holdings are idle or in lower valued uses more frequently than holdings of profit-seeking institutions [Minasian (117)].

B. Models of Producer Behavior

A model of producer behavior that focuses on the structure of rights is also useful for explaining situations where monitoring is effectively altered. For example, a study of productivity in backward economies showed that small changes in the organization of a plant's productive process can significantly increase output and/or reduce costs. An extremely important aspect of this evidence was the lack of application by managers of similar firms of the techniques responsible for the large productivity gains [Kilby (89)]. This outcome is not surprising since the basic constraints in these organizations (except for increased monitoring during the demonstration period) were not altered by the introduction of the new production techniques. Even more striking was the "tendency for the demonstration firms themselves to slip back to their old ways" (p. 305). A resource rights interpretation of producer behavior can explain the large increases in productivity in the demonstration firm, the lack of application elsewhere, and the return to the predemonstration techniques. In fact, the study comes very close to suggesting that rights to use resources (operating environment) is an important factor for explaining the large gains.

III. PROBLEMS IN DERIVING DIFFERENCES IN OUTCOMES

Propositions concerning differences in average behavior among organizations with varying degrees of appropriability are more ambiguous when monitoring costs are low. For example, several studies of nonprofit organizations suggest that both customer and employee outputs will be of higher quality than those found in their proprietary counter-parts [Alchian and Kessel (10), Nicols (125), and Newhouse (124)]. These results are usually derived by explicitly (or implicitly) specifying that $\bar{P}_1 < P_1$ and/or $\bar{P}_2 < P_2$ in Eq. (8), and by implicitly assuming that the governing authorities who impose the controls *do not alter rights in a way that would upset this type of prediction*. But this need not be the case. Governing authorities, for example, could impose more specific, stric-ter controls over employee-purchased outputs where infractions are easier to detect and leave other outputs effectively unconstrained. Cer-tain activities such as time devoted to on-site jobs, acquisition of assets, and use of vehicles or supplies will be relatively easy to monitor. Other activities, such as "business" trips, professional meetings, and off-site activities, are more difficult to monitor, since the output yielded by these activities is not as easily identifiable. Consequently, in nonproprietary enterprises there will be more costly business trips (or other activities that involve high monitoring costs) and fewer lost hours at on-site pro-duction locations when compared to their proprietary counterparts. Furthermore, under certain conditions, it has been shown that govern-mental units will produce lower quality outputs than their proprietary counterparts [Lindsay (101)]. Consequently, before unambiguous differ-ences in the average behavior among producers are derived, certain auxiliary assumptions will often be necessary.[19]

The problem of specifying these auxiliary assumptions becomes espe-cially important when resources offer two or more input services simul-taneously in one bundle. Governing authorities may be able to identify and easily control one form of input services, but when resources offer combinations of input services, effective monitoring is more difficult. For example, consider the implications about the quality of employee-purchased outputs, such as physical surroundings, working conditions, nepotism, and other amenities derived from reductions in the exclusive right to net income in nonproprietary organizations [Alchian and Kessel (10), Nicols (125), and Newhouse (124)]. Some of these employee-purchased outputs are provided by unbundled resources such as the quality of the carpets used in offices. In such cases it would be relatively easy for the governing authorities to place controls on these inputs. Consequently, propositions about these activities will first require deri-vation of implications regarding the existence or nonexistence of specific constraints on them. Such constraints would also have to be deduced from the incentive structures under alternative monitoring or produc-tion function conditions. When resources offer multiple input services, such controls will be more difficult to institute; hence it is not surprising to observe simultaneously both confirmations and rejections of the pro-position that nonprofit and mutual nonproprietary organizations will choose higher levels of nonpecuniary services for members. A more careful derivation of the hypotheses to be tested could therefore explain both sets of observations.

Another example of the problems associated with incomplete specification of the total set of effective constraints is the proposition that nonprofit organizations such as hospitals respond less rapidly to new opportunities [Newhouse (124)]. This may be the case, but one must further specify the conditions affecting the constraints which are applicable to those organizations, including financing schemes and monitoring activities by the governing authorities. Without these or other assumptions, one could just as easily predict that nonprofits will be *more* willing to seek opportunities, both profitable and unprofitable, since these managers will bear little of the costs of failure. Or one might well predict that the enterprises have fixed budgets at levels significantly above costs of providing existing Q_1 and Q_2. Thus G^r $(\bar{Q}_1, \bar{Q}_2)$ in Eq. (8) may specify $Q_1 < \bar{Q}_1$ and $Q_2 < \bar{Q}_2$ with $P_1Q_1 + P_2Q_2 - RX \geq 0$. By choosing higher risk alternatives, or new opportunities that yield net positive revenues in the future, the nonprofit organization may be able to satisfy these constraints and keep revenues equal to costs in the budget period. Auxiliary assumptions are also necessary for other implications concerning intertemporal outcomes. The effective constraints in government, for example, understate the true discount or interest rate, and estimating procedures for costs are systematically biased downward and for benefits are biased upward [De Alessi (53)]. These constraints imply that relatively more investment activities will be observed in governmental enterprises. Unambiguous predictions on intertemporal allocations may not occur, however, when some aspects of the constraints are ignored or incompletely specified. For example, since many government decision-makers lack access to capital markets and often must pay the full capital costs out of an annual appropriation, the net result of these forces is to restrict some investments rather than to increase them [Clarkson (43)].

Sometimes it is necessary to identify precisely the objectives of some particular class of nonmanagerial resource owners. Owners of real property, for example, may set "rents" such that a "nonprofit" organization maintains its status for tax purposes and all accounting profits become rents. Under existing tax laws (for example, quick depreciation schedules, capital gains), such schemes often allow greater returns than a profit-seeking status would yield, even after adjusting for costs of organizing and operating this tax-dodging device. In such cases, organization under the nonproprietary status could systematically increase the wealth constraint and lower the effective price of many employee-purchased outputs when decision-makers were also property owners.

In such conditions, behavior in the "nonprofit" agency might result in allocative consequences very similar (or identical) to those in or with full appropriability. Unfortunately, one must also be careful in applying such models to other resource owners. For example, a recent model of nonprofit hospitals predicts that physician-controlled hospitals will yield short-term outcomes identical to profit-seeking firms [Pauly and Redisch (130)]:

> The only difference between this [orthodox profit-maximizing] model and the physician-profit maximization model of the hospital is that in the latter it is the physician input, rather than the nondebt capital input which obtains economic profits, the residual income. (p. 90)

These results are derived primarily from the nature of physician control over the many forces that contribute to medical care, including outputs (number and type of patients admitted), inputs (capital equipment), and the production process (specific activities). There is, however, a competing hypothesis, with empirical confirmation, that explains why physicians desire control over hospital and other nonphysician inputs; and this hypothesis yields very different outcomes for nonprofit and for profit hospitals when physicians are not also property owners. In this approach, physicians are viewed as seeking to control most nonphysician inputs, such as hospitals, nursing hospitals, and drugs, in order to maximize their derived income [Shalit (150)]. When nonphysician inputs can be substituted for physicians' services, maximization of physicians' group (cartel) income implies some control over potential substitutions. Physicians have the incentive to constrain the choice of input combinations so that nonphysician services are no longer substitutable for physicians' services at some point. At this point, an increase in the relative price of physicians' services would not cause substitution away from their use. In nonproprietary hospitals control over input use would be easier and, although physicians may be expected to seek the lowest cost combinations of the chosen level of nonphysician inputs, there are strong incentives for physician-operated, nonproprietary hospitals to choose overall input combinations different from those used in proprietary hospitals. Consequently, in order to discriminate between these two competing hypotheses of producer behavior, it is necessary to specify in more detail the constraints in Eq. (8) and to derive the resulting implications.

IV. INPUT USE AND TOTAL COSTS

Maximization of the stockholders' wealth in proprietary institutions implies that for each resource, x_i, the decision-maker chooses an amount of x_i, such that $\partial \pi^0 / \partial x_i = 0$, or:

$$\left(P_1 + Q_1 \frac{\partial P_1}{\partial Q_1}\right) \frac{\partial Q_1}{\partial x_i} = \left(R + X \frac{\partial R}{\partial X}\right) \frac{\partial X}{\partial x_i} - \left(P_2 + Q_2 \frac{\partial P_2}{\partial Q_2}\right) \frac{\partial Q_2}{\partial x_i} \quad (12)$$

for all i, where the term on the left side of the equality denotes the marginal revenue product of consumer outputs, and the term on the right side denote marginal net pecuniary payments to resource owners (marginal factor cost less marginal revenue product of employee-purchased outputs).[20] Even when a proprietary organization is owner or stockholder managed, wealth maximization is difficult. This is because the decision-maker or manager must simultaneously (a) identify combinations of customer outputs and employee-purchased outputs, (b) divide employee tasks among alternative operations of the firm, (c) coordinate the interdependent rewards and costs of each operation, and (d) monitor individual tasks to enforce promised behavior to maximize the wealth of the organization. When the enterprise is not owner-managed, the presence of positive information and other transaction costs provides increased opportunities for maximizing the decision-maker's utility and implies additional differences in outcomes among proprietary firms producing similar outputs.

Evidence collected for different managerial compensation schemes for a national franchise restaurant operation is consistent with the implication that the effective cost to managers of not maximizing stockholder wealth falls when the link between compensation and performance is weakened. Using data from an article which studied various franchise restaurants during periods of franchisee-owner (F.O.) operation and company-manager operation, one can construct a simple test [Shelton (152)]. In this test franchisee-operators are compensated by the full residual claim (that is, $\alpha = 1$) or $\bar{\pi}^m$ (F.O.) $= 1.00\pi^o$ in Eq. (6) and the company managers (C.M.) are paid a salary plus a bonus averaging 15 percent of the residual claim (that is, $\alpha = .15$) or $\bar{\pi}^m$ (C.M.) $= 0.15 \pi^o + S$ (salary). Furthermore, there is no known a priori reason to believe there would be a difference in sales under the two operations, especially since "the management of the franchising company believes, in fact, that its operations are so thoroughly supervised and organized that a franchisee is selected only from people who have not had experience in the restaurant industry" [*ibid.*], p. 1254. Omitting the observations from one company because they included a Fourth of July weekend and using only paired observations (choosing equal numbers of franchisee-owners and company managers), one finds no significant difference between the means of the sales figures [$F(1,43) = 0.74$]. In addition, there is no significant difference between the variance of sales for franchisee-owner and company manager. However, because the company manager has a lesser ability to appropriate the net income of the operations, the model predicts that there would be greater variability of input selection with the salary-bonus system. The ratio of profits to sales can serve as an indicator of input selection since differences in reported profits (sales minus costs) imply different combinations of inputs (the cost of an output measured by the quantity of inputs times their respective prices, which are assumed to be constant). Since the ratio of profits (sales minus costs) to sales has greater variance under the salary-bonus compensation system, the variability of inputs used must be greater under this system. Variance of profit/sales for the franchisee-owner is 54.6 and for the company manager it is 98.6 ($n = 22$ for both systems), a difference that is significant at the 10 percent level.

When the nonproprietary constraint is binding, input use will also generally differ between proprietary and nonproprietary enterprises. From Eqs. (9) and (12) the optimum use of any resource in the nonprofit organization is given by:

$$\frac{d\pi^0 (n)}{dx_i} = (1 - \lambda) \frac{d\pi^0}{dx_i} - \lambda \ (\bar{P}_1 - P_1)\frac{\partial Q_1}{\partial x_i} = 0 \qquad (13)$$

for all i. When $\bar{P}_1 - P_1$ is negative (trustees of the organization specify lower prices for customer outputs), the second term in Eq. (13) implies increased use of the resource x_i. Furthermore, the manager has an increased incentive to choose combinations of resources that provide relatively more of those Q_1 outputs which provide utility.

More importantly, when the trustee-specified prices and outputs in the constraints $[\bar{P}_1Q_1 + \bar{P}_2Q_2 - RX$ and $G^r(\bar{Q}_1, \bar{Q}_2)]$ in Eq. (8) are equal to those of the unconstrained wealth-maximizing firm (and they are binding), the solution to Eq. (8) is not unique. This implies that proprietary and nonproprietary organizations which produce "identical" outputs will not necessarily choose the same combination of resources. In particular, there will be greater variability of resource use in nonproprietary organizations when compared to their proprietary counterparts.[21] This is not surprising, given the attenuated appropriability of both costs and rewards (from organizational activities) within nonproprietary enterprises. First, interdependencies among operations make the determination of the overall use and coordination of resources a difficult task in any organization. Second, positive information and other transaction costs imply that all marginal conditions will not be satisfied, even in wealth-maximizing institutions.[22] Third, the lack of a single, all-encompassing, overriding equivalent to the wealth-maximization constraint found in proprietary enterprises implies that the determination and enforcement of rules, regulations, and procedures governing the overall use of resources to produce efficient outcomes will be more costly in nonprofit institutions. Finally, the inability and lack of incentives of the governing authorities of nonprofit firms to reward managers for reducing future costs also increase the probability of deviations from the lowest cost combination of resources for producing any output. Consequently, the effective organizational constraints of nonproprietary firms generally will be less correlated with the true opportunity costs of using resources than those in for-profit enterprises [McKean and Minasian (116)]. The precise magnitude and direction of deviations from the least-cost combination of resources, however, usually will be indeterminate without more detailed information or assumptions about any particular enterprise.[23]

The variability of input use may lead one to conclude that the total cost of producing similar outputs will be higher in nonproprietary institutions than their proprietary counterparts [Frech (67) and Bays (20)]. Total costs will not necessarily rise, however, unless the outputs are identical and the factor prices are equal for both proprietary and nonproprietary organizations. For example, Lindsay has hypothesized that if the output characteristics contain a substantial amount of "invisible" attributes (that cannot be effectively monitored), the average cost of a government enterprise output will generally be less than the average cost of a proprietary enterprise producing for the same market. This implication, of course, ignores the greater availability of input use for producing the visible attribute [Lindsay (102), p. 1068]. Equally important, resource owners may offer labor services to nonproprietary organizations at considerably lower prices than to proprietary organizations for the same work [Clarkson (44)]. Thus, higher cost implications from greater variability of input use in nonproprietary organizations require an additional assumption that the wage rates do not significantly differ between these enterprises or that labor costs are a small proportion of total costs.

The simultaneous existence of invisible output attributes, higher monitoring costs, and managerial compensation schemes that are less correlated with changes in organizational wealth also implies there will be different constraints on decision-makers' use of inputs. In order to reduce consumption of certain employee-purchased outputs by decision-makers, trustees or other governing authorities of nonproprietary organizations will impose stricter rules and procedures on managers for some decisions than those usually found in proprietary enterprises. Thus, managers may be required to pay all employees with the same characteristics, such as degrees held and years of experience, an identical salary (single salary schedule) regardless of expected productivity. In other cases, a specific price different from the competitive price may be placed on a particular resource, x_i, resulting in the inefficient use of that resource.[24]

V. THE USE OF "MAXIMANDS" VERSUS CONSTRAINTS

In the analysis developed in this paper, behavioral implications concerning producer behavior are derived by identifying alternative constraints on producer choices rather than by specifying alternative managerial "maximands" (which are often associated with different preference functions).[25] For example, instead of specifying a quantity-quality maximand for administrators of nonproprietary hospitals [Newhouse (124)], the analysis would focus upon differences in the constraints facing utility-maximizing administrators of nonproprietary organizations. Of course, merely specifying constraints without linking them to some institutional or resource-rights arrangement will not also generally improve understanding of managerial behavior.[26] In one study, for example, a constrained optimization model for a nonprofit agency was proposed [Carlsson, Robinson, and Ryan (32)]. In this model an objective function (level of service) and associated constraints (budgetary appropriation and job position requirements) were assumed. Although the comparative static properties of this model produce some interesting results when the constraints are binding, they fail to indicate the conditions under which a nonprofit agency will have such constraints. Without such identification, the model's usefulness for understanding behavior is severely weakened.

Sometimes the necessary institutional arrangements and associated constraints are presented implicitly requiring little modification of an author's model for deriving differences in behavior. In Becker's (21) discrimination model, for example, individuals are assumed to have "tastes for discrimination." The relative amounts of discrimination occurring in competitive versus monopolistic industries, union versus nonunion markets, and government versus nongovernment agencies are then determined by different theories of individual behavior. Becker derives a lower cost of engaging in discrimination in "nontransferable" monopolies than in competitive industries by considering a random sampling procedure from a continuous distribution of potential employers with identical productive opportunities; on the other hand, he derives differences in discrimination between union and government organization by postulating a majority voting model. Neither explanation of the effective constraints, however, is explicitly derived from the resource right characteristics of monopolies, unions, or governmental agencies. An alternative approach would be to identify the distinguishing effective constraints and then to derive the implied cost of each option facing individuals in these organizations, in order to determine the resulting differences in behavior. Each of these organizations might be classified according to its organizational form. Hence the derivation of the resulting effective sets in monopolies, unions, and governmental agencies may yield different costs between discrimination and certain other activities from those found in competitive, nonunion, and nongovernmental enterprises. This approach has the advantage of showing more clearly the fundamental determinants of the trade-offs and of behavior. More importantly, it embodies a more rigorous and systematic application of economic theory.

VI. CONCLUSION

In this paper a generalized theory of producer behavior for profit-seeking and nonproprietary enterprises was developed by integrating the theorems of utility maximization with the effects that alternative rights to the use of resources have on managerial constraints. In addition to those differences in outcomes created by the use of nonidentical resources, by differences in employee or managerial preferences, and by positive information costs, the theory predicts that both outputs and input use (for the same output) will be altered by changes in the rights to appropriate rewards (and costs) from the enterprise's activities. The effective managerial prices of both customer and employee (fringe benefits) outputs are derived for different changes in resource rights. The theory also predicts that when an output contributes to managerial utility *and* can be jointly consumed and/or involves high monitoring costs, differences in outputs between proprietary and nonproprietary organizations will result. When such conditions do not exist, precise information about the nature of the change in resource rights and the costs of monitoring managerial behavior are required to identify differences in outcomes. In addition, the size and direction of both the wealth and the substitution effects attributable to changes in decision-maker constraints from alterations in the proprietary status are generally not predictable without knowledge of output attributes, monitoring costs, and organizational form.

Theorems about producer behavior, however, can be greatly expanded without precise knowledge of individual preferences, production functions, and monitoring costs as long as changes in the effective managerial price of customer and employee outputs are identifiable. Furthermore, because this approach concentrates on the modification of the costs and rewards facing decision-makers, implications of the model will hold even when managers are unaware of or do not seek the new options [Becker (23)].

More importantly, this model shows that enterprises with weakened appropriability to the net returns of the organization will exhibit more variability of input selection in producing the same output than their proprietary counterparts. This resource rights or ownership inefficiency may be a significant factor in explaining differences in costs and overall performance among enterprises producing similar products. If so, perhaps the appropriate measure of "X-inefficiency" is some measure of the change in resource or property rights [Leibenstein (96, 97)]. The paper also suggests that efforts devoted to identifying the relationship between resource rights and institutional constraints (assuming similar managerial utility functions) will increase understanding of producer behavior more than specifying alternative organizational "maximands" (and testing for different tastes). Finally, the utility-maximization approach to the theory of producer behavior adds to our understanding of why different institutions are chosen.

FOOTNOTES

The author is professor of economics, Law and Economics Center.

Louis De Alessi, Donald L. Martin, Roland N. McKean, Roger Sherman, Earl Thompson, and members of the Law and Economics Center Workshop provided several helpful comments and suggestions on an earlier draft of this paper.

1. By varying the absolute and relative mix of market and nonmarket income, Becker (24) has derived several revealing implications about the behavior of individuals supplying labor services. See also De Vany (58).

2. See Machlup (105) for a menu of alternative managerial hypotheses based on differing managerial tastes.

3. See Furubotn and Pejovich (70) for many of the studies that link organizational constraints to managerial incentives.

4. The pecuniary payment to the input owners is the opportunity cost of the resources less the value of the outputs "sold" to employees or other resource owners.

5. These relationships will not be made explicit in order to keep the formation of the model and associated implications as simple as possible.

6. The wealth function is assumed to be single-valued, concave, and twice-differentiable with respect to X.

7. Unless otherwise stated, $\partial P_1/\partial Q_1 = 0$ and $\partial P_2/\partial Q_2 = 0$. Earl Thompson made a number of very useful comments in this section.

8. The major reason that managerial preferences deserve special recognition is that the decision-maker often has the residual authority (after satisfying certain constraints) to choose outputs and the particular combination of resources used to produce them. One should also recognize that this specification is far from complete: (a) each class of output consists of a vector of outputs that offer different packages of utility-producing characteristics, and (b) outputs may be offered in inseparable combinations. Thus the firm's production of commodities (goods or services) often contains two or more bundled or tie-in consumer outputs (e.g., the physical good and the service) or combinations of customer and employee outputs (e.g., congenial service staff).

9. This assumption is equivalent to the classical owner-managed wealth-maximization model. Much of the discussion here is drawn from Clarkson (41, 42).

10. U^m is assumed to be a single-valued, convex, twice-differentiable utility function and the consumption of commodities by the manager is assumed to have no effect on prices, that is, $\partial P_1/\partial Q_1^m = 0$, $\partial P_2/\partial Q_2^m = 0$, and $\partial P_3/\partial Q_3^m = 0$.

11. $\partial Q_2/\partial x_i$ would be a negative quantity if the resource owner were a troublemaker.

12. A more thorough discussion of the differences in inputs (for the "same" output) as a consequence of nonidentical or differently priced resources can be found in Stigler (160).

13. See Lester (98) for a more complete discussion of differences in nonmoney benefits taken by employees.

14. Earlier analyses of utility maximization by managers under profit-seeking conditions were generally limited to the trade-offs between money income and leisure. See Scitovsky (148) and Piron (135).

15. For a discussion of information and transactions costs in explaining individual behavior, see Stigler (161) and Alchian and Allen (8).

16. An employee who receives Saturday and Sunday as days off is purchasing days off for a lower effective price (if money wages are identical) than the employee who receives Tuesday and Thursday as days off (if Saturday and Sunday are generally preferred to Tuesday and Thursday as days off).

17. See Jensen and Meckling (83) for a discussion of some of the more important reasons for variations in ownership structure.

18. This case was chosen for illustrative purposes only. Similar implications can be derived by altering $\bar{P}_2$ or specifying $G^r\,(\bar{Q}_1,\,\bar{Q}_2)$.

19. In price theory, for example, the theorem concerning welfare losses from monopoly must implicitly assume that the monopolist does not engage in perfect price discrimination.

20. When the producer faces price-taking conditions in all output and factor markets, Eq. (12) simplifies to:

$$P_1\,\frac{\partial Q_1}{\partial x_i} = R\,\frac{\partial X}{\partial x_i} - P_2\,\frac{\partial Q_2}{\partial x_i} \qquad \text{for all i.}$$

21. See Clarkson (41, 42), Frech (67), and Moore (120) for empirical studies (and confirmations) of the variability hypothesis in nonproprietary enterprises.

22. See Whinston (185) for a complete description of the firm as a decentralized decision-maker and the problem of externalities among separate operations of the firm.

23. If one assumed that *all* governing authorities chose the same subset of activities to monitor, variability of resource use for those activities may actually fall. It is unlikely, however, that the same activities would be chosen.

24. This can be shown as:

$$\Pi_\theta^0\,(n) = P_1 Q_1 + P_2 Q_2 - RX - \lambda(P_1 Q_1 + P_2 Q_2 - RX - R_i^\theta X),$$

where R_i^θ = resource prices when trustees establish the price, r_i^θ, for resource x_i.

With such constraints (and $\partial R/\partial X = 0$), resources are used so that:

$$\frac{dx_j\,(n)}{dx_i\,(n)} = \frac{r_i}{r_j} - \frac{\lambda}{(1-\lambda)}\,\frac{(r_i^\theta - r_i)}{r_j},$$

and the change in organizational wealth from increased outputs becomes:

$$\frac{d\Pi_\theta^0\,(n)}{dq_i} = (1 - \lambda)\,\frac{d\Pi^0}{dq_i} + \lambda\,(R_i^\theta - R)\,\frac{\partial X}{\partial q_i}.$$

From $dx_j(n)/dx_i(n)$, the effective organization price of customer and employee-purchased outputs that use x_i falls (rises) when r_i^θ is greater (less) than r_i (the competitive resource price). Consequently, this form of constraint will either encourage (or discourage) expansion of organizational outputs that use x_i. When r_i equals the allowable rate of return on capital, the above yields the familiar and well-documented regulatory constraint. See Averch and Johnson (18) and Bailey (19) for a complete discussion of this constraint.

25. This approach was suggested by Simon (154).

26. The study of the behavioral implications of alternative institutional constraints is not new. One can, for example, view Adam Smith's *The Wealth of Nations* as an investigation of the effects of various sets of effective constraints on institutions, ranging from apprentice-ship programs to the provision of services by public agencies. In most cases, Smith (156) investigated the effective constraints (or sets of options) facing individuals and derived the resulting behavior from these institutional structures [Rosenberg (140)]. There is, however, an important distinction between deriving implications about individual behavior from differences in institutional arrangements and deriving them from differences in incentive systems. The former approach, which was used by Smith, predicts the particular kind or set of options to be expected with each institutional arrangement. Behavioral implications are then derived from the identified trade-offs facing the individual. On the other hand, studies of alternative incentive systems, which were used more often by Smith's followers, do *not* make a priori predictions of the type of effective constraints to be expected in the institution—they start out by assuming particular incentives. For example, they might investigate the behavioral effects of compensating workers on an hourly or piece-rate basis, without indicating what forms of organizations would yield these compensation systems.

ROSE BOWL VS. HONG KONG:

THE ECONOMICS OF SEAT PRICING

Steven N.S. Cheung, UNIVERSITY OF WASHINGTON

It is often observed that in various entertainments better seats tend to be underpriced. I do not refer here to the trivial case where a uniform price is charged on all seats so that the better seats are allocated on a first-come basis. Grading and separately pricing seats is costly. Rather, I refer to the case where seats are graded and price separately, with numbers on tickets to match the seats chosen by customers and the customers often ushered to the seats assigned. Here, the underpricing of better seats is puzzling because separate pricing, once adopted, would entail no higher cost if the better seats were priced even higher. Underpricing better seats, in the sense that more expensive tickets tend to sell out faster or more frequently than cheaper tickets, often generates the impression that the show owner is forgoing easy money. Indeed, the pattern and regularity under which this "underpricing" takes place

Economics of Nonproprietary Organizations
Research in Law and Economics, Supplement 1, pages 27-49
Copyright © 1980 by JAI Press Inc.
All rights of reproduction in any form reserved.
ISBN: 0-89232-132-6

rejects explanations couched in terms of price elasticity or incorrect anticipation of demand.

In this paper, I examine two hypotheses based on constraints of a nonprofit organization that have been advanced by others to explain why better seats tend to be underpriced. Next, I propose a third hypothesis based on profit or wealth maximization, testing it in the third section with observations obtained from Hong Kong movie theaters— organizations about as profit-oriented as one could find.

In the concluding section, alternative hypotheses are evaluated and the "profit" hypothesis is generalized. This generalization is important: in a world complicated by transaction costs, behavior other than pricing may be used to restrain the behavior of competitors so that these costs are reduced; one effective way to induce the functional nonprice behavior is to cut price.

I. TWO NONPROFIT HYPOTHESES EXAMINED

The first hypothesis is advanced by Alchian and Allen (8) in their reference to the Rose Bowl football game, in which they argue that the (separately priced) tickets are *generally* underpriced. The reason offered is that in maximizing utility, members of the Rose Festival Association tend to set prices so low "that more seats are demanded than are available." The price decider is presumed to have several options for gain: he may (unethically) resell tickets, he may buy "tickets for himself more cheaply," or, most important of all:

> The excess demand for tickets enables him to grant favors to certain selected applicants for tickets. . . . Favorable treatment for certain people will enhance his utility. His prestige is increased: he is invited to the best places, clubs, and circles; and even when he buys a car or furniture, past favors are fondly and effectively recalled. (pp. 162–163)

The underpricing of tickets in general is not, of course, unique with the Rose Bowl game, and different situations may call for different explanations. The Shilshole Bay Marina in Seattle, a city-operated "nonprofit" organization, has a seven-year queue for a boat slip. Here, favoritism is not evident and the reason for the underpricing seems to be that while the resident tenants' protest against a substantial rise in rates carries weight in the use of a nonprivate property, discriminatory pricing against new applicants is unconstitutional and the slips are nontransferable. Whatever the explanation, underpricing behavior associated with nonexclusive property rights is relatively easy to understand: underpricing is a way of sharing income among a delineated group of nonexclusive claimants.

To explain the observed underpricing of all tickets for some pop concerts, such as those given by the Beatles or the Rolling Stones, is less easy. The fact that excess demand routinely occurred precludes inaccuracy of prediction as the cause. Perhaps the sponsors relish the publicity of overnight camp-outs as customers wait for the ticket windows to open. Or, since wild cheers seem essential to pop concerts, perhaps louder screams can be expected from those who choose to sleep out than would come from those willing to pay higher prices for tickets.

However, the point at issue here is not why, in some cases, seats in general are underpriced. Rather, our main concern is why better seats tend to be underpriced relative to inferior ones. This type of underpricing may be measured in any one of several ways: the higher frequency with which better seats are sold out; the predictability, in specified situations, that the better seats will sell out first; or, in the event of a full house and reselling of tickets, the fact that better seats will then go at a higher price ratio relative to inferior seats than prevailed during the original ticket sale.

Returning to the Rose Bowl game, Alchian and Allen extend their argument to the underpricing of better seats in particular:

> Let's strain the analysis a bit further. If there are several kinds of seats, which seats will be underpriced? Primarily the kind that the manager and association members would want. These are the best seats. Market-clearing prices will more likely be charged for the inferior seats that go to people who are neither students nor alumni. (p. 163)

Implicit here is that the manager and the association members may want the best seats for themselves, or that in the event of "unethical" resale the better seats will entail lower transaction costs for the same gain, or that favors are usually granted to those who would have purchased the best seats (presumably the influential or the well-to-do).

Another interesting hypothesis for the same phenomenon was put forward to me verbally by Professor Levis A. Kochin. Kochin noted that better seats also tend to be underpriced in operatic productions. Here, the nonprofit organizations allocate the better seats to customers in accordance to their donations, which are tax deductible. When part of the ticket price is converted into donation, all parties thus gain at the expense of the government or other taxpayers. Since donors are usually rich and would want better seats, these are therefore underpriced. Tax evasion is thus one profit motive for forming a nonprofit organization.

I do not know the magnitude of such arrangements in the production of operas, but my own experience in obtaining tickets to concerts in Chicago suggests the same pattern: that better seats are underpriced and that donation is often required to obtain the best ones. A donor friend in Chicago informs me that the same (or very nearly the same) best seats are often allocated to people who have donated significantly different amounts. This opens the possibility that donation may be an effective way of separating customers for price discrimination. It would appear that this technique is comparable to the case of education, where tuition is overpriced but where scholarships are granted in varying amounts. Of course, in the underpricing of better seats, both price discrimination and tax evasion may enhance the seller's advantage; thus Kochin's argument is not rejected.

My main quarrel with Alchian and Allen, and with Kochin, however, does not lie in the logic of their arguments. Rather, the chief weakness is that the constraints they prescribe for a nonprofit organization are so unclear that the hypotheses yield no refutable implications. There is not enough information to determine the price structure for seats of different quality. In Kochin's donation hypothesis, one wonders why the price of seats to donors is not reduced to zero. Donors to charity shows in Asia are often made honorary members of the sponsoring organization and permitted to attend free of charge. On the other hand, for other "charity" or church activities exorbitant prices are printed on the tickets (which may then be useful as evidence for tax deduction).

The hypothesis of Alchian and Allen fares no better in this respect. If tickets are used to buy favors, then the favors would seem to be more clearly transacted if the tickets were given away freely. And if it could be arranged that prices printed on tickets differed from those paid by the "inside" members, then either unethical reselling or favor transacting would seem to suggest that the printed prices for better seats would be overstated. When I was a tutor for student athletes at UCLA, I was impressed by their easy access to Rose Bowl tickets: each athlete seemed to have been allotted some predetermined (but varying) number at a zero price.

I am not suggesting here that Alchian and Allen, as well as Kochin, may not be correct: certainly, under some constraints their arguments would hold. But it is not clear what specific constraints they suggest will have to be altered so that the better seats will no longer be underpriced. One might be tempted to infer from their reasoning that if the Rose Bowl game were played for private profit, or if donations were not tax deductible, then better seats would not be underpriced. In such a case their hypotheses would be refuted, since the underpricing of better seats is definitely not unique with nonprofit organizations. But, as we shall see in the concluding section, this test is no test at all.

II. A PROFIT HYPOTHESIS FOR THE UNDERPRICING OF BETTER SEATS

When I visited Hong Kong in 1975 I wanted to watch an important soccer game. I called an influential friend several hours before the game for some tickets. He called back an hour later, apologizing that he could not obtain good seats on such short notice and that for important games he should be informed two days in advance. Knowing what this friend could do, I had no doubt of the prevalence and effectiveness of the underpricing.

In a place like Hong Kong, regardless of the guise under which an organization is coined, "nonprofit" is the last thing to come to mind. The question then arose: Under what circumstances would the underpricing of better seats be consistent with constrained wealth maximization? Seeking an answer, I asked myself the simple question of what would happen if the price of better seats were allowed to rise. Some of the better seats then would not be sold. But would these unsold seats remain unoccupied? Quite unlikely, since after the game started some spectators holding tickets to poorer seats would simply walk over to occupy the unsold better seats. This violation of rights, of course, would not occur if the better seats were fully occupied. In effect, ticket holders would be utilized to protect their rights against others. This might indeed be the least costly way to enforce the rights to seats, and should this saving exceed the loss in income resulting from a cut in price to induce a sellout of better seats, the underpricing becomes a result of constrained wealth maximization.

Let us formulate the above hypothesis more carefully. Suppose a movie theater has a fixed number of seats and that standing is not allowed. If the theater charges a uniform price for all seats, how is this price determined? And will all seats be necessarily sold?

One may be inclined to think that in the absence of a full house, the marginal cost of serving an extra customer is nearly zero; then the uniform wealth-maximizing price is simply that of unitary elasticity. One may further think that if attendance is properly anticipated, perfect price discrimination will ensure a full house. This line of analysis is incorrect. The "elasticity" argument is based on uniform seating and does not apply that simply to seats of varying qualities. Furthermore, when many theaters show the same movie simultaneously, an approximate price-takers' market prevails.

Seats may be vacant even if attendance is correctly anticipated, although incorrect anticipation may itself result in pricing which leads to vacancy or excessive demand. Neither "perfect" competition nor perfect price discrimination will ensure a full house. The reason is that at a zero ticket price there may not be enough customers to fill the theater. As Professor Gary Becker (24) was prompt to remind us, a viewer's time is an important part of the total cost of seeing the show—for some movies this alone may be too high for too many. Since demand fluctuates among performances, one condition essential for attaining a full house each time would be the capability to vary the total number of seats. In general, this would be prohibitively costly. Given the variability of shows over time, survival in competition does not require that the house always be full.

Assume that in the absence of a full house the marginal cost of serving a customer is zero. Wealth maximization implies that if a uniform ticket price is charged it will be one which maximizes total gate receipts. The determination of this price is complicated by the fact that the early customers will occupy the best seats they can find, and late customers will face the choice of only inferior and less valuable seats. Thus, the higher the uniform price (hence fewer customers and more available choice seats), the more valuable is the ticket to a customer; the converse also holds. In other words, if we are to plot a "demand" schedule for all seats of varying qualities subject to the payment of a uniform price, this schedule will have a steeper slope than one where all seats are identical. Even in a price-takers' market, the "demand" schedule for all seats of varying quality facing a single theater will have a negative slope. In determining the uniform price, the theater owner therefore must take into account the effect of occupation of better seats upon other viewers' willingness to pay. Thus the price which maximizes the rectangular area under our special "demand" schedule bears a unitary elasticity which requires a different interpretation than its standard usage.

Other things equal, the income of the theater will increase if seats are graded and priced separately by quality. This increase in income is generated by two factors. First, in the absence of a full house, the appropriate grading and separate pricing of seats will increase attendance; customers who would decline to pay the uniform price for inferior seats will now pay the lower price. Second, whether or not a full house is attained, much of the queuing for better seats under the uniform-price arrangement will now be eliminated, and this saving in waiting cost will be shared by both the theater and the customers. But the separate grading and pricing of seats is a costly process. The seats themselves must be numbered; tickets must be printed specifically to match available seats; purchasers will tend to pause at the ticket windows in making their selection; and ushers with flashlights will be needed, to avoid confusion in seating. These nontrivial costs must account for the policy of uniform pricing adopted in most theaters in the United States.

In the strictest sense, no two seats in any theater are exactly alike. Thus in the absence of transaction costs every seat would be graded and the prices finely differentiated. In practice, however, the costs of transacting dictate that seats will be separated only into a few broad sections. Otherwise, the would-be purchaser faces a prohibitively time-consuming choice within the enormous range of price-seat options. Imagine a theater of 1,200 seats, where each customer is buying only one ticket. If he averages a mere fifteen seconds in deciding within the complex matrix of options, if only two seconds are needed for marking the ticket and eight seconds for making change, still ten ticket windows will be required if all the tickets for a performance are to be sold in fifty minutes. Granted that many customers may buy more than one ticket, this saving may be more than offset by the increase in time for decision-making and the adding of several different prices, and by the fact that some customers would walk away when realizing that none of the remaining choices conforms to their preferences.

It is far simpler to divide seats into several broad sections, with a different uniform price for each section, separate section windows, and a sign to indicate when a particular section is sold out. How then are the number of seats in different sections and the respective uniform prices to be determined? Suppose good and poor seats in a theater are divided into only two sections, and assume for the moment that customers willingly stay in their assigned seats. Consider first a monopolistic case. In the absence of a full house both sections may have vacant seats. Here the division of seats needs no alteration; the uniform price for each section is jointly adjusted to maximize total receipt. Note that if the price of the better seat is raised, the demand for the poorer seat increases; conversely, a price reduction which draws customers into the more desirable section will lead to a decline in demand for the inferior seats.

The maximization of total receipts requires that the marginal receipt from each section be equal. (Under the assumption of zero marginal cost of serving an extra customer in the absence of a full house, this marginal receipt will be zero.) It is, of course, possible that, given the seat division and prices, one section may be full while the other has vacant seats, or that one section has been filled as a result of price adjustments. In this case, the maximization of total receipts requires that the full section be expanded, with its price adjusted upward or downward, to regain the equimarginal condition. And to the extent that the theater is not full, the receipt-maximizing price structure also implies that any further extension of the better-seat section will leave seats vacant in that area. In the event that a full house is expected (that is, all seats are filled), all prices will be adjusted upward until the first vacant seat is expected with any further price rise in each section. The maximization of total receipts here must also meet the condition that further reclassification of an extra seat will result in either its being sold at a lower price or its remaining vacant.

In a price-takers' market the above reasoning is altered in two aspects. First, if all theaters are unexpectedly full, then each may adjust its prices subject to the cost of making these adjustments. That is, a theater with a lower cost of making adjustments than others may do so as if it were a monopolist. Second, if the competing theaters are not full, then price structure and the classification of seats are restrained in each theater not only by the costs of making adjustments but also by competition. We separate these two constraints because of an inherent implication: if seats in different theaters are not identical, then some sections of seats in some theaters may predictably be full, yet no adjustment will be made regardless of the costs of such adjustment (transaction). This is because the raising of prices for the full section is restrained by the availability of similar vacant seats in competing theaters.

Whether under monopoly or competition, the determination of prices and of seat divisions becomes quite a different matter if the costs are significant in restricting customers to their purchased seats. Some who are entitled only to cheaper seats will try to move into better ones. In this case, given the price structure and seat division described earlier, the pattern of purchase tends to increase the number of unsold tickets for better seats, although after the show starts the unsold seats may not remain empty. In the absence of a full house, and if there is wide divergence in the quality of seats, this problem may become so severe as to produce a situation where charging an overall uniform price yields a greater income.

The theater may enforce seat rights in a number of ways, each entailing a different cost. Ushers may be instructed to check the tickets of seated customers, making occasional corrections and embarrassing those who have cheated. Yet this process is a nuisance to the honest customers which may reduce their willingness to pay. For this reason such checking is rarely practiced, or applies only to obvious suspects. A second method is to erect barriers, making it difficult for customers to move from one section to another. But such construction is often costly and may interfere with the view of the stage; still more important, it generally freezes the division of seats, preventing temporary reclassification which may be desirable. As we shall see, in cases where such compartmentalization has been resorted to, we find a clear test of implication.

Our hypothesis here rests on the premise that in general the least costly method of enforcing seat rights is to make sure that the better seats are fully, or almost fully, sold so that the mere presence of seated customers wards off prospective violators. This goal can be achieved by reducing the price of the better seats, by reducing their section size, or in general by a combination of both. In any case, the better seats will thus have a greater tendency to be sold out, generating the impression that they are underpriced.

How are price structures and seat division determined under this arrangement? The case is not interesting if the theater is expected to be full and customers are turned away, since any adjustment in price would necessarily be upward. Assume, then, some unsold tickets are expected in both sections (although the theater may unexpectedly become full and no sudden change in prices can be made). Suppose that under the earlier pricing scheme, abstracting from the cost of enforcing seat rights, of 600 classified better seats only 550 will be sold and occupied. Now given the enforcement problem, let us suppose the theater seeks to make adjustments to ensure that the better-seat section will be fully sold. Consider first only the reclassification of seats. Suppose the initial 600 better seats are now reduced by reclassification to 550. With the seat-enforcement problem introduced, however, these 550 seats will not be fully sold. Two factors account for this result. One is that with 50 of the previously good seats now reclassified, some customers will shift their purchase to the cheaper tickets. Second, given the enforcement problem, others are now buying inferior seats in the expectation of moving to better ones. Therefore, reclassification of 50 seats will not alone suffice to attain a sellout in the better section. Indeed, it is possible to construct a situation where the number of the previously classified better seats has been reduced to zero to ensure no unsold tickets in this section. In this extreme case, the loss of total gate receipts is the difference between the total of the earlier separate pricing (which sold 550 of the 600 classified better seats) and the total of uniform pricing for all seats (note that the uniform price will be higher than the earlier price for poorer seats). This loss in total gate receipts may be partly, fully, or even more than fully, compensated by the saving in the costs of grading and pricing seats separately.

But suppose that, to enforce seat rights through reclassification alone, a reduction of the better seats to 400 will yield a sellout of this section. The total receipts from the better seats will now be reduced by 150 seats (recall that 550 good seats were sold in the absence of the seat-enforcement problem). If the uniform price of the inferior seats remains unchanged, of the 200 better seats now reclassified as "inferior," 150 will be sold even if the uniform price of the inferior seats rises as a result of the improvement in overall quality of the block (it will necessarily remain lower than the uniform price of the better seats). So far, the increase in receipts from the inferior seats cannot offset the decrease in rceipts from the better seats; total receipts decline. Of the remaining 50 seats reclassified as "inferior," some or all may be sold at the lower price. But other than the definite sale of the 150 reclassified seats, sales in the poorer section will not exceed the original number; hence vacancy in that area must increase. The reason is that should the reclassification of the 50 vacant seats from superior to inferior lead to an increase in receipts, they would have been so classified without the seat-enforcement problem. Therefore, the total receipts from reclassification due to the enforcement problem must decline.

The decline in income resulting from the reclassification may, of course, be mitigated by a simultaneous reduction in price for the better seats. Following the above numerical example, any reduction in price will result in the sale of more than 400 better seats. But will the price of better seats be cut to such an extent that their sale will exceed 600 and an upward adjustment to more good seats be indicated? The answer is, No. The price will not be cut even to the point where sales of more than 550 good seats would be encouraged. The reason is that when that many good seats have been sold as a result of the price cut, total receipts would actually be increased by a reduction in the number of those seats. Additional simplifying assumptions will help clarify this difficult point.

Recall that because of the enforcement problem, out of the original 600 better seats fewer than 550 would be sold. Suppose that if the uniform price of the better seats is reduced 15 percent, 550 will now be sold. To simplify, assume that both the price of the inferior seats and the total number attending the show remain unchanged. With the 15 percent price cut, a reclassification of 50 better seats will fill the better-seat section with all honest customers; in the inferior section vacancy will increase by 50 seats. The seat enforcement problem has been solved at the cost of a reduction in total receipts for the theater equaling the 15 percent decline in revenue in the sale of better seats. This adjustment in price alone may result in a larger or smaller loss in total receipts than would the reclassification of seats alone, depending on the responsiveness of purchasers to the cut in price.

Suppose now that with 550 better seats sold, reducing the price a trifle more will result in one more better seat sold, whereas raising the price a trifle will sell one seat less. Since by our simplifying assumption that one more better seat sold will produce one more vacant seat in the inferior section, the additional price cut yields (1) a loss in revenue equaling the trifling price cut for each of the 550 seats and (2) a gain of the difference in price between a better and an inferior seat. The total receipts for the theater, however, necessarily fall; that is, (1) is necessarily greater than (2), otherwise the adjustment would have already been made under the original pricing arrangement without the seat-enforcement problem.

This additional net loss stemming from the further price cut would be larger, other things equal, the larger would have been the original reduction necessary to attain the sale of 550 better seats (i.e., the 15 percent in our illustration). Consider now the converse. A small raise in price will yield (1) a gain of the small increase in price for each of 549 seats and (2) a loss of the difference in price between a better and an inferior seat for the one converted into the inferior section. Here, (1) in general is larger than (2), since with the 15 percent price cut already in effect, a trifling rise in price is moving toward the original price structure. This net gain would be smaller, other things equal, the smaller the price reduction which was necessary to attain the sale of 550 better seats. Barring corner solution, the net gain generally will become negative before the price is raised back to the original level. Thus, to attain a sellout of better seats as a means to enforce seat rights, wealth maximization implies that in general both the price and the number of better seats will be adjusted—in our example the better seats will be reduced to somewhere between 400 and 550 and their uniform price reduced by some amount up to 15 percent.

The above solution follows a fundamental economic principle: if there are multiple margins of adjustment to attain a given end, ignoring the cost of making the adjustments and barring corner solution, wealth maximization implies that all margins will be adjusted. The total income of the theater will, of course, be less than when seat enforcement does not present a problem, but, given the problem, it will be higher with the adjustments than without. If occupancy is left unchecked, a uniform price for all seats may result. Though this leads to a further decline in receipts, the arrangement saves the costs of adjustments and of grading and of separately pricing seats. But grading or separate pricing will be retained if these costs do not outweigh the decline in receipts. The apparent underpricing of better seats is, therefore, the result of constrained wealth maximization.

III. TESTS OF IMPLICATIONS

Before we put some implications to test, an apology is in order. For a number of reasons I had selected movie theaters in Hong Kong for empirical investigation, and as a chief source of data I sought the seating charts used by each theater there. On these charts, which become waste paper after the show, each seat is crossed off as sold. Friends were asked to make contacts with the theater owners to save the charts for me—a bold request which presumably would be granted under gentle persuasion. But a new development diverted me to an investigation of information costs and the same friends were asked, instead, to contact some jade dealers. The theater investigation was thus sidetracked until about two weeks before I left the colony, during which time I made about sixty evening visits to some twenty different theaters, studied the variations of prices, and glanced at seating charts through ticket windows. Since these visits were intended only to satisfy my own curiosity, no notes were taken. I now write from recollection of hasty estimates made over a year ago, and the facts reported below are necessarily casual and undocumented.

There are perhaps more movie theaters per square mile in Hong Kong than in any other city in the world. They may be roughly divided into two groups, as showing first-run or second-run movies. The prices for first-run shows are nearly double the others, timeliness being only one reason. The price differential is also due to the nature of second-run theaters, where one learns to expect blotches on the screen, a rumbling sound track, a malfunctioning air conditioner, or even the theft of one's shoes![1] It is common practice for any movie, particularly a popular one, to be shown simultaneously at several theaters in different districts. A film is usually run four times daily, and some theaters additionally offer a noontime showing of old movies.

All theaters grade their seats and price them separately, the price structure appearing remarkably similar within each of the two groups. In general, the seats are divided into four sections: two downstairs and two upstairs. Downstairs, the back stall is more expensive than the front by almost double. This discrepancy is understandable, since the extremely high rentals of the city dictate that the front seats be very close to the screen. The most desirable seats of all are upstairs in the highest-priced loge and second-best dress circle areas. Each customer decides not only on a particular section but on a specific seat.

Apparently because some theater-goers feel it important to have tickets in hand before they attend the show, tickets are printed and sold in advance. Thus it is difficult for a theater to alter its prices if demand turns out significantly different from predictions. However, the prices determined in advance may vary from one movie to another. An unvarying price schedule is maintained for most movies, except that very much higher prices may be charged for those which are exceptional either in reputation or in length.

Whereas the prices of seats, once in print, are costly to change, it is not so in the classification of seats. Indeed, the relatively convenient reclassification of seats helps to explain the total lack of alteration in prices which have been determined in advance as well as the quantum jump in prices for exceptional movies. There is one seating chart for upstairs and one for downstairs. The preprinted tickets indicate only the section and price, with the seat number written in by hand once the purchaser makes his choice. On the seating chart, the classification of seats is usually delineated by a red pencil line, which the seller may draw anywhere he sees fit. Thus a customer, dissatisfied with the front stall consisting of the front seven rows, may come back the next day and find the same stall consisting of only the front three rows!

In view of these general facts, we now test several implications of the hypothesis put forth in the preceding section.

(1) Although better seats tend to be sold out first, or tend to sell a greater percentage, the pattern should not hold when the turnout is exceptionally poor. Poor overall attendance encourages the purchase of cheaper seats only to occupy the better ones. A study of upstairs and downstairs charts separately shows that the loge and back stall are always filled or nearly filled when the overall attendance is around 80 percent (this appears to be a "normal" attendance). When the overall attendance is in the neighborhood of 50 percent or less, the best-seat section in each floor has the lower percentage of sales. To test the implication further, I visited two theaters offering noon showings of old movies, because of reports that these generally have the poorest attendance. In each case it was found that for noon shows (only) a uniform price prevailed for each floor.

(2) Whereas viewers on each floor can move freely from one section to another, they cannot change from one floor to another, because tickets are checked and torn at separate entrances. Given this physical constraint, our implication is that the pattern of underpricing better seats will not apply as between floors. Our observations reveal that although downstairs seats are cheaper, they tend to sell slightly better than seats upstairs. Except in the event of poor overall attendance, the back-stall area seems to be a consistent winner in sales. Thus, although loge seats tend to be "underpriced" relative to the dress circle, all seats upstairs seem to be somewhat "overpriced" relative to those downstairs.

The latter phenomenon also is apparent in the pricing of airline tickets: the first class usually has a larger percentage of vacancy than coach seats. One plausible explanation is that the availability of empty seats increases the value of the seats occupied nearby and, given that section rights are enforced, the vacancies permit a raise in the price of the seats sold. The same end might be served by wider seats and more open space; but the additional seats serve to meet increased demand at exceptional periods.

(3) One theater was found to have a special design which provides another test: the so-called "upstairs" is merely a platform elevated a few steps within a seating hall with a common entrance. Viewers can con-

veniently move from one area to the other; and here, the ratios of the relative prices of upstairs to downstairs seats are found to be about 20 percent lower than in other theaters.

(4) One might be inclined to think that, according to my hypothesis, the anticipation of full attendance for a hit movie would increase the relative-price ratios of better to poorer seats in each floor. Yet this implication is complicated by a tendency to raise all prices in the same situation. Given that a higher price structure, once set, would remain unchanged throughout the entire run, wealth maximization implies that prices should be raised to the point where vacant seats are anticipated for some shows. Thus better seats again tend to be underpriced. A comparison was made between the standard price ratios (of seats on each floor, not between floors) and the ratios of prices as raised for hit movies. It was found that the latter ratios are only slightly higher (about 2 percent).

However, the implication on seat reclassification is confirmed. In about 15 observations where theaters were experiencing turn-away crowds, it was found that front-stall seats were usually reduced by about one-quarter. An extreme case was observed during the first-run showing of *Towering Inferno*. One theater eliminated the front stall and extended the already increased back-stall price all the way to the front. Thus with a higher cost for changing prices than for adjusting seats, coupled perhaps with unanticipated demands, full attendance may produce a situation where the variance of prices is reduced to zero.

IV. CONCLUDING REMARKS

In this paper we consider three hypotheses intended to explain the phenomenon of the underpricing of better seats. Of these, the third is tested and the evidence fails to reject it. Barring evidence to the contrary, this tested hypothesis must for now be accepted as valid. Can the other two (the hypotheses related to nonprofit situations) be valid, too?

One may be inclined to think that since better seats are also underpriced in profit organizations, the nonprofit hypotheses are falsified. However, to say that a certain arrangement of rights implies a certain outcome and therefore that a change in the arrangement will produce a change in the outcome, is to commit the fallacy of denying the antecedent. It is true that following a change in the arrangement of rights, *some* outcomes will change; but this may not apply to the observation at hand. The same factors causing the observation may be present under different arrangements of rights, or the same observation may be caused by different sets of factors. Thus, in a trivial and restrictive sense, to say either that "property rights matter" or that "property rights do not matter" may each be correct. However, the matter quickly becomes significant when, under the guise of triviality, economists argue the irrelevance of property rights in determining behavior.

The constraints confronting any organization are enormously complex. In fact, the drastic simplification of constraints necessary for the interpretation of behavior often presents an insurmountable challenge. And when we sometimes manage to reduce them to size, it is essential that the specification be sufficiently accurate so that alterations of constraints which imply different outcomes can be specifically made. One interpretation of the view of Alchian and Allen is that members of a nonprofit organization can take cash openly only at certain costs which are not present in profit organizations. This may well be true, and an alteration of these costs may cause the better seats to be not underpriced or even overpriced. But with the nature of these costs being unclear, it is difficult to make any specific alteration for hypothesis testing. One interpretation of Kochin's view is that a nonprofit organization presents a less costly tax refuge than some other arrangements. This, too, may well be true; if so, the ambiguity lies with the costs of different arrangements at the margins. Why should the better seats (or any seats) command a positive price, or why should "nonprofit" be not extended to other types of entertainment? In either case, information is insufficient to determine the price structure and seat classification, hence testable implications are absent. This is not to deny, however, that both these hypotheses may be correct in essentials.

When one departs from the textbook tradition, one discovers numerous observations wanting explanation. Among these is a class of observations which appear inconsistent with wealth maximization and in which legal or regulatory constraints may play important roles. Certainly the Rose Bowl organization is not quite the same as Hong Kong theaters. But behavior apparently inconsistent with wealth or profit maximization has often been observed in what are called "profit" organizations.[2] Here, the problem is more troublesome, for we have now a contradiction in terms.

I do not wish to claim that my seat-enforcement hypothesis provides a key through which the contradiction is fully resolved: namely, that behavior inconsistent with profit maximization is often apparent rather than factual, or that when it comes to making money, businessmen have more imagination than economists. After all, the underpricing of better seats is a trivial phenomenon. But for the class of observations concerned, a hypothesis as clearly refutable as the proposed has been difficult to come by, and we should do well if we could draw generalizations from what started out to be a special case.

In the standard textbook tradition, constrained maximization is confined to adjustments in prices and quantities. Beyond this tradition, the introduction of the costs of making transactions not only necessitates different price-quantity adjustments but brings to light other associated behaviors. While transaction costs determine behavior, they are also determined by behavior. Thus an overall view of the economic system must recognize that the arrangement under which economic activities are carried out is itself a matter of choice, consistent with constrained maximization. In the difficult and important area of analyzing arrangement choices, our seat-enforcement hypothesis contributes a new dimension for consideration: that by means of a reduction in price, customers may be used to restrain the behavior of other customers, and that the loss from the price cut may be more than compensated by the saving it generates in transaction (enforcement) costs.

It is well known that competition tends to reduce the costs of transactions, usually stated in terms of bids or offers made by actual and prospective competitors. But competition is not necessarily confined to prices or quantities. Any other behavior which will reduce the costs of transactions will generally be incorporated in the functioning of the entire system of competition. Thus, where transaction costs must be considered, the determination of prices and quantities cannot be fully understood without investigating the system as a whole.

Restricting ourselves to the use of customers against customers, we may turn to two other factual examples in Hong Kong to further clarify the generality of the argument. The first example is the allocation of tables in restaurants during rush hours. It is typical that in Chinese restaurants (tea houses), customers seeking a table during lunch hours do not wait in line or in a lobby. Rather, even in first-class restaurants, they are allowed to grab the first empty table in sight. Standing rudely beside customers who are lunching, they impose such a nuisance that the restaurant must take this into account in setting lower prices for the menu. However, the enormously high rental of space in the city (sometimes as high as US $6.00 per square foot per month) means that table occupancy is at a premium. It is very costly to meter the time that a customer remains at a table, and letting him use the space until its marginal value of time to him reaches zero may mean only half as many can be served. Thus the method adopted is simply to let standees drive away the diners in a shorter time.

A second example is found in the pricing behavior of the Hong Kong Land Investment Company, the largest and often regarded as the most efficiently managed land developer in the colony. Unlike most other competing developers, Hong Kong Land constructs premises primarily for lease and at rentals acknowledged to be about 10 percent lower than the market. In a monumental court case fought between Tsang Fook

Piano Company and Hong Kong Land,[3] the opposing lawyer questioned the manager of Hong Kong Land as to the truth of the assertion that their rentals were significantly below the market. The manager replied that it was the company's policy to maintain a "healthy queue." We may interpret the purpose of the healthy queue as a restraint on the behavior of resident tenants. Given the enormous number of rental units owned by the company and the higher rental costs of placing managers in live-in quarters, such a competitive check on undesirable behavior may reduce management costs to the point of more than offsetting the cut in rents. Any litigation is costly, and matters such as arrears in rent or damage beyond "ordinary wear and tear" often present no clearly enforceable rule in law. Thus a simple eviction becomes the best alternative, and a substantial queue makes that threat convincing.

Faced with competition, one's behavior often depends on that of his competitors. The determination of price is one response to competition, and an important one indeed. But it is not the only one. All contracting parties may gain, if price can be reduced to encourage restraints on behavior. This paper has shown that "behavior which restrains behavior" may be effectively induced by the simple expedient of a reduction in price.

FOOTNOTES

The author is indebted to Yoram Barzel, Levis Kochin, and Dean Worcester for their helpful comments.

1. Chinese humor requires some clarification. I refer here not to the theft, which is certainly present in any theater, but to the fact that in second-run theaters the customers like to take off their shoes when watching the show.

2. For a critical survey of the literature on the subject, see Alchian (3).

3. Transcript of the hearings of this case is available in the Hong Kong Tenancy Tribunal, under No. H.E. 33/68.

DELIVERED COMMENTS

Ross D. Eckert (University of Southern California).   On the last occasion that I had to discuss a conference paper, I was assigned an exceedingly weak item in which I found a variety of errors. The good guy that I was, I made extensive line by line comments on the paper which the author on that occasion took to heart as I had innocently hoped he would. For my pains, I was rewarded about six months later with a letter from the director of the conference, who was also the editor of its forthcoming conference volume. He told me that the author of that paper had so greatly reworked the item that my comments were no longer valid, and he then inquired if I would be willing to go through the process again. Since I saw no end to the possible number of iterations to this procedure, I politely declined and realized that I had learned a very good lesson. However, that lesson need not be drawn upon today. The high quality of both of these papers does not call for it.

The strength of Clarkson's paper lies in his approach to a generalized theory of producer behavior that includes the treatment of alternative rights to gather the rewards from managerial activity and the implications of these rights for resource allocation under various circumstances. These alternative right structures can yield results that may seem inexplicable or inconsistent or paradoxical with economic theory unless, as Clarkson stresses, all or at least most of the effective and important constraints are known and understood. The freshest point in the paper is that proprietary status alone is generally insufficient to yield an unambiguous implication as to the size and direction of consumption activity in the goods that are purchased within the firm by managers or other employees. Generally, more information is required concerning the nature of the outputs, whether they are joint or exclusive, their full costs, and the form of monitoring adopted. Clarkson's own study on proprietary versus nonproprietary hospitals is a good example of the detailed investigation of constraints that is required before results of research, at least in this area, can be given much confidence. Let me add, as a footnote, my own recent experiences with large nonproprietary hospitals that I think make Clarkson's point well, although I have a very incomplete sample of such organizations' activities. It is not unheard of in hospital billing offices to collect double payments from insurance companies if a patient has more than one insurance policy, and total payments by insurers sometimes exceed 100 percent of billings. One particular hospital that I am familiar with, within the same month, closed its coffee shop and gift shop to *cut* associated losses, but planned to expand certain emergency services which *produced* very large losses. Behavior of this sort is consistent with Clarkson's point: a nonprofit institution may be cost conscious in some areas but may engage in cost-increasing activities in other areas. Clarkson suggests that we inquire as to just which constraints dominate each situation.

Clarkson proposed a variety of arguments or alternative explanations for dilemmas of this kind. He first says that there could be monopoly elements in the purchase of inputs by firms that are competitive in output markets and vice versa. This argument could explain the fact that General Motors, for example, does not sell Chevrolet franchises to dealers, but that Kentucky Fried Chicken does; yet both organizations monitor subsequent exchanges of franchises between dealers. His second argument for explaining the paradox is that taxes affect the exchanges of goods within firms and between firms. This alters the attractiveness of certain transactions relative to others for both proprietary and nonproprietary firms. Third, he suggests that we know very little about the structure of management compensation schemes in firms, and that these schemes could significantly influence behavior. This subject also has received relatively little professional attention, although Clarkson gives citations to two recent studies that sound very interesting. His fourth argument is that there are monitoring costs that could be high enough in some cases to eliminate effective constraints imposed by government regulation of profit. Unless these monitoring costs are recognized, one might assume, naïvely, that evidence should be found in favor of utility-enhancing relative to profit-enhancing activities simply because the firm was subjected to regulation. These constraints, however, may in fact turn out to be so weak, owing to the high costs of monitoring, that very standard wealth-maximizing behavior is observed in spite of the fact that the firm is nominally subjected to regulation. I will not, however, speculate as to which of these possibilities explains the hospital behavior that I alluded to earlier, without first investigating all the detailed constraints as Clarkson proposed.

Steven Cheung's paper is an excellent demonstration of the value of economic analysis generally. But I think that Cheung has not, after all, set aside the Alchian and Allen hypothesis concerning the behavior of the nonproprietary firm. My reasons are two. First, that theory, we must remember, argued that *all* the seats are underpriced, but especially the better seats are underpriced. Whatever the reason for underpricing the better seats in the proprietary situation, underpricing can still occur in the nonproprietary seats for the reasons that Alchian and Allen give. So when Cheung says that the chief weakness of the Alchian and Allen hypothesis is that the constraints they describe for nonproprietary organizations are sufficiently unclear that their hypothesis yields no refutable implications, I think he is inaccurate.

Second, I question whether Cheung actually has "tested the several implications" of the hypothesis he puts forth. The empirical content of his paper consists mainly of casual judgments from personal first-hand observations (and mental notes) about vacancy rates and seating patterns. I am not criticizing this procedure *per se*; his detection of the likely importance of the boundary that the theater manager draws between the preferred and the less preferred seats, and the fact that this boundary tends to change with the nature of the performance and the anticipation of demand, is an astute observation. The full-scale testing of hypothesis is often so expensive and time-consuming that economists must adopt, at least in certain cases, various rules-of-thumb for deciding which scientific statements are worthy of further investigation and which statements appear to be justified on the basis of general observation. Such guidelines, I suspect, are also adopted in other disciplines. Nevertheless, it is probably inaccurate to consider these to be tests of hypotheses, especially when we have little idea of the likelihood that the results that Cheung remembered could have arisen purely by chance. This is especially important where Cheung notes that the favored seats, in some situations, sold at rates that were only "slightly" different from the other seats. In these cases it may be that the evidence "supports" his hypothesis just "slightly."

Cheung's paper has two virtues, however. First, he reminds us that equilibrium may be achieved through adjustments in quantity rather than price. Second, he has engaged in preliminary empirical work only *after* obtaining a thorough understanding of the nature of the constraints that are at work, those that work in the direction of wealth maximization and those that do not, and that was what Clarkson's principal conclusion recommended that we do.

H.E. French III (University of California at Santa Barbara). My comments today are in two parts. First, I will discuss Steve Cheung's and then Ken Clarkson's papers. Cheung's main point is that much behavior that looks irrational to observers is really wealth maximizing. Many errors are made by casually assuming that businessmen with their own fortunes at stake are stupid, and they make mistakes that an economics undergraduate could correct. The sins of pride committed by economists are impressive.

Cheung's paper makes the point forcefully in explaining why the best theater seats often sell out first. This is based on a simple and beautiful insight that keeping the seats full saves on costs of enforcing higher prices for better seats. But there are some problems with the paper. Cheung asserts that underpricing the better seats is consistent with a perfectly competitive market. But price-taking assumptions imply that theaters could fill all the seats at the going price schedule which relates price to quality. With all seats full, they would never have an enforcement problem. So the environment must be one where some sort of price searching or imperfect competition exists.

The same point arises in a different context in Cheung's example of a Hong Kong rental firm underpricing apartments. He argues convincingly that the firm does this in order to threaten tenants with ejection if they destroy property or fail to pay rent. The landlord's idea is to maintain a healthy queue—indicating to current tenants that they can be replaced with low search costs on the part of the rental firm. Apparently irrational behavior is once more shown to be wealth maximizing behavior, given certain transactions costs. This is a valuable demonstration.

While such pricing policies are very interesting and Cheung's positive analysis is probably correct, he again describes the policies as consistent with perfect competition. But, if the rental firm were truly operating under perfectly competitive conditions, it could replace the errant tenants at low cost. The fact that there are search costs to finding new tenants implies the existence of a bilateral monopoly. There is a range of rents below the current ones where the firm would not find it profitable to incur the costs of replacing the current tenants with new ones.

The apparent intention in characterizing these situations as perfectly competitive is to imply that they are optimal. The description implicitly appeals to the well-known theorems identifying competitive equilibrium with Pareto optimality. Since the situations are not actually perfectly competitive, Cheung's argument is misleading in two ways.

First, optimality provides a positive bench mark. The statement that a certain equilibrium is optimal in the conventional sense indicates that a set of marginal equalities relating to production and utility are met. In the present cases, these marginal equalities are not met.

Second, Cheung's assertions indicate that there is no government policy which can improve efficiency, since the equilibrium is already competitive, thus optimal. Thus, *laissez faire* would seem to be called for. However, in reality, there may be policies which could improve efficiency. For example, it may be that optimal policy would involve some slight tax or subsidy of theater seats. There is no guarantee that the private maximizing activities of the firms will lead precisely to optimality.

As a practical matter there is no doubt sufficient competition, both actual and potential, to prevent deviations from optimality from becoming very large. And the costs of operating governmental policy are great enough to indicate a *laissez-faire* policy. Nevertheless, it is incorrect and misleading to dismiss the welfare issues by describing the markets as perfectly competitive. Further, the detailed examination necessary to discover the welfare economics of the markets and pricing policies described by Cheung might lead to interesting insights into the workings of the markets.

I will now discuss Ken Clarkson's paper. Ken makes two substantive points. The first one is that looking at constraints on decision-makers in different types of nonprofit firms is more useful than assuming different objectives to explain different behavior. And the second point is that it is very difficult to get specific implications for behavior because the owners or trustees of a nonprofit firm impose auxiliary regulations on managers. This occurs in profit-seeking firms also, but is more common in nonprofit firms because of the greater difficulty of monitoring the managers.

Certainly Civil Service rules for hiring can be interpreted this way. I am sure that government secretaries would be very different in appearance if auxiliary constraints on hiring did not exist.

Clarkson presents a formal model deriving the prices faced by the manager for his own consumption of various goods produced by the firm. It is a good idea to model these complex situations in a formal way. However, there seem to be a number of problems with the actual model. A straightforward interpretation of the model does not allow analysis of the interesting managerial behavior discussed by Clarkson.

For example, the verbal discussion of the "nice working conditions" as an item of in-firm consumption is fine. However, this economic good is not handled well by the formal model. Specifically, the quantity produced by the firm is equal to the quantity of "nice working conditions" consumed *by the manager*. In a realistic situation, such an identification would lead to a manager of a large firm consuming millions of dollars worth of "nice working conditions." In reality, most of the goods such as "nice working conditions" are implicitly sold to the employees as a local public good and are not even observed by the managers.

The verbal discussion presents the firm as a price-searcher in some of the goods sold to employees (e.g., location). But in the formal analysis, the firm is a price-taker in all markets.

Formally, the firm is portrayed as a multiproduct company dealing in competitive markets. This has implications for the prices faced by the manager. Ken derives a complex expression for these prices. However, given the competitive nature of the firm, this expression simplifies to the competitive price. Consider a manager who decides to supply a unit to himself of his own firm's output. He does not add inputs and increase outputs as Clarkson's expression suggests. He simply takes one of the units and supplies one less to the market. Does the manager of Mobil Oil care if he puts Mobil gas in his car or Arco gas? I would say the answer is no, and that is what the formal model says.

Now I turn to the substantive parts of his paper. I fully agree with the value of looking at constraints on decision-makers rather than assuming different objectives as is often found in the literature. But I think Ken's emphasis on the difficulty of deriving specific implications for behavior results from looking at the problem at the level of the manager. For many cases, especially examination of the differences in behavior in profit- and nonprofit-seeking firms, it is more fruitful to look at the constraints at a higher level in the firm—that is, the level of the *top* decision-maker. This might be the board of trustees rather than the manager, or the dominant stockholder in a profit-seeking firm. Here constraints are simpler because these are the individuals who impose the complex ones. The difference in behavior produced by adding a nonprofit constraint is easier to analyze at this level.

For example, take the simplest case. Suppose one wants to compare nonprofit- to profit-seeking insurance firms. At the top decision-maker level, the only difference between the two types of firms is that the decision-makers are allowed to retain the residual in the profit-seeking firm, but not in the nonprofit firm. This implies that the top decision-makers in the nonprofit firm will consume more nonpecuniary goods and less income. However, if one were to look at specific nonpecuniary goods consumed by individuals below the top decision-maker level, as Clarkson does, things get very complicated.

To predict that a mid-level manager will have lower money income and thicker rugs in a nonprofit firm, one needs to know the various auxiliary constraints imposed by the trustees on managerial behavior. They may have made a specific rule limiting rug thickness. Further, some of the auxiliary rules which are so vital for analysis at this level may be unwritten. At best, analysis of specific features of behavior at levels lower than the top decision-maker requires painstaking analysis of the actual internal constraints of the firm. While I believe that such analysis would be interesting and useful, the basic features of the differences between nonprofit- and profit-seeking organizations are far easier to study at the top decision-maker level.

MANAGERIAL CONSTRAINTS: DISCUSSION

Clarkson. I would like to respond to some initial comments on the paper while they are fresh in everyone's memory. My model was criticized for allowing managers to consume all of the production. But a careful reading of Eq. (3), characterizing managers' consumption, will note that there is a superscript m on all consumption variables to distinguish them from total production of commodities. Therefore, the q_i produced and the q_i^m consumed in the model are not the same. With regard to the implications concerning public goods, they are derived by focusing on the change in the total wealth constraint since it is assumed that there are no direct or indirect charges to managers for public goods. Furthermore, differences in price-taking and price-searching conditions are handled in Eq. (12).

Finally, I wanted to comment on the difficulties of using this model for trustees. The model, as it is specified, can be modified and applied to anyone who is placed in the situation of being constrained by rules and regulations. Thus the model can be expanded to the trustees as long as we identify the nature of the constraints facing them. It is also possible

Economics of Nonproprietary Organizations
Research in Law and Economics, Supplement 1, pages 51-58
Copyright © 1980 by JAI Press Inc.
ISBN: 0-89232-132-6

to analyze the behavior of a majority stockholder in a corporation as long as the appropriate constraints are identified.

David Davies (Duke University). The definition of proprietary and nonproprietary organizations seems awfully broad. I think you are saying that a nonproprietary enterprise is defined as an organization whose owners or trustees cannot fully appropriate the costs nor the rewards associated with the activities of the organization. I would guess that much more than 40 percent, maybe 80 percent, of all economic activity might be included in that definition. Government corporations, like TVA, might well fit under this definition also.

Clarkson. Yes, I think that's right. In fact if you look for an empirical counterpart to the organization that has none of these restrictions, we would probably not find any proprietary enterprises. We should recognize that this definition is specified as ranging from the pure proprietary to the pure nonproprietary institution, whatever that might be. This definition is very much like that used for public goods.

Roland McKean (University of Virginia). I think most cases illustrate Clarkson's major point, that the constraints are very often hard to unravel. I think there are some constraints which tend to push government toward more expenditures on buildings, and some that cut in the other direction. I was therefore surprised to hear, if I understood him correctly, that he feels there is a net push away from public buildings. Perhaps it's true about replacement of certain kinds of machinery and capital equipment, but I think, unless you look pretty searchingly at the constraints, it's pretty hard to come up with a generalization about investment.

Clarkson. I think there is a confusion that results from the distinction between stocks and flows of building services. I am not prepared to state that, in the long run, there will be an underinvestment in public buildings. When the government is running large deficits, however, investment in public building will be slowed down. For example, in recent years backlogs of 60 or 70 public buildings have not received appropriations after GSA approval. This is because the full capital cost, which in some cases is much more than their annual appropriation, must be paid in a single budget period.

McKean. In some of your earlier research, wasn't it the case that once you ran into a constraint that caused the government to replace trucks or automobiles more rapidly than the lowest cost replacement cycle?

Clarkson. Yes, several administrative agencies were advocating a one-year replacement cycle for automobiles used in the government interagency motor pool. Their position was based on cost/benefit analyses which showed that a one-year replacement cycle was relatively less costly. There were a lot of problems with these analyses, but the single most important one concerned a comparison of the initial purchase price with the resale price at the time of disposal. The resale price was taken from the "blue book," which reflects all excise taxes. The initial purchase price, however, excluded excise taxes. Therefore, the optimal replacement policy from the agencies' point of view was actually one day, because they could buy a vehicle without paying excise tax and then sell it on the open market at the blue book price.

Henry Manne (University of Miami). You suggested there will be more costly business trips in nonproprietary enterprises, or other activities that involve higher monitoring costs, but fewer lost hours at on-site production locations when compared to their proprietary counterparts. I don't understand why there are fewer lost hours.

Clarkson. The lost hours are defined as hours when individuals are not physically present at the job. For example, a recent *Wall Street Journal* article reported that some Department of Agriculture employees were present at their job location, but only had a candy bar and feet on their desks. This is an extreme case, but it dramatizes that monitoring actual output rather than inputs, such as hours spent on the job, is relatively more costly in nonproprietary organizations.

With regard to business trips, proprietary organizations can compare the revenues or the contracts that the individual person brings in, so that you have some kind of measure of actual performance of the individual employee. In the case of governmental bureaus, the employee who was sent to Hawaii to check on the food stamp program may return with the information that a large number of individuals are buying food with their stamps. For this reason, it is possible that nonproprietary organizations will reduce all travel rather than try to monitor it. Thus we want to concentrate on the relative costs of monitoring and not on the absolute costs.

Donald Martin (University of Miami). I have a fundamental statement to make about Clarkson's model. It purports to be a generalized theory of economic organization. Perhaps this claim is its main weakness, in that it attempts to do too much. To accomplish its task, it requires a tremendous amount of detailed information about administrative, legal, and informal constraints. He continually reminds us that you really have to know a great deal more about the actual constraints operating on decision-makers before you can make statements about behavior. I'm not saying that his warning is unjustified. I am saying that it is a methodological weakness of the model. A model is supposed to abstract from reality, to economize on resources in making predictions. Perhaps we have a model that requires a nonoptimal amount of detailed information for it to operate. Since I used this model for my own work, I am subject to the same criticism.

Clarkson. I am suggesting that there is an appropriate mix of theoretical models and institutional information. To date, most analyses have been significantly biased in favor of the pure axiomatic approach and have ignored the constraints of the organization. Without such knowledge we are prone to error in our analyses. Nonproprietaries, for example, are a mixture of a lot of different organizational forms. Thus, in the same city you have church, community, and other nonprofit hospitals. In my research on hospitals I found that the "other" category was often owned by physicians, and in many cases, those physicians owned another corporation that held the assets of the hospital. In these cases the lease payments to the corporation that owned the hospital corresponded very closely to what might be called profits. If we use that organization as a representative nonprofit organization, I think that we could all agree that its behavior would be relatively similar to proprietary enterprises.

John Moore (University of Miami). One difficulty in this field is that we don't have a satisfactory general theory of monitoring costs. Our hypothesizing tends to be *ex post* in many cases. I think that some progress could be made in that direction.

Let me turn to a more specific question I have about Clarkson's paper. The paper states that inefficiency due to monopoly may be understated, because firms are likely to be price-searchers for at least some employee-purchased outputs. When I saw that statement I put a question mark next to it because I wondered how we could know such a thing beyond simply asserting it. These transactions don't take place in the market where we can observe results.

Clarkson. That's a hard one. First of all, we could look at all the employee-purchase outputs that are sold under relatively competitive conditions such as insurance policies, and just exclude those outputs. Estimating the demand curve for the other employee-purchased outputs would be relatively difficult, because you would have to find situations in which the firms were relatively similar, yet provided different amounts of vacation hours or other outputs.

Mark Pauly (Northwestern University). I have two comments. First, the statement was made that for some fringe benefits like insurance, because there is a market, the firm might be a price-taker. For other benefits, however, like working conditions, it will be price-searcher. Presumably, the reason why insurance is provided as a fringe benefit is usually because there is some tax advantage to having the employer pick up the premium rather than having it paid out of pocket. This suggests that there is a divergence between what the person would pay in the market and what he must pay for it as a fringe benefit. Therefore, there is still going to be a substantial margin for price-searching behavior even for goods sold in those kinds of competitive markets.

The second point I wish to make relates to a number of observations made in the paper, empirical observations, about expected differences in behavior between nonproprietary and proprietary firms. It should be pointed out that one must be careful about such comparisons, because there is an identification problem which can be quite important. If we question why one firm may be organized differently from another firm, there are at least two reasons. It may be due to the corporate structure of the firm, whether it is proprietary or nonproprietary; but it may also be due to the kind of output that the firm produces. The nature of the output may affect the type of organization. If we look at the distribution of the nonproprietary form of organization across the products produced in the economy, we observe that it is not random. You tend to find many more nonprofit firms in the business of fixing up bodies than you do in the business of fixing up dishwashers. This suggests that there is some association between product characteristics and organizational form. Not all output differences are easily discernible. Therefore, empirical differences in behavior between a nonprofit and a for-profit hospital, or between a nonprofit and a for-profit research organization, may be due to unobservable differences in the kinds of output produced, rather than due to the organizational form itself. But how can you tease out the particular influence of the organizational form? I think that you have to look for something exogenous. You have to find, somewhere, some set of rules which state that, at this place, you can only organize this activity in nonprofit form. This should avoid the identification problem and reduce ambiguity.

Earl Thompson (University of California—Los Angeles). I am concerned about the testability of Clarkson's (and others') hypotheses about differences in nonproprietary and proprietary institutions. In particular, are nonproprietary organizations going to have thicker carpets or are they going to have prettier secretaries? and so on. It seems to me that these hypotheses are essentially untestable. The reason is that if we could easily identify overconsumption by managers, someone else could also easily observe this behavior. Economists, we should assume, are not better informed than the managers or the trustees of the organization. As a result, overconsumption would have been prevented by quantity or quality constraints set up by the trustees. If trustees are running an efficient organization, we should never be able to observe employee overconsumption. I think the only reason we are trying to test this particular implication is that we are in the habit of testing our hypotheses, but in this instance, I think we are wasting our time.

On the other hand, it seems to me fairly easy to test the general hypothesis that there will be lower salaries in the nonprofit organizations to compensate for nonpecuniary rewards. The competitive labor market would, in effect, be saying, if you've got thicker carpets, etc., you are going to have lower salaries. So, this difference is observable. The relevant question concerns the value of such information. Why would anybody pay money for it? I'm suggesting that there is an economic policy that is implied by this analysis. It is, simply, that we should subsidize salaries. Subsidize the pecuniary payment of salaries to managers, and then tax the number of workers, so that the revenue effect is canceled.

Stephen Pejovich (University of Dallas). Has anyone noticed any systematic difference in depreciation schedules between proprietary and nonproprietary firms?

Andrew Whinston (Purdue University). I'm on a university committee at Purdue looking at decision-making within the university. One of our findings was that the university does not depreciate its assets. I have the impression that many other universities do not depreciate facilities, computers, or buildings, a factor creating many problems in the budgeting process. The reason is because universities have to go to the state to get money for new buildings, whereas private companies would be likely to depreciate assets so that when a building is no longer useful, they actually have accumulated money to replace it.

Frech. I am familiar with some research that tries to calculate profit rates for nonprofit hospitals. It has foundered on the attempts to measure depreciation. It was discovered that many hospitals do not bother doing it, just as many universities do not. There is no depreciation on the books at all. They are carrying 100-year-old equipment at its original cost.

Eckert. The University of Southern California, which is a private institution, does not establish depreciation charges, but it does assign an overhead rate to each unit of the university that varies with the nature of the activity. It also assigns an implicit rent charge for space, which is factored into each department or school's overhead charge. This rate varies between different departments.

William Meckling (University of Rochester). I think there is some misunderstanding about what depreciation actually does. It does not, of course, provide funds at all. Indeed, depreciation is a fairly new phenomenon in accounting, and it was invented in order to protect creditors of private firms. One of the reasons you do not observe depreciation in noncapitalist firms is simply because they do not have a creditor problem. The creditor problem is the following. If you have a contract where some group of owners or stockholders have some residual claim on the assets, and the board of directors has the right to pay out what are called profits to those stockholders, you can make those profits be anything you want them to be if you don't take into account depreciation in the accounting statement. You can, in effect, transfer wealth from the bondholders to the stockholders. That is why depreciation was invented in accounting, and why you don't observe it in nonproprietary institutions.

On a completely different topic, I want to discuss the use of utility functions instead of other maximands for analyzing the behavior of organizations. In the end, you cannot have multiple objectives if you want to talk about human behavior, since you must use a single maximand. But using a utility function for an organization runs into the problem of whose utility function you are talking about. That is the difficulty I have in dealing with Clarkson's paper. I don't understand whose utility function is being maximized. If your example is nonproprietary hospitals, whose utility function is being maximized? One of the most interesting questions in examining nonproprietary institutions is how do you explain which constraints are imposed on a nonproprietary organization, not simply taking those constraints as given. For example, based on some stories about the University of Miami told to me last night, there is at least as much difference in constraints and management policies between the state universities and private universities in the way they are managed as there is between private universities and private firms. My own experience with private universities is that they come very close to maximizing present value. And I might say that, in the case of private firms, there is a lot of theory now which says that maximizing present value is, under some quite general conditions, equivalent to maximizing the utility to stockholders. As long as the stockholders do not get direct utility out of the activities of the firm, and as long as the firm's activities are independent of the utility of the stockholders, then maximizing the present value of the firm is in fact equivalent to maximizing stockholders' utility.

Clarkson. I think that it is necessary to understand how people would behave when you change the constraints by weakening proprietary interests. The utility function that we are concerned with in my model is the utility function of the particular decision-maker.

McKean. Steve Cheung mentioned that restaurant pricing is one way of getting the patrons to move on fairly quickly; another is to have new customers standing around sort of making a nuisance of themselves. In most cases where customers' tastes and incomes vary, you expect to encounter a variety of options such as those found for automobiles. You don't expect to find one optimal automobile, you expect to find a different number of designs and sizes. I would think in most situations, unless there is a very strong cultural tradition operating, you would expect to find some restaurants in which customer queuing is used, others that charge higher prices and don't have the nuisance of people hovering over your table. He also mentioned supermarket queues, and I just want to add a very trivial point to that. Some supermarkets cut down the number of cashiers very sharply at off-peak hours so that you get approximately the same size queue all the time. Thus you do have adjustments taking place to alleviate the kind of discrepancies that Cheung discussed.

Cheung. With reference to the term "nonprofit firm," in Clarkson's paper, I really don't know what he means by that term. If you asked a lawyer or an accountant, they would know what it means because it has some IRS definition, but it is not very relevant for economics.

I also do not see why, when trying to explain behavior, Clarkson makes a point of having people shift from wealth or profit maximization and utility maximization. They are the same! I mean you may spend the money on a beautiful female companion outside work, or you may hire a beautiful secretary.

Armen Alchian (University of California—Los Angeles). I would like to reinforce a point Meckling made earlier. He avoided use of the term nonprofit and spoke about noncapitalistic firms. I know he wanted to emphasize the distinction between capitalizing the future consequences of present actions and the nonprofit status. The former is present in proprietary firms and is not present in nonprofit firms. This is the distinction that I bet will be *the* difference in explaining the nonproprietary firm. The example that I think will be useful in emphasizing that point in teaching is to ask my students how the university would be affected if their entry rights to the university were altered so that they could be sold. At first they will sit there dumbly and not know what to say. But pretty soon they begin to realize that if they can sell those rights, that university is going to change enormously as someone becomes "an owner." In this context, the word capitalistic is more revealing than the words proprietary or nonprofit.

MUTUAL ORGANIZATIONS

HEALTH INSURANCE: PRIVATE, MUTUALS, OR GOVERNMENT

H. E. Frech III, UNIVERSITY OF CALIFORNIA—

SANTA BARBARA

Are mutual insurance firms as efficient as stock firms? How do they compare to the nonprofit service organizations (Blue Cross and Blue Shield, primarily)? Spiller (159) found a hint—mutual life insurers have been growing more slowly than stock firms in recent years. Pfeffer and Klock (134) argue similarly that: "The long run trend of the industry is in the direction of more stock companies as the advantages of other forms are eroded by legislation" (p. 379). On the other hand, Blair, Jackson, and Vogel (27) argue that mutual health insurers' costs are lower than those of stock firms.

The question is not idle. Mutual insurers dominate the life insurance line (or product type). Of the top ten firms, seven are mutual (*Best's Review*, June 1976). In property-liability insurance, mutuals are not dom-

Economics of Nonproprietary Organizations
Research in Law and Economics, Supplement 1, pages 61-73
Copyright © 1980 by JAI Press Inc.
All rights of reproduction in any form reserved.
ISBN: 0-89232-132-6

inant, but still form an important part of the industry. Of the top ten companies, four of them are organized as mutual firms (*Best's Aggregates and Averages*, 1976, p. 24). Further, in health insurance, Blue Cross and Blue Shield nonprofit service firms write almost half of the business (Sourcebook, 1976). Current governmental tax and regulatory policy is biased in many ways in favor of nonprofit insurers of both the mutual and service organization type [Frech (66, 67), Samprone (143)].

In a previous paper, I found profit-seeking (stock) insurers to be more efficient than a group consisting of mutual and other nonprofit firms (mostly Blue Shield firms) in processing claims for physician services insurance under Medicare [Frech (67)].

This paper presents a refinement of that earlier work, designed to examine the specific issue of mutual insurer ownership rights and efficiency. First, the theory relating the type of ownership to the firm's efficiency will be briefly summarized. Then, past empirical studies will be surveyed. Next, the data resulting from the Social Security Administration's (SSA) natural experiment will be examined. The last section will summarize the results reported in my earlier study (*ibid.*) and then present the new analysis which is aimed at mutual insurers in particular.

I. THEORY: THE PROPERTY RIGHTS THEORY OF THE FIRMS

The property rights theory of the firm [Williamson (188, 189), Alchian (2), Alchian and Kessel (10), Alchian and Demsetz (9), Furubotn and Pejovich (70), Frech (67, 68)] relates the type of ownership rights in the firm held by the top decision-maker to the behavior of that individual and thus to efficiency. Private property rights are compared to attenuated rights.

Under private property rights, the decision-maker has the right to (1) decide about the use of the firm's resources, (2) keep the residual (total revenue minus contractual costs), and (3) capitalize any wealth gains of the firm by selling his rights.

As property rights are attenuated for a nonprofit firm, the decision-maker cannot keep the residual nor can he sell the rights to future income flows.

Attenuated rights lead to different behavior than private property rights in two ways. First, the attenuated rights effectively reduce the price of nonpecuniary amenities (pleasant offices and colleagues, prestige, short working hours, greater output) to the decision-makers. This leads to choice of lower firm wealth and more nonpecuniary benefits. Second, the attenuated rights reduce the gains and increase the costs of the takeover of poorly managed firms.

The result of these reinforcing effects is that, in the words of Alchian and Demsetz (9), p. 790: "One should, therefore, find greater (management) shirking in nonprofit . . . enterprises." The implication for our work is that nonprofit insurers will exhibit lower levels of efficiency.[1]

II. PAST EMPIRICAL STUDIES

In spite of the intuitive appeal and apparent importance of the analysis, relatively few attempts have been made to measure empirically the impact of alternative property rights specifications on costs of operation. The ones which have been undertaken suffer from the problem that the output is not quite held constant, nor controlled for in the analysis. The result is some degree of ambiguity concerning the independent influence of property rights structure versus the difference in costs of supplying different products. Another important weakness in much of the work is a lack of statistical testing.

In a study of stock (private property) and mutual (nonprofit) savings and loan associations, Nicols (126), p. 265, found mutuals to have 20 to 60 percent higher expenses than the stock savings and loan associations in California where both forms are legal. Some characteristics of the product (number of mortgages, loans made and new savings) were adjusted for by regression analysis. However, many dimensions of product (for example, location and number of branches) were ignored. Statistical significance of differences was above the 5 percent level. More suggestive is the fact that the market share of mutuals declined from 58.1 percent to 33.7 percent in California from 1950 to 1964 in spite of a regulatory environment favoring the mutuals (*ibid.*, p. 60).

Davies (50, 51) compared the labor productivity of the two interstate airlines of Australia, one private and one governmental, and came to the conclusion that the private one is 13 percent more efficient. This comparison is particularly interesting because the Australian government tries to treat the two airlines approximately equally even to requiring virtually identical airplane fleets. However interesting, this is an imperfect measure of the effects of the property rights differences for two reasons. First, both airlines are regulated very rigidly by the government. In terms of our theory then, both firms are characterized by somewhat attenuated property rights, regardless of the formal legal situation. A very detailed study would be necessary to find the actual differences in constraints. Second, the sample of two firms precludes tests of the statistical significance of the observed differences.

Clarkson (41, 42) compared various measures of behavior for profit-seeking versus nonprofit hospitals. He found many fascinating and strongly statistically significant differences in the manner in which the two types of hospitals are managed. First, hospitals with attenuated property rights were much more likely to have detailed internal rules and regulations constraining behavior of employees. Second, nonprofit hospitals exhibited far greater variation in input choices than private property ones.

The study had two important problems from our viewpoint (which do not detract from its importance or quality). First, the output of profit and nonprofit hospitals differs. Nonprofit hospitals tend to be larger, to produce more research and teaching (of nurses and physicians), to provide a wider menu of services, especially experimental ones, and to provide more philanthropic medical care. Although size is held constant in Clarkson's work, some (though clearly not all) of the differences can be attributed to different output.

The other problem is that Clarkson did not directly measure or compare efficiency or cost. However, it is possible to make inferences concerning the relative efficiency of nonprofit and profit-seeking hospitals from Clarkson's results. If there is a unique cost-minimizing factor proportion, and one assumes the distribution of actual factor proportions center on the efficient one, then the observed greater variation for the nonprofit hospitals implies higher average operating costs.

In a survivor analysis, Spiller (159) compared the growth rates of mutual and stock life insurance companies over the period between 1952 and 1966 and found statistically significant differences in the growth rates of the firms, with the stock firms growing faster. This is an interesting study, but the complex and nonneutral regulatory structure of the insurance industry makes it dangerous to attribute the observed differences in growth entirely to different property rights structures. Notably, many firms enter and grow as stock firms only to convert to mutuals when they become large. Presumably the incentives for this behavior come from the regulatory environment.[2]

Houston and Simon (79) attempted to measure the independent impact of stock versus mutual corporate form in their study of economies of scale in life insurance. They found no significant differences in administrative costs between mutuals and stocks. However, output is not held constant in this study in an important respect. Mutual insurers are much more likely to use the "direct writing" method of sales. This entails the use of salaried employees as salesmen, rather than the independent agency system common to stock firms. The latter is a higher cost method [Joskow (84), Samprone (143), Pfeffer and Klock (134)]. Thus, the comparison is meaningless because of uncontrolled variation in the type of output.

Blair, Jackson, and Vogel (27) investigated the scale economies in health insurance administrative costs for a large sample of insurers operating in the private market. They found that stock insurers had higher costs than mutual firms, in contradiction of our theory. However, since they were dealing with market insurance, their study had problems similar to those of Houston and Simon—the same uncontrolled variation in output. Mutual insurers are much more likely to sell their insurance by the less costly direct writing method. This paper avoids this problem and finds just the opposite result. Thus, the advantages of the natural experiment provided by the SSA's contractual arrangements with private insurers can be seen clearly.

Another problem with the Blair, Jackson, and Vogel paper is that operating cost is divided by premiums written. In the case of mutual insurers, this figure is inflated because premiums include an expected dividend to the policyholder. The correct divisor should be net of dividends.

All of these studies suffer from problems in the standardization of either the output or the regulatory environment. This study examines the data on Medicare processing by intermediary firms of differing property rights structures. This provides a natural experiment, where the data allows one to attribute differences in performance to differences in property rights structures. The specification of output and the legal environment are determined by contract with the SSA which provides for reimbursement based on "reasonable" costs, including adjustment for size of firm.

One study other than the current one and Frech (67) makes use of data from this Social Security natural experiment. This is a small part of the work of Vogel and Blair (175). In regressions holding scale constant like those of Frech (67), they find that commercial insurers (including mutual insurers) have lower costs than Blue Shield plans (p. 106). This is consistent with the results reported here, but the specification of the regressions is different than those in Frech (67) and the fits are not as good, even though more variables are used. Further, the classification differs. Mutual insurers are grouped with profit-seeking ones, rather than with Blue Cross insurers. And speed and accuracy of processing is not addressed.

III. EMPIRICAL RESEARCH ON HEALTH INSURANCE—BACKGROUND

A. The Natural Experiment

The SSA contracts with private health insurance firms for claim-processing services on a "reasonable" cost basis. These firms deal directly with medical care providers and consumers. A government report on the Medicare program states that "the carriers' principal function is to determine whether charges are allowable (reasonable) and to make payment" [U.S. Department of Health, Education, and Welfare (174)]. Thus, the carriers have no role in such common insurance activities as classification of risks, determination of benefit packages, and sales promotion. The narrowness of the service and its contractual (rather than market) determination are important advantages. Unmeasured variation in type of service is likely to be very low. Carriers are selected directly by the secretary of HEW. They are granted geographic monopolies. This virtually eliminates variation in the medical complexity of claims.

As is obvious from the large variation in the data on the costs and performance, firms and their geographic monopoly regions were not selected on the basis of competitive bidding. Further, no carrier has been dropped for poor performance. Since the selection and retention of intermediaries was not based on cost minimization, efficiency cannot be inferred from survivorship.[3]

B. Industry Structure

The health insurance industry, from which Medicare intermediaries are chosen by the SSA, is largely made up of three types of firms: ordinary profit-seeking insurers, mutual insurers, and Blue Cross and Blue Shield nonprofit firms which provide physician and hospital insurance, respectively.

By the argument of the "theory" section above, the nonprofit insurers should be unable to compete with the more efficient profit-seeking insurers. Therefore, the survival of the mutual and Blue Cross–Blue Shield firms deserves some comment.

In the case of the mutual firms, it appears that their form allows them to undercut the regulated insurance price by paying dividends to insurers [Kimball (90), Samprone (143), Pfeffer and Klock (134)]. Further, reserve requirements are generally less onerous for mutual insurers, although this advantage is being reduced by legislative actions (*ibid.*).

Blue Cross and Blue Shield firms survive because of quite strong regulatory and tax advantages in most states [Frech (66, 67)]. In many states, Blue Cross and Blue Shield firms pay no taxes on property or premium income, while profit-seeking and mutual firms must pay such taxes. Premium taxes alone average about 2 percent of gross premium volume. In the majority of states, special laws have been passed granting tax and regulatory advantages to the Blue Cross and Blue Shield firms. Recent work by Frech and Ginsburg (69) shows the Blue Cross market share to be quite sensitive to these tax advantages.

IV. EMPIRICAL ANALYSIS—PROFIT-SEEKING FIRMS VERSUS ALL NONPROFIT FIRMS

In this part of the paper, I will first summarize the results reported in Frech (67), then discuss the new comparison, separating the mutual insurers from the service organization, nonprofit insurers, largely Blue Shield firms.

A. Relative Performance: Comparison of Means

The data presented in Table 1 give the means, standard deviations, and statistical significance level of the difference in means for average cost per dollar processed, average processing time, and errors per dollar processed for nonprofit and profit-seeking Medicare Part B intermediaries, based on data from the SSA [HEW (174)].[4] Nonprofit firms include Blue Shield, one government agency, one prepaid group practice, and mutual (owned by policyholders) firms. As one can see, the superiority of the private property firms is striking. The probability of these performance differences occurring by chance is apparently very low. The grouping of all nonprofit firms together masks some very interesting differences in the types of firms. And these differences in structure are related to important differences in performance.

B. Scale and Performance

The differences reported in Table 1 are striking. With the efficiency differences so great, it seems very unlikely that they can be explained

Table 1. Medicare Processing Performance and Ownership: Profit-seeking versus All Nonprofit Firms

Type of Firm	Cost (per dollar processed)	Other Dimensions of Performance	
		Average Processing Time (days)	Errors (per $1,000 processed)
Profit-seeking firms	$0.0715	18.70	0.1844
(SD: N=12)	(0.0178)	(10.34)	(0.0717)
Nonprofit firms	0.1039	33.59	0.4426
(SD: N=60)	(0.0331)	(19.83)	(0.7576)
Approximate *t*-value for difference of means	4.908	3.565	2.706
Degrees of freedom	29.9	31.3	70.9
Statistical significance (one-tail test)	<.0005	.0009	.005

Note: If variances are assumed to be different and unknown, the appropriate test statistic is an approximate *t*-value [Yamane (190), pp. 522–524].

simply by differences in scale between the two types of firms. However, since the Medicare processing activities of the profit-seeking firms are larger in scale (both in total dollars processed and in the size of the average claim), it would be useful to determine how much of the differences can be attributed to scale differences. Exploration by regression analysis indicated that some, but not all, of the differences in efficiency could be explained by differences in scale.

V. MUTUAL INSURERS VERSUS OTHER NONPROFITS: A NEW COMPARISON

A. The Property Rights Structure of Mutual Insurers

Mutual insurers are legally owned by policyholders. However, as Hetherington (75) and Pfeffer and Klock (134) have argued, this ownership is a legal fiction. Management may terminate a policy, thus wiping out the ownership interest of the policyholder. On dissolution of the firm, the policyholder has only limited rights to the net worth of the firm. For example, in Wisconsin the policyholder can receive only the aggregate premium he has paid plus interest. The residual goes to the Wisconsin state school fund [Hetherington (75), p. 1076]! The legal obligation of the mutual's management is limited to performance of the insurance contract. It is not fiduciary in character. That is, there is no duty of loyalty as there is toward stockholders in stock firms.

On the matter of control, the lack of real ownership rights of the policyholders is equally apparent. Legally, the policyholders elect the directors who control the firm. However, there are no requirements to solicit proxies, so that in practice, a very small number of policyholders vote. For example, in the Metropolitan Life Insurance Company election of 1967, fifty-one policyholders voted, out of over 22 million eligible (*ibid.*, p. 1079). The legal quorum requirements are not very exacting. In Wisconsin, the presence of ten policyholders is required; the requirements for public notice are minimal.

Clearly, the rights of the legal owners, the policyholders, to either the residual (profit) or to control the firm and select the management are very weak.

The next candidates to be considered as the owners, or top decision-makers of the mutual insurer, is the management. In Hetherington's words (p. 1091):

> To the extent that ownership means the ability to use and to make and implement decisions affecting a business, the owner of a mutual organization is its managerial establishment. To the extent that such an establishment is free of the possibility of outside interference or removal, it occupies a proprietary position to a degree not

possible to its counterpart (hired management) in a stock corporation. Realistically, the only aspect of ownership which a mutual management clearly lacks is the proprietary right to profit.

A similar description may be found in Pfeffer and Klock (134).

However, in practice we find that the management does have some access to the profit—not as completely as a stock corporation's shareholders, but more completely than the typical nonprofit firms.

B. Management Mechanism for Sharing in the Residual (Profits)

There are a number of mechanisms through which management may share in profits and thus attain more complete property rights in the firms. The most obvious is through salary and pensions. Clearly, if the firm is earning a large income and accumulates a large surplus, it can pay management higher salaries and provide more generous pensions. In this respect, it will be less limited than other nonprofit firms (such as Blue Shield plans). The reason for the difference is that the other nonprofit firms enjoy greater regulatory and tax advantages and thus are under closer watch by the state governments. For example, Blue Cross and Blue Shield firms avoid property taxes and pay smaller premium taxes in most states than either mutual or stock health insurers. Mutual and stock firms are usually treated identically, with the exception of the corporate income tax [Frech (66)].

More interesting and potentially more powerful ways for the management to claim some of the profits are found in corporate relationships with stock firms. These can take three forms, with roughly similar effects. The first and most obvious is the management contract. In this arrangement, the management forms a stock corporation and contracts with the mutual firm to provide management services. The management fee can then be set in such a manner as to allow the management corporation to shift some of the profits to itself, if the mutual has good results. Furthermore, this arrangement allows the management group to sell its ownership rights "by the sale of the stock of the management entity, which carries with it *de facto* control of the insurance company" [Hetherington (75), p. 1092]. This type of contract is similar to those used by investment advisory companies in relation to mutual funds.

Still another method for management to obtain a share in the profits of the firm is through contractual and ownership relations with other insurance companies. It is very common for mutual firms to own stock firms. For example, State Farm Mutual Automobile Insurance Company, a large mutual, controls State Farm Fire and Casualty Company, but does not own all of the stock (*Moody's*, 1976, p. 1932). The key element is that ownership of the stock firm by the mutual be *incomplete.*

Consider the possibilities for an incompletely owned stock firm. If the mutual has very good experience, it can, by the adjustment of the transfer payments between it and the stock firm, raise the value of the stock. If those who control the mutual are important stockholders in the firm, they can use this process to share in the mutual's profits.

Alternatively, the mutual can be dominated by *de facto* representatives of a stock firm which supplies inputs to the insurer. Nicols (126), pp. 159–170, finds this to be important for Mutual Savings and Loan firms. An example would be a bank which sells securities to the mutual for its portfolio and perhaps manages the portfolio. For this case, the management group participates in profits through the pricing of inputs sold to the mutual firm.

For our purposes, the effect is the same—incentives for careful management are stronger because the effective owner has some access to the profits of the mutual.

To summarize this section, the real owners of mutual insurers apparently are able to share in the good fortune and/or fruits of good management of the firm, in spite of the legal fiction that the policyholders own the firm. This ability is greater for mutuals than for other nonprofit firms which are more strictly regulated due to tax and regulatory advantages. On the other hand, the ability of mutual owners to share in the profits is more difficult, less complete, and more costly than similar sharing for the shareholders in a stock corporation. Thus, the top decision-makers of mutual firms would seem to have somewhat attenuated property rights, but not as attenuated as the rights of other nonprofit firms. The expected efficiency of the mutual firms would fall between that of the stock insurers and the other nonprofit firms.

C. The Empirical Results

The question of the comparative efficiency of the mutuals can be easily examined with the data generated by the natural experiment of the Medicare system, described above. The results for the performance of the three types of firms are summarized in Table 2.

We see that performance of the mutual firms falls between that of the most efficient stock firms and the least efficient other nonprofit firms in the dimension of cost, and also for processing time.

In the dimension of errors, the mutuals' performance is even worse than the other nonprofit firms. The next objective is to examine the statistical significance of these results. This is done in Table 3, where an approximate *t*-test is used to make pairwise comparisons of the mean values between the stocks and mutuals in turn, between the mutuals and the other nonprofit firms.

Table 2. Ownership Rights and Medicare Claim Processing Performance

Type of Firm	Cost (per dollar processed)	Other Dimensions of Performance	
		Average Processing Time (days)	Errors (per $1,000 processed)
Stock insurance firms	$0.0713	18.70	0.1844
(SD: N=12)	(0.0178)	(10.34)	(0.0717)
Mutual insurance firms	0.0875	29.88	0.5623
(SD: N=13)	(0.0175)	(10.52)	(0.7026)
Other nonprofit firms			
(largely Blue Shield)	0.1080	34.50	0.4132
(SD: N=53)	(0.0348)	(21.49)	(0.7740)

Source: U.S. Department of Health, Education, and Welfare, Social Security Administration, Bureau of Health Insurance, *Memorandum: SMI Carrier Operations: Selected Workload and Cost Data, January-March 1970*, Washington, D.C., July 7, 1973.

Mutuals have higher (22 percent) costs than stock firms, but lower (19 percent) costs than the other nonprofit firms. These comparisons are very strong statistically. Some of the difference between the mutuals and other nonprofits is doubtless due to the mutuals' larger scale. The mutual insurers are about the same size as the stocks.

Thus, the notion that mutual firms have somewhat attenuated property rights is confirmed by the comparison to the stock firms. But the idea that there are mechanisms through which the effective owners of the mutual firms can appropriate some of the residual (profit) of the firms is apparently also confirmed. Mutuals are substantially more efficient than the other nonprofit firms where the ability of the top decision-makers to share in profits is weaker.

As we turn to the other dimensions of performance, we find the general pattern is repeated. Mutuals are clearly inferior to stock firms in both processing time and in errors. In these dimensions, the mutual firms performance is closer to that of the other nonprofit firms than it is to the stock firms. In fact, the differences between the mutuals and the other nonprofit firms are not statistically significant at reasonable levels of accuracy. The differences in the dimension of errors take on the incorrect sign. However, the lack of precision of the estimate indicates that little confidence can be placed on the result.

Comparing stock firms and other nonprofits, one sees striking and statistically strong results. Other nonprofit firms incur costs 51 percent higher than the stock firms. The differences are greater in the other dimensions. Other nonprofits take 84 percent longer to process claims and make 124 percent more errors. Given the analysis of this paper, it is

Table 3. Ownership and Performance:
Statistical Tests

Category		Cost (per dollar processed)	Other Dimensions of Performance	
			Average Processing Time (days)	Errors (per $1,000 processed)
Profit-seeking insurers vs. mutual insurers	Approximate *t*-value for difference of means*	−2.266	−2.692	−1.931
(Profit-seeking minus mutual)	Degrees of freedom	24.85	24.90	12.32
	Statistical significance (one-tail test)	.017	.005	.041
Mutual insurers vs. other nonprofit insurers	Approximate *t*-value for difference of means	−3.014	−1.031	.6722
(Mutual minus other)	Degrees of freedom	40.23	43.13	21.04
	Statistical significance (one-tail test)	.004	.17	**
Profit-seeking insurers vs. other nonprofit insurers	Approximate *t*-value for difference of means	−5.210	−3.529	−2.112
(Profit-seeking minus mutual)	Degrees of freedom	36.28	39.36	55.93
	Statistical significance (one-tail test)	<.0005	<.005	.021

*Under the assumption that the variances of the two means are unknown and unequal, the appropriate test statistic is the approximate *t* [Yamane (190), pp. 522–524].
**Difference of means takes on incorrect sign. Significance level for a two-tailed test is .25.

not surprising that this comparison between the stock and other non-profit firms reveals the largest differences and most reliable statistics. These firms have the greatest differences in property rights structures.

VI. CONCLUSION: THE RELATIVE PERFORMANCE OF MUTUAL INSURERS

Examination of the actual property rights structure of mutual insurers indicates that their real owners are their managements or other firms, and that these owners do not have full private property rights. Thus they are expected to perform less efficiently than the stock insurers. And that expectation is borne out.

However, it appears that the mutual insurers' owners have a number of possibilities open to them to share in the firms' profits. Their rights are not as attenuated as those of other nonprofit firms (principally Blue Shield). Thus, the mutuals are expected to perform better than the other nonprofit firms. In terms of costs, this is clearly so although partly due to scale differences. For the other performance dimensions, the evidence is less clear and statistically weak.

FOOTNOTES

The author is associate professor of economics, Department of Economics.

An earlier version of this paper was presented at the Center for the Study of American Business, Washington University. Thanks are due to the participants at that seminar and also to Paul B. Ginsburg, Joseph C. Samprone, Jr., and Sam Peltzman for valuable comments. I am grateful to the University of California-Santa Barbara-Academic Senate Committee on Research for a small research grant and to the Robert Wood Johnson Foundation for support in the form of a faculty fellowship in the Economics Department, Harvard University.

1. If nonprofit insurance firms are less efficient, one may wonder how they can survive against the competition of the lower cost profit-seeking firms; see discussions in Frech (66, 67), Pfeffer and Klock (134), and Samprone (143). Nonprofit firms receive tax and regulatory advantages from state government policies.

2. See Kimball (90) for insight into the complexity of Wisconsin insurance regulation, as an example.

3. For more details on the nature of the relationship of the Social Security Administration to the independent intermediaries, see Blair, Ginsburg, and Vogel (26), U.S. Department of Health, Education, and Welfare (174), and Vogel and Blair (175), p. 73, 74.

4. A nonprofit firm with very poor performance was deleted from the sample because of incomplete data on errors.

UNIONS AS NONPROPRIETARY INSTITUTIONS

Donald L. Martin, UNIVERSITY OF MIAMI

The empirical revolution that has swept the economics profession since the Second World War has permeated almost all subdisciplines of the subject. The study of the economic impact of trade unions has been a prime target of the new empirical techniques. Yet, unlike the study of almost all other conventional economic institutions, such as firms, industries, and unionized factor markets, these empirical efforts have proceeded without a broadly accepted economic theory of the behavior of the trade union.

The absence of an economic theory of the trade union is not for want of trying. Scholars since Smith (156) have searched for an explanation of union behavior within the confines of economic theory. Others, not so constrained, have pursued such explanations into political theory [Atherton (17)]. The biggest stumbling block for economists, however, has been the answer to the deceptively simple question asked by Dunlop

Economics of Nonproprietary Organizations
Research in Law and Economics, Supplement 1, pages 75-109
Copyright © 1980 by JAI Press Inc.
All rights of reproduction in any form reserved.
ISBN: 0-89232-132-6

(62) some thirty years ago. "What do unions maximize?" Given an objective function, it is possible to derive logical implications that, from an otherwise bewildering collection of facts, will serve to identify data relevant to the empirical examination of the economic impact of the trade union. The response to Dunlop's question by economists and students of industrial relations has been disappointing, to say the least. The profession has generated an embarrassingly large number of maximands.

From time to time, it has been suggested that unions maximize the wage bill [Dunlop (62)], the wage rate per member [*ibid.* and Simons (155)], the utility of the membership [Fellner (65), Cartter (34), and Atherton (17)], the rents generated from union monopoly power [Dunlop (62), Powel (136)], the size of the membership [Dunlop (62)], the probability of the union's survival [Ross (141)], Atherton (17)], "the economic welfare of the membership" [Ross (141)], and the difference between union receipts and expenditures [Berkowitz (25), Atherton (17)]. Still others have suggested that unions are *satisficing* rather than maximizing institutions [Reder (138)]. This cornucopia of maximands is itself evidence of the profession's failure to develop an operational model of the trade union comparable to the model of the profit-maximizing firm. It is the purpose of this paper to demonstrate that this failure is largely attributable to insufficient recognition of the role institutional arrangements play in determining opportunity sets that constrain behavior and, indeed, in identifying the maximand relevant to that behavior. In so doing, a new theory of the trade union will be introduced and a number of testable implications will be derived.

Profit is the maximand in the conventional theory of the firm because it is assumed that final decision-makers have economically enforceable *private property* rights in the assets of the firm and in its residual earnings. The institution of private property does more than bestow exclusive rights on individuals, it also operates as a constraint on their behavior. It serves to make more costly than otherwise those choices that fail to maximize wealth for the holders of such rights. In other words, *it is the private property assumption that translates the interests of utility-maximizing owners into behavior that is consistent with wealth as an organizational maximand of the firm.* Perhaps because these assumptions and their implications have rarely been made explicit in the theory of the firm, as it applies to conventional forms of economic organization, it should not be surprising that the relevance of property rights, or ownership characteristics, has eluded scholars attempting to explain the behavior of less conventional organizations, such as labor unions.

Knowledge of the ownership characteristics of trade unions is crucial in deducing union behavior from economic theory. As will be shown, differences in ownership characteristics imply differences in organizational maximands and in organizational behavior. This paper develops a model of union behavior based on the structure of property rights in American trade unions.

Section I contains a discussion of the role of monopoly power at the trade union level and of the relevance of property rights in exploiting that power. Section II presents an analysis of union behavior under nonproprietary assumptions, and Section III concludes with a review of the implications of the analysis and its extension to behavior not discussed in previous sections.

I. MONOPOLY RENTS AND CHOICES AFFECTING UTILITY

The role of the trade union in society is often described in multidimensional terms. It is at once economic, political, egalitarian, revolutionary, educational, and fraternal. Yet no one can doubt that the source of the union's ability to serve these roles is due, in large part, to its comparative advantage in affecting the terms of trade (both pecuniary and nonpecuniary) in the labor market. This advantage derives from legally sanctioned restrictions that unions impose on the contractual freedom of individuals who would otherwise supply labor services competitively to employers of union members.[1] These restrictions are defined by the *exclusivity* of bargaining rights held by the union within some specified jurisdiction and the right to strike.[2] As the sole bargaining agent for its members, the union is insulated not only from the competition of rival unions' representational claims (and the demands such claims would make on resources), but also from the threat posed by independent bargaining on the part of individual union members. In this sense, an exclusive bargaining right is a resource that facilitates the exercise of collusive behavior among workers, that is, monopoly.

Together with the strike, exclusive bargaining rights make the union an instrument for the production of monopoly rents, available for appropriation by some or all of the membership.[3]

A. Production and Composition of Rent

The model that follows owes much, in terms of inspiration, to Clarkson (45).

Monopoly rents may be expressed in a variety of pecuniary and nonpecuniary forms that are reflected both in the remuneration package, arising out of collective bargaining, and in the services provided directly to members by the union.[4] The firm sometimes has a comparative advantage in providing specific on-the-job or job-connected goods which are consumed by its workers. Consequently, the employer is not indifferent to the composition of the remuneration package exchanged for labor services. This suggests that, in addition to the "normal" cost unions face in attempting to improve their terms of trade with employers, the latter will offer differential resistance to alternative remuneration packages of equal market value. Thus, some remuneration packages for which the union might bargain will be more costly to secure and yield smaller rents than others.

We define the total of union rents appropriable to incumbent members as ρ_T, the present value of the residual given by the discounted sum of pecuniary and nonpecuniary differentials resulting from the exercise of union monopoly power less the value of resources committed by the union in supplying services to the members. That is,

$$\rho_T = \left[\overline{W(mH)} - \hat{W}(\overline{mH}) + \sum_{1=1}^{m} (P_1G_1 + P_2G_2 - P_1Q_1 - P_2Q_2) - FX \right] R, \tag{1}$$

where:

$\overline{W}$ = contract wage rate matrix, containing the wage rates ($\overline{w}_i$) paid different members over (n) time periods;

$\overline{mH}$ = contract man-hours. The product of contract employment for different members ($\overline{m}$), and contract hours ($\overline{H}$), where $\overline{H}$ is a matrix containing ($\overline{h}_i$) hours per worker-member[5] over (n) time periods;

$\hat{W}$ = a matrix composed of wage rates (w_i) for different members in their best alternatives over (n) time periods;

P_1G_1 = market value of a matrix composed of g_i goods at p_i market prices (p_ig_i), produced by the union or firm under collective agreement and consumed by members *on the job*;

P_2G_2 = market value of a matrix composed of g_i goods at p_i market prices (p_ig_i), produced by the union or by the firm under collective agreement and consumed by members *off the job*;

P_1Q_1 = market value of a matrix composed of q_i goods at p_i market prices (p_iq_i), that would have been produced by the firm and consumed by employees *on the job without union contract*;

P_2Q_2 = market value of a matrix composed of q_i goods at p_i market prices (p_iq_i), that would have been produced by the firm and consumed by employees *off the job without union contract*, e.g., firm-sponsored bowling teams;

F = a matrix composed of resource prices (f_i) faced by the union in producing rents over (n) time periods;

X = a matrix composed of resources (x_i) employed by the union in producing rents over (n) time periods;

$R = [1 - (1 + r)^{-n}]/r$, where
r = uniform discount rate, and
n = number of periods during which rents will be received.

Given that rents are, in part, a function of the selection of G_i goods by the union and of employer resistance associated with some selections, the production of rents is subject to the following constraints:

$$\beta(G_0, G_1, G_2) = Z(X), \text{ and} \tag{2}$$

$$-\frac{\overline{dmH}}{dW} \frac{\overline{W}}{mH} = n, \tag{3}$$

where Eq. (2) is the production function for rent with respect to all goods yielding rents, including G_0—the matrix of those goods that general purchasing power (wage payments) will buy outside the firm and union. Equation (3) is a "wage" elasticity of labor demand in terms of man-hours for members. More accurately, Eq. (3) may be interpreted as a *variable labor cost elasticity of labor demand,* calling attention to the fact that remuneration per man-hour includes variable nonwage payments as well.[6]

The creation of rent implies a relative scarcity of rent-yielding jobs. The scarcity value of these jobs depends on the form(s) in which rents may be appropriated. Under closed shop or even union shop conditions, membership in effect represents an access right to such employment. If exclusive rights to rent-yielding jobs, *job rights,* were assigned individually to incumbent members (e.g., in the form of union cards) and were specified and enforced as their alienable property, the cost of pursuing rent-affecting policies that failed to maximize the net present value of a job right would be greater than if transferability were prohibited. This follows because transfer rights imply the immediate capitalization and appropriation of future rents into present prices, while an absence of such rights implies that rents can only be appropriated when and where they are generated. Given an uncertain life and job tenure, for any given member, nontransferability suggests a lower opportunity cost to ignoring the future consequences of present actions. To the extent such actions affect rent maximization, it will be less costly than otherwise not to pursue them.

B. Choices Affecting Utility

Since workers usually must be physically present on the job to deliver their product, the working environment (in both its tangible and intangible forms) is a source of utility to them. Purely as a result of difference in tastes among members, the set of utility-maximizing environmental characteristics[7] for any given worker-member could be different from the set that maximizes rents for the group. This suggests that where members can affect union decisions, a model that accommodates preferences will yield a richer set of implications.[8]

Toward this end, we introduce a utility function for a given member:[9]

$$U_m = (G_0, G_1, G_2) = U_m(g_1, \ldots, g_{k+n+s}). \quad (4)$$

Members, while under contract, derive utility from three classes of goods. The matrix G_0 represents $g_1, \ldots, g_k$ (including leisure) consumed off the job over (n) time periods and acquired through general purchasing power (that is, wage payments). These are the goods individual members purchase with $(\overline{Wh})_m$ income.[10] Matrices G_1 and G_2 are goods (including in-kind payments) consumed, respectively, on the job $(g_{k+1}, \ldots, g_{k+n})$ and off the job $(g_{k+n+1}, \ldots, g_{k+n+s})$, and associated with the union's efforts to create rents. We take as axiomatic that members maximize utility irrespective of the ownership characteristics of their particular organization. For each member, the choice theoretic structure that bears on union policy objectives may be written:[11]

$$\text{Max}\phi = \theta U_m(G_0,G_1,G_2) + (1-\theta)U_m(Q_0,Q_1,Q_2) = \quad (5)$$

$$\theta U_m(g, \ldots, g_{k+n+s}) + (1-\theta)U_m(q, \ldots, q_{k+n+s}).$$

Subject to: $0 \leqslant \theta_m \leqslant 1$, $\quad (5.1)$

$$\rho_m + R[(\hat{W}\overline{h})_m + Y] - R[(P_0G_0)_m + (P_1G_1)_m + (P_2G_2)_m] = 0 \quad (5.2)$$

$$R[(\hat{W}\overline{h})_m + Y] - R[P_0Q_0)_m + (P_1Q_1)_m + (P_2Q_2)_m] = 0. \quad (5.3)$$

The symbol θ_m in Eq. (5.1) is the probability that a given card holder will retain his job, over some specified period, as a result of union policy objectives. This probability is a function of the variable labor cost (or wage) elasticity of demand for union members, the number of employed members, the percentage increase in variable cost attributable to union labor, and the seniority coefficient associated with the card holder. The latter measures the effect of seniority status on the probability that a given member will retain his job.[12] Equation $(1-\theta)$ is the probability of losing a union job and consuming Q_i goods in the absence of a union contract on some other job.

The variable ρ_m is the net present value of the stream of rents appropriable to any given union member; and $\rho_m = \delta\rho_T$. Where all employed members share rents equally, $\delta = 1/m$. More likely though, older members or more skilled members enjoy a higher δ than younger or less skilled members. In expression (5.2), $(\hat{W}\overline{h})_m$ is the segment of a member's total wage earnings attributable to competitive opportunity costs at contract hours, $\overline{h}$. $(\hat{W}\overline{h})_m$ in Eq. (5.3) are a given worker's total earnings in the absence of a collection contract. The variable Y, in both

Eqs. (5.2) and (5.3), represent all nonwork associated wealth possessed by the individual. $(P_0G_0)_m$, $(P_1G_1)_m$, $(P_2G_2)_m$, $(P_0Q_0)_m$, $(P_1Q_1)_m$, and $(P_2Q_2)_m$ in Eqs. (5.2) and (5.3), respectively, have been defined above.

Utility maximization requires that $\partial\phi/\partial g_1 = 0$ for all $i = 0, \ldots, j$, or:

$$\theta \frac{\partial U}{\partial g_i} - \lambda \left\{ \alpha \frac{\partial \rho m}{\partial g_i} - p_i \right\} = 0 \tag{6}$$

where the union member retains his employment under union contract. And

$$(1 - \theta) \frac{\partial U}{\partial q_i} - \lambda p_i = 0 \tag{6'}$$

where a member cannot maintain employment under collective contract and must accept work elsewhere. We will concentrate on utility maximization in the former case, expression (6), which yields the condition that:

$$\frac{\partial U/\partial g_i}{p_i - \dfrac{\partial \rho_m}{\partial g_i}} = \frac{\partial U/\partial g_j}{p_j - \dfrac{\partial \rho_m}{\partial g_j}} \tag{7}$$

where $\partial U/\partial g_i = \partial U/\partial G_i \cdot G_i/\partial X \cdot \partial X/\partial g_i$ and where $[p_i - \partial \rho_m/\partial g_i]$ is the difference between the market price of g_i and the change in a member's wealth that would arise from his union's efforts to produce more (or less) G_i goods.[13] It is the *effective price* of consuming a unit of g_i. Where $\partial \rho_m/\partial g_i$ is greater than zero, this price is lower than if $\partial \rho_m/\partial g_i \leq 0$. Where $p_i = 0$, goods with $\partial \rho_m/\partial g_i > 0$ will be consumed until the marginal returns to further consumption are negative, rendering the denominator in Eq. (7) positive.

II. A NONPROPRIETARY MODEL OF UNION BEHAVIOR

There are countless books and articles describing union institutions at all levels and across many separate organizations. These descriptions clearly establish that, except for some filial preference arrangements,[14] the intent of unions has been to prohibit and penalize individual and unauthorized transfers of membership status by incumbents to would-be unionists. Explicit private property in union membership exists only in the breach.[15]

Why haven't unions included the right to transfer title to memberships in the bundle of rights associated with membership status? At least two explanations suggest themselves. First, additional memberships in a union of nonhomogeneous workers increase the probability of pecuniary and nonpecuniary externalities. The physical characteristics,

personality, religion, and political convictions of a stockholder in a public corporation are less relevant to other owners than they would be to
members of a private club or a union. Members of the first group do not
work or socialize with each other, whereas members of the latter groups
usually do. If would-be unionists are capable of heaping pecuniary (e.g.,
by violating the "standard rate") or nonpecuniary damages on incumbents, these potential damages are viewed as collective or public. The
price an individual incumbent member is willing to accept for his union
card may be much less than the sum of the losses imposed on other
members by the sale of that card. Before the other members would
honor the rights attached to a transferred card, a majority of them would
have to be compensated for any losses they anticipate as a result of the
transfer. The costs of transacting such side payments, if they could be
determined accurately (members would be prone to exaggerate damage), most likely would be prohibitive.

Secondly, private property rights in membership cards create a
pecuniary conflict between any individual member and the collection of
members. For example, a retiring member, or one who is leaving the
union's jurisdiction, would be interested in capturing at least some of
the rents he would have received had he stayed on. Sale of his card to a
newly hired worker would achieve this. Alternatively, if the new worker
were issued a *new* card instead, rents could be extracted from him
through initiation fees, dues, and wage differentials in which the remaining members could participate, however modestly. This suggests
that unless incumbent members can be compensated for each and every
transaction involving the transfer of membership status from an existing
member to a would-be member, alienability in union cards (i.e., private
property) will be resisted by the great majority of the membership.
Given the above two explanations, a policy of nontransferability may
not be surprising.[16]

Where membership status is transferable, it will be subject to close
scrutiny by the collective. This suggests why union cards, where alienable, have been limited to family members on death or retirement of the
incumbent holder. "Keeping it in the family," so to speak, economizes
on the cost of information that is associated with investigating the
characteristics of would-be applicants and screening new members.[17]
Once it is recognized that job rights are costly to transfer, the cost of
nonrent-maximizing behavior is lowered, and the correspondence between the maximization of rents and the maximization of utility is
loosened for every union member. Without transferability, members
with preferences more consistent with the maximization of rent must
incur higher costs to induce members with other preferences to pursue
rent-maximizing behavior. Moreover, they have less incentive to do so if

they themselves are handicapped in appropriating the full rents supplied by such actions.

The choice theoretic structure for a given union member as it relates to the objectives of union policy was given by expression (5) above. Specification of the ownership characteristics of a given union should not affect the form or content of the utility function of any given member of that union, whether the union is taken to be composed of members with identical preferences, or, more realistically, whether the utility function, for the purposes of analysis, is taken to reflect the preferences of the *median voter* in that organization. Consequently, expression (5) is adopted for the analysis of the nonproprietary union discussed below. On the other hand, the ownership characteristics of a particular union are relevant to the form and content of the function that constrains utility-affecting behavior by any given union member. This suggests that the utility constraint as expressed in Eq. (6) above must be modified to account for the configuration of property rights among union members specific to a given organization. Let expression (8) represent the constraint on utility maximization in a nonproprietary union:

$$[\alpha \rho_m + R\{(\hat{W}\bar{h})_m + Y\}] - R[(P_0 G_0)_m - (P_1 G_1)_m - (P_2 G_2)_m] = 0. \quad (8)$$

This is identical to expression (5.2) except for the addition of α, where α is an index that measures the effect that particular ownership configurations have on the rent-maximizing incentives of members.

If a given individual may participate fully in any rents generated by the union immediately upon acquiring membership status, if he can transfer (for a consideration) the right of access to a rent-yielding job to any willing recipient, and if the costs of enforcing his claim are nonprohibitive, α takes the value of 1.[18] Here the scarcity value of a union card is closest to ρ_m^*, the maximized present value of the stream of rents a given card owner can expect to appropriate over n periods, *ceteris paribus*. If rents are unassignable, or if enforcement costs are prohibitive and members may not even participate in rents *as they occur* over time, α has a value of zero; this is also the scarcity value of a union card.[19] Between these two extremes are numerous permutations and combinations of possible ownership configurations that give α a value greater than zero but less than one.[20]

The effective price of any g_i good is now expressed as $p_i - \alpha(\partial \rho_m)/\partial g_i$, and Eq. (7), the condition for utility maximization between any two goods, may now be written as:

$$\frac{\partial U/\partial g_i}{\partial U/\partial g_j} = \frac{p_i - \alpha \dfrac{(\partial \rho_m)}{\partial g_i}}{p_j - \alpha \dfrac{(\partial \rho_m)}{\partial g_j}}. \quad (9)$$

A. Some General Implications

1. In the extreme case where $\alpha = 0$, and *no* rents may be appropriated by members, the mix of goods for which members wish to bargain will not be influenced by any rent-enhancing opportunities associated with them. For example, assume in Eq. (9) that $\partial\rho_m/\partial g_i = 0$ and that $\partial\rho_m/\partial g_j > 0$. Now compare the effective relative prices between g_i and g_j where $\alpha = 0$ and $\alpha = 1$. In the proprietary case, $\alpha = 1$, the ratio of effective prices favors the consumption of rent-enhancing goods g_j. In the nonproprietary case, $\alpha = 0$, consumption is influenced by the ratio of market prices only, and the cost of *ignoring* rent-increasing possibilities is lowered.

2. If job rights are nontransferable and only *current* rents are captured through pecuniary and nonpecuniary elements in the collective agreement, the value of α is greater than zero but less than one. To the extent that some policy choices, as expressed in the utility function of the median member-voter, yield more of their benefits in future periods than other policy choices, the α assigned to the former will be smaller than the α assigned to the latter. Thus, in the nonproprietary case, the *effective price* of future-oriented goals will be relatively higher than the price of present-oriented goals. This suggests two more reasons, in addition to the obvious benefits of general purchasing power in an exchange economy, why unions usually emphasize wage increments relative to other rent sources in collective bargaining agreements.

First, increments in current wage rates are sources of *current* consumption.[21] A value of α less than one has made this choice less expensive than otherwise.[22] Second, some sources of rent have the characteristics of *collective goods*. The wage rate bargain for all working members is an element with collective good properties. Any given member sees the price to him of his union negotiating a wage increase as equal to zero (or at least lower than the value of the wage increment to him), especially if he expects no strike call. In expression (9), let g_j be the collective good and let g_i be the private good in the bargaining package for which he will have to pay some explicit price p_i. Then, by comparison, members of unions with a lower α[23] will view private goods as relatively more expensive than collective goods. As a result, these unions may be expected to put relatively greater emphasis on collective-good components (including wage rates) in the bargaining package.

3. Finally, if membership is not transferable, the classification of collective bargaining objectives will tend to ignore the more general interests of unknown would-be members and reflect relatively more of the idiosyncrasies of the existing membership as reflected in the revealed preferences of the median voter. To the extent that union members are

not identical, median-voter preferences across unions need not be identical, and the components of bargaining packages of different nonproprietary unions within the same industry or of different unions across industries should evidence relatively wider variation, *ceteris paribus*. [24] Thus, for example, the ratio of wage to nonwage benefits in dollar terms should exhibit a statistically significant variation across different unions within the same industry or across industries, other things being equal. On the other hand, under proprietary unionism, the ratio of wage to nonwage benefits in dollar terms should exhibit little or no significant variation across unions within the same industry or related industries. The costs to nonproprietary incumbents of ignoring future generations of members are relatively low if the values those would-be members place on union activities are not capturable by incumbents.

B. Changes in Demand and
Union Wage-Employment-Membership Policy

Increases in labor demand signal opportunities to incumbents for increasing rents in both pecuniary and nonpecuniary form. Returning to expression (9), this suggests that the effective prices of all rent-enhancing (rent-inhibiting) elements in each member's utility function are lowered (raised), though not proportionately, relative to their levels before the change and relative to nonrent-affecting goods. In the case of a proprietary union, this implies a rise in membership *at the expense* of the maximum wage increment consistent with employment limited to the incumbent members. [25] The nonproprietary case permits no such conclusion. [26] That is, if rents may not be appropriated from new members or if only a "small" fraction may be so appropriated, the effective price of expanding membership, as a device to increase rents and therefore utility, may *rise* relative to the effective price of other sources of utility associated with no increase in membership. One such source is the increment in general purchasing power implied by the wage increase that would limit employment to the existing membership.

A diagram may show this result more clearly. Assume incumbent members (me) face labor demand DD and marginal revenue MR. The union's average and marginal costs of performing collective bargaining services, policing agreements, and other such tasks for varying numbers of members are given by AC and MC. These curves include the reservation prices or opportunity costs of alternative numbers of incumbent and would-be members, and this supply function is shown by SS. For simplicity of exposition, the analysis abstracts from all nonpecuniary sources of rent, and membership size is taken to equal total employment in the unionized firm or industry at any given wage rate. [27]

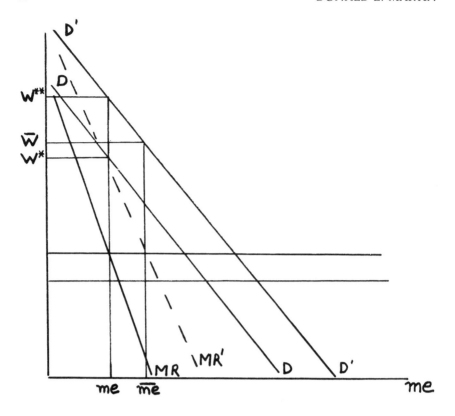

At wage rate W*, rents are maximized and membership-employment is (me)*. This is the outcome expected if incumbents have full proprietary interests in membership. Now compare the results of a shift in demand on the wage-employment-membership policies of proprietary and nonproprietary labor organizations.

If demand were increased to D'D', incumbents would be able to increase their share of rents up to some maximum. Under existing assumptions, the largest rent increment possible is that associated with the wage rate $\overline{W}$ and the membership-employment level ($\overline{me}$). Since members of a proprietary union would be able to appropriate all of this increment through participation in the proceeds from the sale of new membership—or in the case of a temporary increase in demand, through participation in the proceeds from the sale of work permits—they would support an increase in employment to ($\overline{me}$).[28] For similar reasons, a decline in demand would not generate resistance to wage cuts by incumbent members. As long as incumbents may appropriate rent from newer members, it will pay the former to adopt wage policies that minimize the loss in aggregate rent and foster the continued employment of the latter group.

Under nonproprietary conditions, participation in rent increments from the sale of new memberships is greatly attenuated. This implies that the net returns from a wage policy that permits expansion of membership-employment beyond $(\overline{me})^*$ could be smaller than would obtain by setting the wage at W**.[29] This further suggests that it is the nonproprietary, nonwealth-maximizing union model rather than the proprietary model that predicts employment-inhibiting wage increases. This prediction, however, appears to be rejected by experience [Reder (138)].

In response to increases in labor demand, unions appear to pursue policies of wage *and* employment expansion. At least two complementary explanations, consistent with the nonproprietary model, suggest themselves. The first is that *some* employment expansion will occur if pecuniary and nonpecuniary differentials between new and incumbent members are adopted. Journeymen/apprentice wage differentials and seniority wage/hours differentials serve to transfer wealth from newer to older worker-members. These institutions provide a means for incumbents to participate in rents arising from the expansion of employment, thus raising the costs to existing members of ignoring this option when demand increases. However, *future* wage differentials, given a "low" α, will be discounted more heavily than otherwise, and membership-employment will not be expanded to the fully appropriable, rent-maximizing level $(\overline{me})$.

The second explanation for increasing membership-employment beyond $(\overline{me})^*$ focuses on the discretionary role of union managers and may only be treated briefly due to space limitations.[30] Several factors encourage union managers, in the face of increased demand for labor, to bargain for wage rates and other remuneration that have the effect of expanding employment and membership beyond existing levels. Managers of most unions receive salaries that, in part, are positively associated with the membership size of the unions they administer and the value of organizational assets; see Taft (164), pp. 105–116. Since the initiation fees and dues of most unions are either fixed by constitution or subject to change only at the will of a majority of members, managers have an incentive to expand membership as a source of direct and indirect wealth for themselves. "Large" memberships and "large" treasuries, used to finance expense accounts and to purchase assets, should be sought by leaders at the expense of higher wage rates for incumbents and therefore smaller potential memberships. The sacrifice of rents, otherwise captured by incumbents, does not directly affect managers at the margin because they do not directly share in them. This suggests that, even if the salaries of managers did vary directly with the rents obtained by rank-and-file members, managers would still find it attractive—at the margin—to trade *some* of this reward for both "somewhat" higher executive salaries associated with larger memberships *and* for the nontaxable benefits associated with control over larger treasuries, expense accounts, and trust funds.

The preceding analysis does not suggest, however, that union managers seek to *maximize* either membership or the net revenue arising from essentially fixed initiation fees, dues, and other assessments per worker.[31] Since managers do not have a proprietary interest in these revenues (that is, they may not transfer rights to them or legally use them for personal expenditures that are unrelated to union business), the cost of pursuing growth in membership beyond the size that would maximize net revenues is lower than if such revenues were fully appropriable by leaders. Managers may be expected to expand membership beyond this apparently "optimal" point if larger memberships raise the cost of forming voting blocks significant enough to threaten the manager's political survival. The larger the membership, the smaller the returns to any one member devoting resources to collective action in challenging union management. Moreover, the larger the membership, the more likely it is to have heterogeneous interests.[32] However, larger and more heterogeneous memberships also raise the probability that subgroups within the membership will seek to form their own election units and flirt with rival unions.[33] The prospect of generating these minority election units, as membership is expanded, limits managerial interests in membership maximization as a source of utility.[34]

These comments suggest that the response of nonproprietary unions to reductions in demand will be less flexible than the response of proprietary unions. In the latter case, incumbents would agree to wage reductions because they would participate in some of the income that newer members would be able to earn if allowed to retain their jobs. In the nonproprietary case, on the other hand, the cost of such participation is assumed to be higher or prohibitive, and the incentive to adopt a flexible wage policy is considerably lessened. Thus, although seniority-layoff criteria and other such schemes intended to influence favorably the probability of continued employment among incumbent members are implied by both proprietary and nonproprietary ownership arrangements, wage or remuneration flexibility is not. More specifically, the assumptions of the proprietary model unambiguously predict wage and employment symmetry in response to demand fluctuations. Although the wage and employment responses to an increase in demand are less clear-cut under nonproprietary unionism, the model does suggest wage inflexibility in response to a decrease in demand.

C. Strike Policies

Strikes, like negotiations, are costs of producing rents. If unions knew the bargaining package that employers would accept after a strike of some given length, and employers knew the package unions would accept after the same strike, both groups could gain by avoiding the costly contest and settling. The same may be said for the resources both sides expend in lengthy negotiations. But it is precisely because the production of information or knowledge is not costless that we observe such activities. Consequently, a union's bargaining objectives are constrained by negotiation and strike costs.

In one dimension, higher wage rate demands by unions will eventually meet with employer resistance. Multidimensionally, the more valuable the remuneration package demanded by the union, the more resistant the firm will be beyond some level. As discussed earlier, firms will be less resistant to the components of some bargaining packages than to others of equal market value, if the firms have a comparative advantage in meeting the demands inherent in the former relative to the latter.

For members of nonproprietary unions, bargaining packages that threaten relatively greater employer resistance, and thus higher strike and negotiation costs and lower rents, may not be as forbidding as they might be to members of proprietary unions. This is because the cost to individual members of depleting current strike benefit funds (that is, *future* assessments[35] against *future* wage earnings to replenish those funds) is not capitalized into the present value of membership status. Strikes and strike lengths that appear irrational to outside observers, because the increments won are equal to or less than the total costs of the strike, may be perfectly logical if a relatively larger fraction of benefits won is captured currently while a relatively larger fraction of costs is amortized over a longer period.[36] The incentives to ignore the costs of uneconomical strikes are so great that most unions are subject to a two-stage *authorization* requirement: first by the leadership of the local, then by the executive board of the national or international union. Penalties for ignoring this requirement include the withholding of strike funds by the international organization.[37]

In their hypothesis explaining the existence of strikes, Ashenfelter and Johnson (15), p. 36, portray the role of the union leader as "[doing] more than merely represent[ing] the wishes of the rank and file." If the expectations of the rank and file regarding achievable wage increases are much greater than that of the leaders, the latter will attempt to convince the membership to accept a smaller increase. This may be done with or without a strike. The former, however, has the effect of raising rank-and-file's estimates of employer resistance to higher wage demands. Rather than sign an agreement for a lower wage increment and risk political backlash, the leadership is said to favor and *promote* a strike call.[38]

Ashenfelter and Johnson (A/J) fail to explain why rank-and-file members resist the advice of their leadership. In their analysis, they assume a certain expertise among leaders and claim that "the leadership is aware of the possibilities of each bargaining situation..." (*ibid.*). They approvingly cite the experience of federal mediators who claim "... in many situations... [where] the union membership is unwilling to accept the reasonably attainable results of negotiations and is more militant than responsible leadership, a strike may be necessary to drive home the 'facts of life'" (p. 37, *n.* 8). Why the apparent "unreasonableness" on the part of the rank and file, even in the face of more knowledgeable and presumably trustworthy sources? The answer is implied by our nonproprietary model.

"Unreasonable" and "irresponsible" rank-and-file demands are in fact rational for incumbent members, if the present costs of realizing those demands are relatively low. Although wage rates and other demands for remuneration may be modified following the initiation of a strike, so will be the offers of employers. The *estimated* returns to incumbent members, or to a majority of them, may be larger rather than smaller as a result of a strike if the structure of rights to future benefits, and the structure of liabilities to future costs, are clearly recognized.

An analysis of the propensity to strike does not require a distinction between rank-and-file interests and leadership interests, as claimed by the Ashenfelter-Johnson hypothesis, although our analysis of nonproprietary unions implies such a distinction and suggests different conclusions.[39] The implication that derives from our analysis, and that distinguishes it from the A/J strike model, is that unions with higher α's will exhibit relatively fewer uneconomic strikes (and strikes that average longer than the average length of strikes for all unions) than will unions identified as relatively nonproprietary (lower α's), *ceteris paribus*.

D. Nonprice Discrimination in a Nonproprietary Union

One of the implications that may be derived from the analysis of proprietary unions developed in this paper is that, other things the same, nonprice discrimination is less likely to occur in unions with relatively large potential rents and relatively small numbers of incumbent members.[40] The evidence, however, does not seem to support this implication. It is widely believed that craft unions with relatively small memberships and relatively large rents per member [Lewis (100)][41] practice relatively more nonprice discrimination in the form of racial and sexual discrimination among applicants to their ranks than do industrial unions with larger memberships. It has been suggested by Ashenfelter (14) that this observation can be explained by the fact that, unlike craft unions, industrial unions are often found in relatively unskilled labor markets where there is a higher incidence of nonwhite and female workers. Exclusion of the latter two groups from membership would impose a competitive threat to the survival of such unions. Ashenfelter has concluded that, in such circumstances, heavily unionized markets would exhibit egalitarian membership policies; otherwise these markets would be only lightly unionized if at all (the South being an example in point). Merely to observe, however, that nonwhites are better represented in industrial than in craft unions ignores the fact that the former have been known to employ separate locals, separate seniority lists, and separate promotion lists for blacks, and that these separations serve to relegate nonwhites to lower earnings opportunities; see Hill (76).

Given the assumptions of the nonproprietary model, it should be no surprise that nonprice discrimination in membership would be found in both craft and industrial unions. In a nonproprietary union, institutional arrangements make it prohibitively costly to appropriate rents other than those capturable through wage, hours, and benefit differentials. The effective price of buying "desirable" personal characteristics in new members is relatively lower than if all potential rents were readily (inexpensively) capturable. In terms of expression (9), assume that g_i is a personal characteristic that is desired in new members and that is available to all incumbent members at a zero market price. Assume also that, at the margin, $\partial \rho_m / \partial g_i < 0$ and $\partial \rho_m / \partial g_j > 0$. In the proprietary case where $\alpha = 1$, the effective price of g_i is positive and measures the full costs of choosing this personal quality relative to choosing more of g_j (and thus more rents), the private good in the bargaining package. Once the proprietary assumption is relaxed, so that $\alpha < 1$, both numerator and denominator in Eq. (9) fall, *but not proportionately*. The numerator falls relative to the denominator. The result is to lower the relative effective price of desirable personal characteristics, a collective good to members, and more will be consumed at the expense of rent-increasing opportunities.[42] The fact that rents may be directly capturable through wage, hours, and benefit differentials does not in any way alter the above implication. Since membership status is not transferable, differentials cannot be capitalized into the present and thus distant returns will be heavily discounted. The effect is to weaken the connection between nonprice discrimination and loss of monopoly rents.

The objection may be raised that this analysis does not apply to industrial unions because the latter are rarely in a position to exclude undesirable would-be members, if employers have already hired them under union shop agreements. Other things the same, however, economic theory would predict no significant difference in the degree of discrimination exhibited in the membership policies of nonproprietary craft and industrial organizations. In fact, the evidence presented by Ashenfelter and others purporting to identify differential discrimination between craft and industrial unions is less than persuasive. Among other things, it fails to distinguish between *referral* unions, typically craft unions, and nonreferral unions, typically industrial unions.[43] Membership policy under referral unionism is influenced by the power to control the supply of workers to a particular trade or group of trades rather than to a specific firm or industry. Nonprice discrimination, as a consequence, will reveal itself in the *exclusion* of undesirable would-be unionists. On the other hand, nonreferral unions, because their unit of organization is the firm or industry rather than the trade or occupation, seek *inclusivity* in their membership policies. That is, given the level of employment in the firm or industry, industrial unions are motivated—subject to cost constraints—to include all employees as members. In this environment, nonprice discrimination will reveal itself not in terms of the exclusion of nonwhites from the union, but rather in terms of the exclusion of nonwhites from seniority lists and promotion lists favored by whites, and the assignment of nonwhites to seniority and promotion lists promising relatively inferior economic opportunities.

Even if industrial unions were not subject to the threat of relatively large concentrations of nonwhite workers, which forces them toward more egalitarianism, two independent factors suggest that craft unions would exhibit a smaller proportion of nonwhites in their membership relative to industrial unions. The first factor is the nonproprietary character of almost all unions. This lowers the cost of discrimination for both types of union and suggests that discrimination will occur in craft unions. However, and this is the second factor, since discrimination *by exclusion* is employed mostly by craft unions, whereas discrimination in industrial unions takes another less obvious form, the nonreferral union is left with the *appearance* of a more egalitarian posture.[44] This posture is accentuated in those markets where the fraction of nonwhites in industrial union jurisdictions, both prior and subsequent to unionization, is much larger than in the case of craft union jurisdictions.

E. Pricing Membership in a Nonproprietary Union

Modern methods of pricing membership are usually characterized by relatively low lump sum initiation fees, dues differentials between newer and incumbent members, and periodic assessments that ostensibly finance strike funds and other activities [Powel (136), chap. 1]. In addition to these explicit fees and assessments, unions are also known to promote wage, hours, and benefit differentials that discriminate between newer and incumbent members and, as such, constitute an indirect form of initiation fee (*ibid.*). The ownership characteristics of trade unions are relevant to an explanation of these pricing arrangements.

The nonproprietary institutions of trade unions, and the "publicness" of personal characteristics in members, contribute to an explanation of the well-known "underpricing" of their memberships.[45] Earlier writers were struck by the fact that other monopoly institutions charged entry fees that were reasonable estimates of the monopoly rents to be derived from service sales to customers, whereas union fees were only a fraction of potential rents. For example, Becker (22) noted that, while taxicab medallions in New York City were selling for prices that reflected the capitalized value of rents associated with legally limited market entry for cabs,[46] the Glaziers union, with one of the highest initiation fees among American trade unions ($3,000), charged only a small fraction of the estimated monopoly value of membership status.[47]

Several explanations for this anomaly have been offered. One explanation is that there are laws against "excessive" fees charged by labor unions.[48] But "low" fees existed before the Taft-Hartley strictures. Another is that the power of trade unions is generally assisted by government aid, largely associated with the New Deal labor legislation of the 1930s. Such aid may be withdrawn or modified, as in the case of post-World War II labor legislation, where abuses became widely known. To the extent that the monopoly power of unions may be flaunted in the "face of the public" by initiation fees that reflect the high personal gain members can expect from their organizations, public opinion may sour and the aid will be wholly or partially withdrawn. Thus, it is said, fees are kept low.[49] This explanation ignores the fact that other groups rely on government aid in the sense discussed but are content to ignore the possibility of public outrage. Taxi drivers, liquor retailers, broadcasters, and airline owners, among others, *go for the buck!*

Alternately, "low" union fees may arise because of the high cost of capital to would-be members. Cab drivers, broadcasters, airline owners, and liquor retailers all deal in transferable assets that may be used as collateral in negotiating loans to acquire their monopoly rights. Would-be unionists, on the other hand, seek to acquire a *nontransferable* asset. I conjecture that nontransferability results in differences between borrowing rates facing the individual would-be members and the union, as an institution. Without further evidence of financial worth, lending institutions would be less than eager to finance the purchase of a membership. Without such financing, the effective demand for memberships, and the price of memberships, should be lower than their monopoly value. Moreover, even if financing were available, costlessly, would-be unionists would not prepay the monopoly value of nontransferable membership unless they expected to live and work long enough to earn a normal return on their investments. This suggests that unions would have the incentive to finance the purchase of union cards and permit members to pay back the "loan" by some installment plan.[50]

Incumbent members, however, do not have personal claims to the revenue collected by the union from new members, and cannot capitalize such funds into enhanced values for their own job rights. Accordingly, incumbents have limited incentive to structure fees, dues, and other assessments, even wage and benefit differentials, so that the present value of rents is maximized. That is, once multiperiod alternatives and decisions become relevant so that current actions have future consequences, ownership characteristics influence the level and mix of fees, dues, and indirect prices for union membership.

The pricing of memberships in nonproprietary unions will reflect an obvious bias toward immediate and personalized transfers given risk, transaction costs, and the nonproprietary constraints themselves. This suggests three implications. First, membership pricing schemes in nonproprietary unions should result in a relatively larger fraction of payments from newer members to be appropriated directly by incumbents, rather than collected and deposited as general revenues in union treasuries where individual claims are more tenuous. This implication may be better understood if we contrast it with the pricing policy of a rent-maximizing proprietary union. In the latter organization, fees extracted from newer members, as well as dues and assessments contributed by incumbents, would be managed so as to maximize rents. This means that decisions whether to retain rents in the union or to distribute them in some pecuniary manner would be influenced by a comparison of rates of return between investments the union can make to improve rent levels in the future and the expenditures individual members can undertake outside the union. So long as the rate of return is larger in the former alternative, more rents will be retained by the union and invested to increase future rents until, at the margin, the rate of return to further union investment is equal to the rate of return to nonunion-related undertakings by individual members.

Under proprietary unionism, rent distributions to incumbents, made directly from pecuniary and nonpecuniary employer payments as well as from the discriminatory proceeds from the sale of new memberships, would be regulated by the size of dues payments and special assessments as well as by specific pecuniary and nonpecuniary rebates. Thus, given private property in membership status, the risk preference of members, and the costs of maintaining a discriminatory pricing policy for new members, there will be some optimal schedule of initiation fees, dues payments, and rent distributions that is consistent with rent maximization for incumbents.

Returns to new members will be no higher than the normal rates of return on human capital. Returns to incumbents will be determined by the amount of resources devoted to attaining exclusive bargaining rights, the accuracy of their expectations, and the resources devoted to policing rent-dissipating incentives reflected in the existing membership.

Once we relax the proprietary assumption, one important device for capturing rents is forsaken and the returns to pursuing other rent-capturing devices rise. Rents not claimed in the present are not secure if left to the future, because there is no way to capitalize future streams of earnings into present transfer prices. This suggests that members should resist the diversion of current rents to investments for the purposes of producing future rents, unless individual claims can be established in the latter. Consequently, incumbents seek to divert the value of new memberships away from union treasuries and toward themselves by bargaining for wage and hours differentials between senior and junior members that are greater than productivity differentials, by establishing regressive dues schedules among members of different tenure, by different probabilities of job tenure, and by establishing discriminatory and private benefit programs that favor senior members though disproportionately financed by junior members. This suggests a second implication that is also a corollary of the first. Under nonproprietary conditions, incumbents will also seek to retard increases in dues and assessments levied on themselves, behaving as if their rate of time discount were higher than the rate of return to the union for further investments in rent-enhancing activities.[51] Similarly, nonproprietary unions should pay less attention to revenue obtainable from the sales of *work permits* to temporary, nonunion workers beyond the point where they no longer provide a substitute for contributions to union treasuries by incumbents. This is, perhaps, why many unions fail to price work permits to clear the market when they are issued [Lahne (93)].

It is important to remember that the relevant implication is *not* that incumbents will seek discriminatory methods of extracting rent from newer members, since such practices are consistent with proprietary unions as well, but that incumbents will seek to adopt practices that transfer wealth directly and immediately to themselves at the expense of increasing union funds and their own rent prospects in the future.

The bias in nonproprietary unions toward immediate and personalized transfers to incumbents suggests a third implication. The present value of rents extracted from a new member, whether by wage and dues differentials, by lump sum initiation fees, or by a combination of all three devices, should be less than the expected value of the capitalized monopoly rents the union could produce for a new member. At first blush this appears to suggest that nonproprietary unions, unlike proprietary unions, permit newer members to capture and retain some portion of rents generated by union activities. Two factors work to mitigate this conclusion. First, economic theory suggests that nonproprietary unions will adopt policies and practices that are inconsistent with rent maximization. Thus, rents will be smaller than those that could be under proprietary conditions. Second, the queues generated by new members seeking to share in the monopoly rents associated with membership would also create competition among would-be members. Potential rents will be dissipated, and new members would earn no more than normal returns.

To conclude, the fewer the proprietary characteristics of a union, given some level of potential rents, the lower will be the union's fee(s) relative to the present value of expected income per member, the greater will be the union's reliance on personal and direct transfers to incumbents, and the more nonprice discriminatory practices for admission and job assignment will be exhibited.[52]

III. SUMMARY AND CONCLUSIONS

The purpose of this paper has been to apply economic theory to trade unions in order to generate testable implications. The theory and implications presented above have been developed from assumptions about the ownership characteristics of labor organizations. These ownership characteristics have also been useful in identifying the maximand most likely to be consistent with observed union behavior. The nonproprietary nature of membership in labor organizations suggests that unions will not behave as wealth-maximizing institutions. That is, the nonproprietary constraints facing utility-maximizing members suggests behavior that is inconsistent with adopting wealth as the organizational maximand. Utility-maximizing behavior on the part of union members, under conditions of both heterogeneous and homogeneous preferences, yields implications about union bargaining goals and internal policies that are testable at least in principle. These implications pertain to the choice of components of the bargaining package, including the relative weights given to future versus present benefits and to the policy tastes of incumbent versus would-be members. The analysis of nonproprietary unions also yields implications for union policy toward wage flexibility in the face of fluctuating labor demand, toward membership size, and price and nonprice discrimination in the role of memberships. Moreover, the analysis yields implications regarding the attitude of members toward strike policy, including strikes that appear irrational or uneconomic from the point of view of wealth maximization.

This paper has only scratched the surface of what, I believe, is a powerful theory of union behavior. Elsewhere, I have shown that the "Ownership Theory" is capable of generating testable implications about the existence and nature of conflict among members as well as between members and leaders that other writers have observed.[53] The ownership theory of trade unions suggests that the leaders of a nonproprietary labor organization will enjoy greater opportunities to increase their own utility at the expense of rank-and-file members. These opportunities will express themselves in leadership discretion over wage policy, membership policy, the management of union assets, the relative composition of collective bargaining components, and tenure in office. Where the cost of policing union leaders is relatively high, as is expected under nonproprietary arrangements, the preferences of the rank and file will be modified in collective bargaining outcomes by union managerial discretion.

Not all unions have identical ownership characteristics. Some will be more proprietary than others. These differences provide opportunities to test the theory. Obviously, this is the next logical step.

FOOTNOTES

The author is research professor of economics, Law and Economics Center.

This paper has benefited from comments made on earlier versions by Kenneth Clarkson, Louis De Alessi, Arleen Liebowitz, Roger Leroy Miller, and John Pencavel. More recently, the paper has received valuable comments from Dale Collins, Nicholas Kiefer, William Landes, George Neumann, Richard Posner, Melvin Reder, and other members of the Law and Economics and Labor Workshops of the University of Chicago during the Winter Quarter of 1977. However, all errors associated with this paper are the exclusive property of the author.

Research support fundamental to the development of the theory presented below was provided by the Hoover Institution.

1. To the extent that the union has a comparative advantage in the production of some goods, such as grievance services, contract policing, group purchase benefits, and others, the union itself will be a source of rents to the membership completely independent of the benefits arising from any monopoly power it may exercise. This, however, should not

suggest that rents arising from grievance services and the like, performed by the union, are necessarily independent of that power. In fact, it should not be surprising to find unions with relatively more monopoly power providing relatively better or more services to their membership, *ceteris paribus*. Nevertheless, this explains why some unions survive even when their monopoly power in the labor market is nil.

2. Where jurisdiction may be defined by occupation, plant, industry, or location and the right to strike implies the effective right to exclude direct labor substitution by the struck employer.

3. Any employment relationship, union or otherwise, is multidimensional. It includes the wage rate, the workers' productive abilities, the physical working conditions, the quality and number of complementary human and nonhuman resources, the personalities of the parties to the relationship, and so on. Almost all of these elements are amenable to adjustments at the margin. From the union's point of view, the more elements and the greater the extent to which the employer is free to adjust at the margin, the less valuable is its "exclusive" bargaining right. That is, the fewer the elements over which it has exclusive rights in the employment relationship, the less valuable are the set of rights it does possess. This suggests that, in addition to sole representation, the value of bargaining rights is enhanced by mechanisms that would increase the union's control over other margins on which employers make adjustments. One set of such mechanisms that appears particularly popular are union security agreements. For a more detailed discussion of this point, see my manuscript [Martin (110), chap. 3, pp. 4-9].

4. The notion that union monopoly rents include nonpecuniary elements is hardly novel; see Becker (22), p. 209, and Rice (139), p. 592.

5. $\overline{W}(\overline{mH})$ and $\hat{W}(\overline{mH})$ are real disposable claims on general purchasing power and may be expressed in Eq. (1) in terms of the market values of goods that may be consumed ($P_0 G_0$) and ($P_0 Q_0$), respectively.

6. This approach suggests that labor demand elasticities that focus only on money wage rates may appear unstable if variable nonwage payments are important in the remuneration package.

7. These characteristics include many of the nonpecuniary goods that contribute to the composition of rents in Eq. (1) above, such as plant or office lighting and air conditioning, work tools, personal characteristics of co-workers, cafeteria menus, etc.

8. Note that so long as a members' utility is affected by job-related environmental considerations, the negotiability or job rights offers no guarantee that members will have tastes consistent with rent maximization. It does, however, suggest that in this case tastes are more likely to be coincident with rent maximizing than where job rights are not transferable. See Feinberg (64).

9. Since preferences have been hypothesized to be identical, there is a strong temptation to use an aggregate utility function to describe "the union" and its bargaining goals. This temptation is resisted here if only because we will soon be discussing situations where member interests diverge and we wish to avoid the impression, so often advanced by earlier writers, that the union is some entity *outside* the individual preferences of *all* those who compose its membership and chart its policy. See, for example, Atherton (17) and Cartter (34).

10. This particular formulation calls attention to what should be obvious, that members do not bargain for wages *qua* wages, but for the utility associated with the market basket of goods that wages may purchase.

11. The following constraint is formulated in terms of proprietary unionism. That is, members may capture their share of the full capitalized value of any rents produced by the union. A more general constraint on a member's utility-maximizing behavior is presented in the next section.

12. Let $\theta_m = m(1 + \dot{W}\eta)/m \cdot S$. Where m is the number of employed members, $\dot{W}$ is the percentage change in the variable cost per unit of union labor, η is the variable labor cost elasticity of demand for union members, and S is the seniority coefficient. Note that S may vary between 0, where the individual has no seniority, *but others do* (and thus $\theta = 0$) and $m/m (1 + \dot{W}\eta)$, where the individual is in the highest seniority class (and θ is equal to 1).

13. For the purposes of simplicity the subscript m has been dropped from U_m in Eq. (7) and θ is temporarily assumed to be unity.

14. Filial preference appears to be illegal under the Civil Rights Act of 1964. See Phalen v. Theatrical Protective Union 62 LRRM 2689.

15. Aside from the explicit proprietary arrangements in union cards ascribed to Seattle Longshore Unions at the turn of the century [Larrowe (94), p. 88], markets for union cards have been clandestine and, apparently, infrequent [Martin (108, 109)].

16. A third, perhaps less important, explanation for the absence of proprietary institutions in trade unions concerns employer response to union participation in the hiring process. If the employer has relatively little discretion in the hiring process, as in the case of hiring halls and other referral systems, and if a large variance in employee performance is relatively costly to the firm, the latter will not be indifferent to the characteristics of the employees referred to it. This suggests that any additional hiring costs imposed on employers will be shifted back onto wage rates and thus affect the potential rents of all union members. Although transfer rights may be valuable to each individual member, their adoption may lower total rents below what they would be if cards were not transferable.

17. Where there is no heir, the card usually reverts to the union, to be awarded by majority vote. See Martin (108).

18. The value implicitly assumed in Eq. (6).

19. This last case suggests the plight of rank-and-file members of a "racketeering" union making "sweetheart" contracts with employers. See Weinstein (179).

20. For the purposes of comparative statics, however, it is virtually impossible to compare different sets of rights in order to determine, a priori, which union has a higher α. On the other hand, it will be possible to identify unions with similar ownership structures save one or two "important" and observable differences (such as whether members have rights to bequeath their union cards to relatives or whether incumbent members share directly in the fees, dues, and other payments new members must tithe to the union), and to make a priori statements about the relative size of α among them.

21. Wage receipts, of course, may be exchanged in the marketplace for *transferable* claims on future consumption.

22. Strictly speaking, α less than one makes *all* current pecuniary and *non*pecuniary sources of rent (of which wage payments constitute only one source, albeit an important one) relatively less expensive.

23. For simplicity, we assume α to be identical for g_i and g_j, although they need not be.

24. Evidence consistent with this implication is presented by Solnick and Staller (158). To my knowledge Clarkson (42) was the first to make this argument as a general implication of nonproprietary organization.

25. The maximum wage increment foregone constitutes the price to incumbents, P_i, of generating rent transfers from membership sales made possible through employment expansion. Of course, beyond some point an additional membership acquired through employment expansion will reduce rents for incumbent members relative to raising the wage rate. Thus, as long as P_i is less than the increment in rent from new memberships, members will support a wage increase less than the maximum.

26. See my manuscript [Martin (110), chap. 3] for an analysis of union behavior under proprietary assumption.

27. See chap. 3, pp. 31–39, and chap. 4, pp. 14–20, of *ibid.* for a detailed discussion of the determinants of membership policy under proprietary and nonproprietary unionism.

28. This result is particularly interesting because it has often been alleged that "... the typical union does not regard demand for more labor than the *current* membership can supply as evidence it has set the wage rate too low, *as would an income maximizing union*" [Reder (138), pp. 350–351]; italics supplied.

29. This is a case to which, I believe, Reder's remarks seem most appropriate.

30. A more detailed discussion of the following point is found in chap. 5 of my manuscript, *op. cit.*

31. The net revenue maximand is adopted by both Berkowitz (25) and Atherton (17). See chap. 2 of my manuscript, *op. cit.*, for a critical examination of their models as well as other models of union behavior.

32. To my knowledge this is the first time such an argument has been used to explain at least some of the leadership's interests in the growth of the organization. See Ross (141) for the standard argument. This argument also suggests that leaders will be less inclined to favor racial and other discriminatory entrance requirements.

33. These units are known as Globe election units. See *Globe Machine and Stamping Company*, 3 NLRB 294 (1937). The proliferation of these units has been the experience of the International Typographical Union. See Atherton (17), pp. 95 and 96.

34. Membership maximization might require actual cuts in contract wages to sufficiently expand employment and appropriate cuts in membership fees to subsidize additional memberships. These efforts would be particularly costly to leaders.

35. The word assessment is used broadly here to include various forms of financing strikes.

36. This point should be kept distinct from any common pool—free-rider—implications that derive from a collective strike fund.

37. An *N.I.C.B.* survey of 194 national union constitutions representing over 17 million union members revealed that in 53 percent of these organizations, representing over 10 million workers, two-stage strike authorizations were required before strike benefits would be distributed. See *Handbook of Union Government Structure and Procedures, N.I.C.B.,* Studies in Personnel Policy No. 150 (n.d.).

38. "... although contrary to the membership's best interest" (15), p. 37. The leadership in the A/J model is said to promote strikes in order to inflate rank-and-file underestimates of employer resistance to wage demands, as an alternative to securing agreements for lower increases without a consensus.

Although the A/J model makes much of it, it is difficult to see, operationally, how leadership may be separated from membership. To the extent that the latter must approve strikes by vote, strike calls are clearly expressions of the membership. If a strike can be called without a vote, it still requires the acquiescence of the membership, without which the A/J model leadership will ultimately face political retribution. Thus, holdouts for unrealistic or unreasonable demands, as contracts expire, emphasize a willingness to mount a strike by the rank and file. It may be the case that the leadership has a different estimate from the membership of the ultimate outcome, but that need not mean that a strike may be foisted upon the membership for its own good, as if it were helpless. It should be noted that A/J devote no space to assumptions that would permit union managers the kind of discretion and insulation from rank-and-file retribution that their model claims.

39. The nonproprietary model suggests that union leaders will discourage rather than promote strike calls, especially those that place a *net* drain on union assets. See my manuscript, *op. cit.*, chap. 6.

40. This proposition is not affected by the introduction of nonzero transaction costs

associated with side payments, where they are a function of the size of membership. The proprietary model of union behavior and its implications are discussed in chap. 4 of my manuscript, *op. cit.*

41. There is much to be cautious about in using wage differentials as a measure of monopoly power. See Becker (22) and Rice (139).

42. Although union treasuries may be increased by pricing new memberships to reflect potential monopoly rents, irrespective of ownership characteristics, a member of a non-proprietary model of union behavior and its implications are discussed in chap. 4 of my of a proprietary organization.

43. The referral/nonreferral classification is actually preferred by Ashenfelter (14), p. 97, *n*. 13.

44. This differs from Ashenfelter's view that "craft unions tend to have greater control of the supply of labor and the hiring process than do industrial unions, and *this also will tend to make them more discriminatory*"; italics supplied. Economic theory, under nonpro-prietary unionism, does not unambiguously predict that craft unions will be more dis-criminatory than industrial unions. Rather, it predicts that discrimination will take dif-ferent forms as between the two union types.

45. For evidence and discussion of underpricing see Taft (164), Becker (22), and Pen-cavel (133).

46. The market in taxi medallions is by no means unique. Liquor licenses, broadcasting rights, and airline routes generate monopoly rents for their owners and have been ob-served to command their capitalized values when exchanged.

47. See Becker (22), p. 221. The wealth-maximizing formula used by Becker is $F = by/r \cdot [1 - (1 + r)^{-n}]$; where b = union/nonunion wage differential, y = annual income of a union member, r = market rate of interest; and n is the estimated number of years member expects to be in the union. Note that Becker ignores the dues component of union fees, perhaps because of the difficulties in identifying the rent element in these payments and focusing only on the *initiation* fees of the Glaziers union.

48. The Taft-Hartley Act (1947) and the Landrum-Griffin Act (1959).

49. Legislation prohibiting "excessive" fees was passed in response to reports and evi-dence that "corrupt" unions were bleeding their members by charging exorbitant fees. Although this may only have been rent extraction of the kind discussed above, the legisla-tive response was to corruption in unions and *not* to a revelation of the monopoly value of a union card.

50. Becker, to my knowledge, was the first to point this out. He believes this argument is sufficient to dismiss imperfect capital markets as an explanation of "low" initiation prices. See Becker (22) and Powel (136).

51. Since rent-enhancing investment by the collective raises the value of monopoly rents to *all* incumbents, free-rider resistance to dues increases will be present under proprietary unionism also. However, that resistance will be even greater where future rents cannot be capitalized to the present.

52. Here we refer to racially and sexually separate seniority lists and promotion ladders that have the effect of excluding "less desirable groups" from the more desirable jobs. Although this may be interpreted as merely a form of rent extraction through wage dif-ferentials, it differs in that nonwhites and/or women may never extract rents from *newer members* who are white and/or male, respectively, even though they would be willing to pay for the future right to do so. This opportunity cost is not felt in the nonproprietary union.

53. See chap. 6 of my manuscript, *op. cit.*

DELIVERED COMMENTS

Louis De Alessi (University of Miami). Walter Oi presumably will exercise his comparative advantage in labor economics and focus on Martin's paper. Accordingly, I will direct most of my comments to Frech's contribution to the large and growing body of empirical evidence supporting the usefulness of the property rights approach.

Frech, in an earlier paper, compared the performance of profit and nonprofit (mutual and Blue Shield) firms which process health insurance claims under contract to Medicare. As expected, he found that the nonprofits were less efficient.

In the substantive part of the present paper, Frech suggests that mutuals are characterized by institutional arrangements which permit their managers, relative to the managers of the other nonprofit firms in his sample, to capture more of the residual. Accordingly, they may be expected to operate their firms more efficiently. Frech, however, does not indicate how the residual is affected by processing costs, time, and errors—the three functional variables in his study. This linkage depends upon the form of the compensation, and Frech's observation that carriers are not selected by competitive bidding and that no carrier has been dropped for poor performance is particularly disturbing. For example, it is not clear why stronger claims to the residual would not imply greater incentive to operate "inefficiently" by using low-quality inputs (e.g., trainees) to process claims (yielding more errors), scheduling work in otherwise slack periods (longer processing time), and incurring higher accounting costs but lower or negligible opportunity costs. Additional information regarding how prices are set and how HEW employees select and retain carriers would be helpful.

Frech tested the hypotheses using the raw data from his earlier study, retaining the sample of profit-seeking firms and splitting the sample of nonprofit firms into mutuals and other nonprofits. It is not clear, however, how he controlled for variables other than ownership; this is a particularly sensitive point given Frech's criticism of other researchers on this score. For example, do the criteria used by HEW in selecting and retaining carriers bias the test results? If they do, what is the direction of the bias? How were processing costs, time, and errors computed? What exactly do they measure?

Given the final form of the data, the statistical test applied by Frech to evaluate the hypotheses is powerful. There are nonparametric tests, however, which would have permitted direct evaluation of the hypotheses using the three-way classification of the data. Although the addition of such a test would not have provided independent evidence on the validity of the hypotheses, it would have been helpful in case the data did not fully meet the conditions underlying the parametric test used.

Turning to Frech's introductory remarks, which constitute the bulk of his paper, the purpose and nature of his criticisms of other studies of cost behavior under alternative property rights are puzzling. For example, consider the three objections raised to Davies' study of the Australian airlines. Frech's first objection is that "both airlines are regulated very rigidly by the government." But that is precisely what makes Davies' study striking: the major, crucial difference between the two firms is that the private firm is owned by individuals with explicit rights to at least some of the residual—the very crux of Frech's own paper. Frech's second criticism is that, given a sample of only two firms, tests of the statistical significance of the differences observed are not possible. If the world is unkind enough to provide us with small samples, however, we should not despair. A small sample can be suggestive, and a sufficiently large number of small samples can provide the data necessary for more rigorous statistical studies.

I would like to conclude my review of Frech's paper with a few remarks of more general applicability. First, there is no such thing as a property rights theory of the firm or of anything else. There is simply an extension of the traditional economic theory of individual choice under constraints, with special emphasis on the economic consequences of alternative institutional constraints. I make this point because I wish to distinguish the property rights approach from ad hoc modeling. Second, decisions affecting a firm's behavior typically are group decisions, and these are the outcomes of utility-maximizing choices made by each individual member of the group in pursuit of his own self-interest. To focus attention on the constraints imposed on the top decision-maker, without careful specification of the context, is misleading. One purpose of institutional constraints is to provide a mechanism for resolving conflict within an organization, and a major contribution of the property rights approach is to provide a theoretical framework for analyzing how alternative institutional arrangements affect incentives *within* an organization and thus affect the outcome of the decision process; see, for example, Alchian (7) and De Alessi (55).

I will now turn briefly to Martin's paper. Martin is breaking new ground in an area particularly rife with ad hoc theorizing and impressionistic or judgmental assertions, and I applaud his attempt to bring rigorous economic analysis to bear on the issues.

Most of my comments on Martin's paper relate to the exposition, and I will not bore you with them. I will raise a couple of points, however, just to show that I have read the manuscript.

The definitions of the terms appearing in Eq. (1) are not quite clear to me. Do members pay a zero price for the Q's and the G's? If they do not, where is this price reflected? Are the Q's actually produced, even though not specified in the union contract, or are they goods that would have been produced had there not been a union contract? Are the alternatives at hand union or no union, as seem to be specified in the PQ's and PG's, or a wider range of alternatives, including unions of different form, as indicated by the W(mH)?

The diagram in his paper shows the effect of an increase in demand on the rents obtainable by members of proprietary unions. What is the initial situation and what is predicted after an increase in demand in the case of nonproprietary unions?

The conflict between members and leaders, although discussed by Martin elsewhere, could usefully be clarified in this paper. References to the "union" do not always make clear which groups within the union gain or lose in a given situation.

In conclusion, I would like to emphasize that both papers contribute to our understanding of the workings of the real world. They are a useful addition not only to the property rights literature, but also to general economic analysis.

Walter Y. Oi (University of Rochester).   At the outset, I would like to offer my impressionistic review of the contents of this paper. Martin begins with the question, "What do unions maximize?" Eight alternative maximands which have been suggested by various economists are then summarized. The formal model in Section I of the paper is intended to accomplish two things. First, it defines the concept of union monopoly rents in his Eq. (1). Second, the rent concept is incorporated into a budget constraint in a model of utility maximization by the typical (possibly potential) union member. The model of a nonproprietary union is introduced in Section II via a loosely defined parameter α. The five subsections rationalize such phenomena as (A) the composition of the negotiated union "compensation" package where compensation includes fringe benefits and working conditions, (B) wage and membership policies, (C) the propensity to strike, (D) nonprice discrimination, and (E) membership dues.

The quality of the paper is variable. Although some useful insights are provided in Part II, the evidence is anecdotal and his theory is loose. In the concluding section, the author writes: "Utility-maximizing behavior on the part of union members . . . yields implications about union bargaining goals and internal policies that are at least testable in principle." Perhaps this is so, but I am skeptical.

In my remarks on the paper, I first suggest a slight modification of

Martin's basic theoretical model. I then raise some questions about the usefulness of the analytic model. Finally, I offer some opinions about selected parts of the anecdotal evidence.

In Eq. (4), the utility of a union member depends on three vectors of goods, (G_0, G_1, G_2). Without loss of generality, we can let $G = G_0$ denote the vector of goods including leisure that can be bought with general purchasing power. Let $P = P_0$ denote the discounted expected prices of the G goods. (Hicks in *Value and Capital* uses the practice of discounted expected prices in his intertemporal models. It avoids the need to incorporate discounting of future values and simplifies the notation.) Let $H = G_1$ represent the vector of goods provided "on-the-job" with $\gamma = P_1$ denoting their "prices." Since the author never explicitly deals with the off-the-job "goods" G_2, I shall ignore them here. Let $Q = Q_0$ and $H' = Q_1$ be the counterparts for the nonunion individual. The maximand in your Eq. (5) can then be written:

$$\phi = \theta U(G,H) + (1 - \theta)U(Q,H'). \qquad (5)$$

The budget constraints become:

$$\rho_m + [\overline{WH} + Y] - [PG + \gamma H] = 0; \qquad (5.2)$$

$$[\hat{W}\hat{H} + Y] - (PQ + \gamma H') = 0. \qquad (5.3)$$

Finally, the monopoly rent earned by the union can be written in this simplified notation as:

$$\rho_T = [\overline{W(MH)} - \hat{W}(\hat{M}\hat{H})] + [\gamma H - \gamma H'] - FX. \qquad (1)$$

For the later analysis, it is useful to write an explicit expression for the per capita union rent:

$$\rho_m = \partial \rho_T. \qquad (1b)$$

It will be remembered that γ is the vector of "prices" of "on-the-job" goods provided either by the union contract H or by the nonunion employment contract H'. Discounting to present values is implicit since the arguments of the utility function as well as of the goods vector, etc., contain dated flows.

Concerning the concept of monopoly rent in Eq. (1) (where discounting is incorporated into the wage W and price γ vectors), the total monopoly rent, ρ_T, that is realized by the union can be viewed as the algebraic sum of three components: (a) the earnings differential due to higher bargained wages; (b) the difference in the value of "on-the-job" goods; and (c) the cost of negotiating the other two components. Let me rewrite this as follows:

$$\rho_T = [\overline{W(MH)} - \hat{W}(\hat{M}\hat{H})] + [\gamma(H - H')] - [FX]. \qquad (1)$$

The first component is the one which most easily lends itself to interpretation and hopefully measurement. Recall that $H = G_1$ is a *vector* of OTJ "goods." I have omitted the "off-the-job" goods which I presume are on the order of pension plans, medical insurance, turkeys on Thanksgiving, and so on. The "on-the-job" goods presumably include such factors as more industrial safety, cooler temperatures in the factory, employee recreation rooms, and the like. The author seems to imply that these OTJ goods can accurately be valued at parametric prices γ. If *all* the OTJ goods are on the order of turkeys on Thanksgiving or free lunches, then the assumption may be valid. However, if $H = G_1$ includes industrial safety or recreation rooms, which involve elements of public goods, then a consumer surplus measure of "value" may be more appropriate. Finally, the union through its size may be able to influence γ, the "prices" of these OTJ goods.

Let me first direct attention to Eq. (5.3) for the nonunion state of the world. The budget constraint (again ignoring G_2) can be rewritten in the more familiar fashion:

$$PQ + \gamma H' \le \hat{W}\hat{H} + Y. \tag{5.3}$$

This simply says that outlays on "goods" must be less than or equal to the present value of income. Remember that $\hat{W}$ can be interpreted as a vector of discounted expected wages so that $\hat{W}\hat{H}$ is a dot product producing the present value of wage earnings. Two remarks can be made here:

First, it is argued that Q is a vector of "goods" *including leisure* which can be bought with general purchasing power. If leisure time is valued at the wage rate $\hat{W}$, then $\hat{W}$ must be an element of P, the vector of "prices." If this is so, then Eq. (5.3') must be replaced by:

$$PQ + \gamma H' \le \hat{W}T + Y, \tag{5.3'}$$

where T is the potential time available for work and leisure. Thus, ($\hat{W}T + Y) = F^*$ is the counterpart to Becker's concept of "full income." See Becker (24).

Second, if the "on-the-job" goods H' that are provided by the firm are paid for by the firm, then $\gamma H'$ should *not* be counted as an expenditure. The theory is very imprecise as to how one measure $\hat{W}$, γ, etc.

Turn next to Eq. (5.2) for the union state of the world. If the rent, ρ_m, cannot be transformed into general purchasing power (and if "rights" cannot be sold then it cannot be so exchanged), it cannot be properly included in full wealth that can then be allocated to G,H. The G goods (excluding leisure) can only be purchased with $(\overline{WH} + Y)$, while the OTJ goods H are purchased by the unionized worker's share of the residual after paying FX to get H.

In the formal model, θ, the probability of being in a union state, and α, the appropriability parameter, are treated as exogenous parameters. But when Martin turns to the implications in Section II, it becomes clear that both parameters may indeed be endogenous. Thus, if the union negotiates a very high wage-and-fringes package, θ must decline. It is argued that if α is high (the proprietary union), then the union is more likely to demand more future-oriented OTJ goods. But can't this be turned around? Namely, when the union contract entails more future-oriented goods, there are surely incentives for the union to establish internal membership contracts that raise the value of α. The model is very imprecise about the links from contractual provisions to the numerical value of α. Finally, the implication of the model to interpret various perceived union practices, suggests that the model must be expanded to allow δ, the sharing parameter, to be a function of various factors like X, H, etc.

In Eqs. (6) and (7), the decision variables are taken to be the arguments of the utility function, $U = U(G,H)$, or $U = U(Q,H')$. The typical union member varies his demand for ordinary goods G to maximize U, and, apparently, he also determines the package of OTJ goods H that will maximize his utility. Although X is the vector of inputs used by the union to negotiate wages $\overline{W}$ and fringe benefits H, the union member never explicitly determines X. I suppose that the model implicitly builds this suboptimization into the utility-maximization process, but it is not at all clear that we are satisfying Eq. (2). More importantly, there is nothing in this model which determines the union wage rate $\overline{W}$. If all unions were competitive unions that only provide their members with grievance procedures, formal pension rights, and so forth, then $\overline{W}$ may be exogenous. But, in this event, the utility of being a union member must be equal to the utility of being a nonunion member—Smith's concept of equalizing wage differentials must somehow come into play. The omission of the wage rate as one of the decision variables is, in my opinion, a rather serious flaw in the theory.

The maximand here is expected utility ϕ in Eq. (5). I question whether it is analytically convenient to deal with direct utility functions. Suppose that G contains two elements, leisure L and corn C. Then Q must also include L and C, and the only difference between G and Q is in the equilibrium values of L and C. Given a state of the world (union or nonunion), the individual maximizes his utility. The maximum utility that will be realized, say by the nonunion worker, can then be written:

$$U = U(Q,H') = V(F^{**},P,\gamma) \quad [F^{**} = \hat{W}T + Y = \text{full income}], \quad (4a)$$

where V is the indirect utility function. If θ is truly exogenous, then $(1 - \theta)V(F^{**},P,\gamma)$ will be fixed, and the typical "potential" union member only maximizes the utility in the union state. When we put things in terms of indirect utilities, it becomes clear just what are and are not decision variables that can be manipulated by the individual worker.

In Section II-A, Martin defines a nonproprietary union as one for which $\alpha = 0$. But if $\alpha = 0$, then ρ_m and hence ρ_T and $\delta = \rho_m/\rho_T$ have *no effect* on utility since they no longer influence the union member's budget constraint. What then determines the union wage rate or the composition of the union "total compensation package" which includes $\overline{W}$ and $H = G_1$? In short, the definition of a nonproprietary union leads to the loss of the problem with the bathwater.

The discussion in the last half of II-B is interesting, but fails to clarify the composition of the union employment contract. What determines the length of the contract and how often are contracts renegotiated prior to their expiration? The demand changes here presumably refer to real changes. But the flexibility of money wages will be influenced by the provisions of the contract and the external rate of inflation.

In reviewing Section II-C (Strike Policies), I again have trouble in trying to understand Martin's definitions of a nonproprietary union and of union monopoly rents. Clearly, the wage components of the rent, [$\overline{W}$ − $\hat{W}$], has got to be divorced from the nontraded component, γH − H'). The appropriability parameter α for the wage component (aside from membership dues) ought to be the same for all unions. Martin implies this. In terms of the formal model, the union's assets presumably reside in the nontraded portion, $\gamma(H - H')$. His discussion here is interesting, but more care must be exercised in formulating the theory and empirical tests. The utility function of the leadership must be introduced. Finally, you may want to consult the Ph.D. thesis by Harry Grubert (M.I.T., circa 1968) who (as I recollect) argued that strikes occur in those industries where the wage component of the rents are highest.

The concluding subsection of Part II raises a number of interesting questions dealing with the construction of an optimal pricing policy. The "buyers" in this market are the potential union members, while the "sellers" are the incumbents negotiating through their agents, the union leadership. The author correctly points out that "dues" can be in the form of initial membership fees, monthly dues, or lower wages. The "rents" can be deferred to retirement pensions, steeper age-earnings profiles, and the like. I would like to see the theory here formally developed with reference to particular union employment contracts. To the extent that a contract fixes both wage rates and hours, I suspect that there may be several optimal pricing policies. The empirical test of any hypotheses will be confounded by the sorting of workers across unions. Which individuals are most likely to wait it out to get the positions in proprietary unions?

I am also troubled by Frech's paper. I am troubled that the claims for reimbursement of medical expenditures are supposed to be homogeneous. Yet, when I look at the dimensions of output, in particular the time required to service claims, I notice that the average time taken by firms to process them is thirty-four days with a standard deviation of twenty days. It is not at all clear what these claims are. They could be claims for drug purchases, for chemotherapy, for complicated hospital operations, visits, and so forth. If one is to verify whether or not the charges are allowable and whether or not to make payments, it is evident to me that the complexity of the claim ought to matter.

Since all of Frech's equations are in logs, I worked up an equation in which the left side variable is the cost incurred per day allocated to processing claims; it is a cost per-unit input. I suggest that if the number of days allocated reflects the complexity of the claim, this might be a better measure than the one used by Frech. Using my measure, I find that the cost per day of processing claims is virtually unrelated to the number of claims processed. It is higher for larger claims, and indeed, the nonprofit firms have the lowest cost per day allocated to processing. This is contrary to the hypothesis set forth in Frech's paper. I am disturbed that the same analysis was not repeated in terms of the breakout between mutuals and Blue Cross-Blue Shield. I think we should know more about the nature of these claims. What are the revenues that different classes of firms receive, and what are the costs? Are the costs for the mutual companies and the stock companies net of the remuneration to their managers? These are questions that should be answered if we are to properly evaluate Frech's analysis.

MUTUAL ORGANIZATIONS: DISCUSSION

Martin. I wish to cover several of Professor Oi's points but, before I do, I would like to acknowledge the very fine quality of his suggestions for simplifying the notation and tightening up the theory.

My first comment concerns Professor Oi's reference to the problems that might arise if on-the-job goods include collective public goods. Although reference to valuing such goods is absent from the text, I certainly agree that a consumer surplus measure of value for collective goods would be correct. Later in my analysis, however, I am concerned with the presence of collective goods in the bargaining package but my focus is on the well-known proposition that the value of the *marginal unit* of collective good is zero to its consumer. Thus the $p_i th$ element in the vector P_0 or the $p_j th$ element in the vector P_1 takes on a zero value where the ith or jth good is collective.

Second, I have assumed that firm-provided, on-the-job goods should be counted in the union member's expenditure function because the member can influence the composition of bargaining packages, as be-

Economics of Nonproprietary Organizations
Research in Law and Economics, Supplement 1, pages 111-122
Copyright © 1980 by JAI Press Inc.
All rights of reproduction in any form reserved.
ISBN: 0-89232-132-6

tween wages and on-the-job goods, through voting and he therefore pays for on-the-job goods with forsaken wage rates.

Third, with reference to Professor Oi's suggested utility function, Eq. (4a) notwithstanding, $\overline{W}$ is determined in my model, albeit indirectly. When the median voter chooses between G_0 and G_1, the vector of goods purchased with money wages outside the firm and the vector of goods bargained for inside the firm, respectively, the utility-maximizing combination of G_0 and G_1 simultaneously determines the wage and nonwage goals of the union member. This is because G_0 must be purchased with wages $\overline{W}$. I am afraid this point may have been somewhat esoteric, but determining $\overline{W}$ was certainly an objective of building the model.

Fourth, Professor Oi concludes that a totally nonproprietary union α = 0 destroys the model's ability to determine union wage rates and the composition of the collective bargaining contract. If we assume that union leaders are able to extract *all* rents from members, $\alpha = 0$, and the latter receive competitive wage rates and competitive nonwage income. The problem then becomes one of treating the union as a monopolistic firm with the leaders as the residual claimants. Union contract wages and nonwage income will be consistent with maximizing rents for the leaders who have proprietary interests in the organization. This may be a reasonable interpretation of the racketeering union. If union leaders have no proprietary interests, an $\alpha = 0$ value means that contract wage and nonwage income is identical with that which would obtain in the absence of unions.

Finally, let me make it clear that my definition of a nonproprietary union is any union whose members may not transfer all or some of their membership rights to would-be unionists or otherwise capture the *full* capitalized value of those rights in the present. Some unions may be more nonproprietary than others. These differences should show up in the respective formation of bargaining goals.

Frech. I have three points to make. The first was raised by both discussants. They were wondering what the connection was between the residual that the top decision-makers of these firms get and their performance in this social security type of scheme. The answer to that is that there is no connection. The scheme is a cost-based reimbursement and I argue that if a firm is organized as an efficient claims-processing operation in all of its other business, it is somewhat constrained to be efficient in this line of business which is smaller than its main business. In Sam Peltzman's words, "a fast horse can't walk slowly."

My second point is a response to Walter Oi's observation that the complexity of the claims that are being processed might vary across these firms. That is not a problem because each firm has a geographic monopoly and deals with all of the claims of any sort that arise within its area, so what I've got here is a random sample of *all* of the claims that come from a large geographical area. It therefore seems unlikely that the average complexity of the claim is going to vary dramatically from one area to the next.

The third point relates to my criticism of previous empirical work. I may have overdone it. I think those previous works are good scholarship and very important. In fact, they convinced me that this was not only an interesting theoretical point, but an important empirical point as well. However, I think that the natural experiment that I have used, by the very nature of the way the social security administrator has set up the program, is a useful way to identify a narrowly defined service that is not free to vary in a market. It's a nice experiment.

Earl Thompson (University of California—Los Angeles). I would like to direct my question to something in Martin's paper on unions. According to the received theory on attenuated property rights, I think you would expect that the growth rate in union wages through time would be lower than the growth rate of nonunion wages because the first generation of union workers would essentially sell out the second generation of workers by demanding very high wage rates. This, however, does not seem to be observed empirically. Perhaps you have tested for this?

Martin. No, I have not examined this question empirically but I do know of one piece of evidence that is consistent with the implication you correctly derived from my theory. George Neumann, at the University of Chicago, is investigating the present value of union wage rates over different time periods. He has found that the shorter the discounting period the larger the differential between union and nonunion wages in present value terms. The longer the period, the closer union capitalized wages approached competitive capitalized wages. Although this evidence does not speak directly to your question, it is in the spirit of the question and it is consistent with my theory.

Henry Manne (University of Miami). May I ask, is that not like the implication of turning over the management of an endowment of a university to the faculty? They have greater incentive than the present trustees to utilize it for present oriented interests.

Thompson. Yes. So you would expect then a lower growth rate of those union wages or the returns to faculty in that example.

Martin. I would have said a higher growth rate.

Thompson. No, not among "mature" unions. Starting from mature unions and then letting them run, you should get high wages at the beginning as they're selling out the future generation of union workers and then lower almost competitive wages if the transformation is perfect in the next generation. So I would expect, let us say starting from the '50s, that by the '70s a lower growth rate of union wages relative to nonunion wages would have occurred. I don't think it has. If it has occurred I don't think it is significant. To my knowledge, where there are strong unions, there seems to be relatively normal growth rates in terms of wages.

Manne. Would somebody like to follow up on that? It's an interesting point. Ken Clarkson.

Clarkson. My follow-up is in a more general sense, because Thompson's point is the application of a more general problem. I do not understand why union members cannot avoid many of these problems by forming contracts to reduce mismanagement by leaders. They can, for example, tie union leaders' compensation more to pension funds if the leaders tend to ignore the present. If they are using the pension fund to obtain personal gains, union members can reduce other benefits to leaders. It seems there are ways of constraining union leaders so that they will act more like proprietary institutions.

Martin. I think that's a very different question than Earl Thompson raised. We were talking about the interest of union members and not the distinction between leaders and members policing. There is evidence that leaders are policed in very interesting ways. For example, their salaries are constitutionally determined. Dues, which are a source of revenue for the leaders themselves, are also constitutionally determined or determined by a vote of the membership. The rights to use pension funds, or other kinds of funds for investing in equities, are severely constrained, and constitutions often force leaders to invest in government bonds and hold cash in the bank. I used to think that holding cash in the bank was really a method by which a leader could extract rent from the membership, but in fact it's often the case that these union constitutions are written so as to limit discretion on the part of the leaders. That kind of discretion and those limitations don't appear in such an extreme form in proprietary institutions, where more freedom is permitted in terms of investment decisions or wage decisions. So there are attempts to do that.

Evsey Domar (M.I.T.). I have one specific comment and a couple of general comments about Martin's paper. He says: "In other words, it is the private property assumption that translates the interests of utility-maximizing owners into behavior that is consistent with wealth as an organizational maximand for the firm." I wonder, is it really private property that is so crucial? I can imagine the socialist manager, if given the proper success indicator, could behave very similarly to the capitalist manager. There are two differences that probably should be noted: one, I suspect that the capitalist managers stay in their jobs or at least with the same company longer than their socialist counterparts, and that might account for the shorter time horizon; second, the socialist manager usually deals with excess demand, and that I think accounts for the difference in most of his actions. But if you told him to maximize profits and gave him a bonus as a percentage of the profits, I think he would behave very much like a capitalist manager, even though the enterprise itself belongs to the state.

Martin. You have pointed out a fundamental difference in our understanding and interpretation of the function of private property. It is certainly the case that if I gave the managers of a Yugoslavian firm, for example, a percentage of the difference between current revenues and costs, in any one year, that I could get them to behave as profit maximizers for that year. The distinction is, I think, and I have tried to make it in my paper, that private property gives an incentive to the manager or the owner of the firm or the manager/owner, if you like, to take account not only of his current actions, and therefore current differences between revenues and costs, but of the *present value* of the whole future stream of differences between revenues and costs.

The manager of a Russian firm who shares in current profits but has no rights to the proceeds from the sale of the firm's assets or from what amounts to the same thing, the sale of rights to future profits, will discount the future relatively more heavily than would a person who did have those kinds of rights. That is, compared with a person enjoying proprietary rights in that organization. And so we have a distinction between the decision-maker as profit maximizer in a socialist firm and the decision-maker as wealth maximizer in a capitalist firm.

Domar. A Soviet manager is like every other manager in the sense that he wishes to have a successful career, to have a reputation for being an efficient manager who can get jobs done. The fact that he receives a bonus is just one of the considerations. What he wants most of all is to have a good reputation. That may lead to further achievements, maybe a transfer to Moscow. That, I think, is probably the most important part of his life, rather than the bonuses that he gets. But the bonus is part of the success indicator. The very fact that he gets bonuses indicates he is doing well.

Martin. Fine, but I don't think that his behavior would parallel the behavior of a private property owner, even though he might do exactly what the state wants him to do.

Domar. Even if he has a long time horizon and he thinks of the firm as practically his?

Martin. You may have defined the problem away.

Roland McKean (University of Virginia). Mine is a very general point, directed to Martin. I just want to add another case that he might want to analyze some day, and that is when a nonproprietary union faces a nonproprietary employer. For example, when the Department of Defense gets fully unionized, what kind of behavior can be anticipated as far as the model is concerned?

Martin. I guess I'm to throw my hands up and say chaos. But, of course, we have that case already. There are public employee unions that bargain with government. One party may give away too much while the other party, according to my theory, may ask for too little. Note that both parties have relatively shorter time horizons.

De Alessi. Let's return to Domar's point. The issues of who is doing the monitoring and of how (and how much) to monitor the monitors are relevant to American firms as well. One would predict differences in behavior between managers who receive some percentage of accounting profits and managers who receive stock options, since the latter provide rights to future income.

Steven Cheung (University of Washington). My question is directed to Professor Domar. Suppose you have two farms, the same number of workers, the same amount of land and fertilizer and so on, and each farm has a manager running it. Now suppose in the case of one farm the land is privately owned.

Domar. Owned by a single manager or by a company?

Cheung. It doesn't matter. By a company. The important feature is that it is privately owned.

Domar. I would draw the line at the manager who owns the farm. If he owns it himself, I would expect one set of behavior characteristics that I would put in one category; but if the farm is owned by a company, some stockholders, and there is some board of directors to which he is responsible, then that manager comes much closer to the socialist manager, appointed by an administrator responsible to the ministry, who in his behavior tries to do what the administrator wants him to do. But, so long as the ministry doesn't tell him go ahead and maximize profits, of course he'll behave differently.

Cheung. Yes, but let me try to further emphasize my point. Even under this second type of farm, the manager, in making a decision, is at least guided by relative factor prices in the market. But if you don't have an authentic market for the people, it seems to me that these decisions are much more difficult to make. On a Soviet farm, for example, the greater emphasis will be on administrative criteria whereas for a farm in the United States economic criteria will be more important.

Domar. Actually, the farm is a bad example, because there is much less emphasis on profit there. There are all sorts of constraints which make profits impossible. That is why I suggested a Soviet plant manager. You just have to tell him to go ahead and maximize profits and to make it stronger, give him 10 percent of the profit, and he will behave very much like a capitalist manager.

William Meckling (University of Rochester). I want to take strong issue with that statement because I believe it to be wrong. In the case where we are dealing with a company, there will be some present value of the firm, and if it's traded in an organized market like the stock market, there will be minute-by-minute revelations as to the estimates of the firm's value by potential investors. That will not be true of the situation facing the Soviet manager that Domar talks about. In fact, you have a problem of defining what profits are in those firms in order to reward their managers. The Soviet manager will spend his time figuring out how to make his annual profits appear very big, and in the process he'll eat up the assets as fast as he can—he won't have any reason to replace them. There are a whole set of incentives he will have, which are very different from the set of incentives of the corporation president, given the fact that there is an external capital market for that firm. That's why this capitalization thing is so important.

Martin. That last statement of Meckling's is precisely what encouraged me to look at the ownership arrangements in trade unions.

Armen Alchian (University of California—Los Angeles). Is Professor Domar telling us that there are no private property rights of any strength in our corporate sector, or is he saying that it wouldn't make any difference if there were?

Domar. I'm very much in sympathy with Clarkson's paper. Corporations have a corporate manager, an assistant, say to the president and his officers, but they don't own the company, even if they own some stock. They behave under certain constraints enforced upon them by the directors, who in turn are under some constraints by stockholders.

Alchian. Suppose there was only one stockholder who was the director, and he hired a manager. Are the outcomes different from those if there were many stockholders?

Domar. I imagine the manager would probably be more responsive to that kind of an arrangement.

Alchian. Then, why do ten stockholders relative to one stockholder make any difference?

Domar. Well, they are more difficult to get together in order to influence management.

Alchian. Why is it more difficult when you have stockholders?

Domar. Why are you asking such a question?

Alchian. Because I want to lead you to what the consequences are when you don't have property rights at all. I think you are arguing that it is the same thing. You have more and more shareholders, right? They just get weaker and weaker in that firm, don't they? But is this the same as having voting rights with no effective private interest in the firm? What you're telling me is that socialism or a thousand people owning a firm have the same effect on the manager. You are saying it occurs because the individuals have no interest in the firm. You seem to have been arguing that private ownership makes no difference.

Domar. The individual manager certainly has an interest in the firm.

Alchian. I'm talking about owners not managers. Let me repeat. There can be one stockholder who owns all the stock. You say that is more effective than if there were ten stockholders. If there were a thousand it would presumably be less effective. Right? If you reduce each of those thousand persons' interest in that firm, wouldn't that make it still less effective?

Domar. I imagine that it would make a difference.

Alchian. Well, you seem to have been denying that. You seem to be arguing that property rights make no difference.

Domar. No. What I'm saying is that there are several ways in which decisions can be controlled, and having *private* ownership is just one of them. It's not the exclusive one. There are substitutes.

Alchian. Nobody said it was the exclusive one. The important point of this conference is what are the effects of different kinds of property rights? They're not identical.

Domar. In order to answer Professor Alchian, all I would have to do is take a Soviet manager, train him the way I want to train him, even including a trip to General Motors, and then take him back home and say now I want you to behave exactly the way the president of GM behaves and you will be judged according to "these" criteria with such and such weights. I imagine if I found an intelligent man it could be done.

Frech. No one has the incentive to do what you're suggesting in the Soviet system because no one owns the firm. If you somehow performed your experiment, I am sure you could get the constraints such that the manager would act as if you owned the firm. The point is that in the Soviet system or any nonprivate property system there is nobody with those incentives. That's the point.

Clarkson. The theory concerning the structure of resource rights implies that if we use roughly the same resource inputs, we'll get different outcomes if we have private capitalization of net benefits than if we don't permit capitalization. It is true that you can get the Soviet manager to behave like a proprietary manager if you have five times as many resources devoted to monitoring him. You can probably even get the Soviet manager to look more efficient when measured by resources directly used to produce outputs than a profit-seeking manager, but when you included additional monitoring costs, it would be more costly and inefficient.

Domar. Before we started on this discussion I had intended to say a couple of words about Martin's paper. Before we go any further, let me do just that.

If I were Martin, I would put more emphasis on what the leadership wants, rather than on what the membership wants. I think of the union leadership in terms very similar to what Ken describes as corporate management. That is, union leaders, first of all, want to perpetuate their jobs, which is true of corporate management. They also want to enhance their position with fringe benefits and salaries, again very similar. They are acting under the constraints of a union membership, which evidently votes more often than stockholders do or at least more effectively than the stockholders do, and I think this is probably the way to begin. It is the union leadership that tries to maximize its own wealth subject to the fact that the members have to be kept in some state of satisfaction. Otherwise the union leadership might be thrown out. Some years ago—I hope my example is correct—when the railroads had one of those perpetual negotiations with the railroad unions about increasing efficiency by getting rid of some featherbedding, the railroad offered to reduce the work force without firing a single person now working on the railroad. Only attrition, and nothing else. This suggested to me that the welfare of the union members was well provided for. The leaders refused because they would rather preside over bigger unions than smaller unions.

Oi. No, that isn't it. The social security pay-as-you-go system on the retirement and pension fund was the key. You see, membership size determines the size of the pension fund and the strike fund, and that's where the appropriability comes in. That's the way that the union leaders can get appropriation rents in part.

Martin. I just want to reply to Domar's suggestion. I think that focusing on the behavior of the union leadership is very important; however, space limitations prevented me from discussing it in my paper. I have developed the objective function of the leader in a book-length manuscript that does handle it. Whether or not one should begin with a model of the leadership is quite another story. By focusing on differences in proprietary rights, I was able to discuss why it is the case that a divergence of interest between members and leaders should arise.

Domar. I note that you have some comments to that effect. But you were puzzled, for instance, why union members are not generally permitted to sell a membership card to someone else.

Martin. You mean, of course, why they *choose* not to allow it. After all, the collective can decide that for itself. Members decide to vote or not to vote things for themselves. That prohibition isn't imposed upon them by legislation.

Domar. Would transferable membership rights be against the interest of the leadership?

Martin. Perhaps. But there are lots of so-called democratic unions where the leadership does not have a tremendous amount of power, and they also choose not to have that kind of arrangement. You go from so-called autocratic unions where leaders have a tremendous amount of power to relatively democratic unions, if you permit that expression, where the membership has a great deal more to say about union policy, and yet you see the same kind of configuration of rights.

Donald O'Hara (University of Rochester).   I would like to turn to Professor Frech's paper and specifically to a point that was at least implicitly touched on by Louis De Alessi in his comments. As I understand the structure of the arrangements between HEW and the insurers, the insurers are essentially being reimbursed for their costs in processing these claims, whether or not it is literally a cost-plus contract. If I am correct about that, then I think an extreme interpretation of the data in the paper is that stock insurance companies who have what are called low costs, but what are really low rates of reimbursement per claim processed from the government, are really extraordinarily inefficient at capturing revenue from the government.

Oi.   They're maximizing profits from the other side.

O'Hara.   The same sort of interpretation can be placed on both the error rate and the delay rate in a profit-seeking firm that does some business with the regular public and some business with the government. Such a firm would have incentives to divert managerial resources away from the government side of the business to better serve the part of the business where service makes a difference. So Frech's evidence seems consistent with the idea that, for some reason, profit-seeking firms are not efficient at extracting revenue from the government. I thought the only explanation is what Frech referred to as Sam Peltzman's "fast horse can't walk slow" theory. But then I heard Walter Oi's rearrangement of the regressions. I thought there was at least one of them where the sign was reversed. That is, the cost per day was high rather than low, so I wonder where that leaves us?

Mark Pauly (Northwestern University).   You could think of the numbers that are reported here. Suppose there are really two parts to the cost data Frech reports. One part is paying for the inputs which are used specifically for Medicare business. The profit-seeking firm isn't really concerned with minimizing this. The other part is composed of costs attributable to common inputs that are used in other areas of the firm's output: computer, top level management, and so forth. The firm does minimize these costs. What is being suggested is that to really test Frech's proposition one would want to look at the differences in common costs—costs applied to the common elements across firms— because there we're picking up an effect of the true incentive structure of the firm. We're picking up something which a profit-seeking firm really has an incentive to minimize, and the nonprofit firm, with attenuated property rights, perhaps does not.

The problem, of course, is that the numbers that we could get from the accountants would be arbitrary because of the way that they allocate these common costs. Either they are just rules of thumb which differ across firms, in which case they're not very trustworthy, or even if they use the same rule of thumb, the allocation that they will make will depend upon the magnitude and composition of the firm's other business. For example, the commercials and the mutuals typically offer a lot more than health insurance, whereas the Blues are almost exclusively health insurers. The magnitude and composition of the other business is going to differ between the former and the latter. It seems to me the basic problem is that we are not going to get useful numbers from these HEW figures.

Erik Furubotn (Texas A & M University). I just wanted to ask Professor Frech about the special case that he described in the paper in which the managers of mutual funds were able to secure some ownership rights. In the mutual case you outlined some institutional features that seem to work in the direction of shortening the managers' horizon; others less so. I think you mentioned a management contract. Presumably it would extent only for the tenure of office for the manager. I am not sure how that could be transferred effectively. When some other group of managers take over, after such a transfer, would their objectives necessarily satisfy the original set?

Frech. Let me go back over the comments in reverse order. With respect to the management contract, it brings them the closest to private property rights because mutual owners have created a stock company with this contract that effectively controls the mutual by controlling the manager. So they can capitalize the present value of any improvements they make in the mutual because they can sell stock in the management company that runs the mutual.

Furubotn. These are actually companies, not individual contracts with managers.

Frech. Yes, that is correct. They are companies with long life and normal capitalization. I don't think Professor Oi's cost calculations are relevant, because they take the view that a day of processing a claim is a reasonable unit of output proxy for measuring the complexity of a claim. Given that these firms have geographic monopolies, the average complexity of a claim probably will not vary greatly.

Oi. However, the dispersion in the average number of processing days, for given ownership type, is huge. If you look at your tables, 18 days processing time for the stock companies is a standard deviation of ten. That suggests a variation between zero and 38 days.

Frech. I think the reason for it is that it's really not a very important dimension of output, and within pretty broad limits, nobody cares.

Oi. Perhaps, but if they are all stock companies, and if they are all handling the same kinds of claims, why such a huge dispersion?

Frech. I have no answer.

O'Hara. I would just like to get a definition. Is the average processing time in days the elasped time from the time the claimant comes in the door?

Frech. It is elapsed time.

John Moore (University of Miami). I'd like some clarification on that point myself. If Professor Oi's argument is that elapsed time is serving as a proxy for complexity—and this I think is Ted [Frech]'s point—then Oi's argument would be strengthened if the standard deviations were small and not big.

Oi. No, not at all, because companies have different degrees of complexity. Some companies specialize in simple office call claims. Others have to deal with hospital claims.

Frech. That's not the way it operates. Each firm handles all claims of all sorts within its geographic area. Each firm is getting a certain number of claims for appendectomies and a certain number of claims for office calls. In other words, each one is getting a cross section of all the claims of all the over-65 people for physician services in their area. It's not that these firms are competing in the same area so that they're selecting different types of claims. If that were the case, I would agree, the comparison would be impossible.

Alchian. Does the variance among those firms within those classes have anything queer about it? Were there any extreme outliers? I'm trying to explain that large variance. It does look very large and one would have to agree with Professor Oi that the large dispersion is a very puzzling thing.

Frech. There are some extreme outliers.

Alchain. One or two very large outliers would change it. I'm trying to look for some artifact rather than some economic reason.

Frech. There are some outliers. In fact, there is one that I deleted because the data wasn't complete. It was a Blue Shield firm that had a processing time of something like 200 days.

CHARITABLE
ORGANIZATIONS

CHARITY AND NONPROFIT ORGANIZATIONS

Earl A. Thompson, UNIVERSITY OF CALIFORNIA—

LOS ANGELES

Perhaps the most popularly discussed economic trend of the twentieth century has been the boom in all kinds of observed transfer payments, or, as we shall call it, "charity." Yet economists have had little effect on these discussions. While pure economic theory covers the phenomenon of charity by considering the effects of utility interdependence under perfect market conditions [De Graaff (56), Arrow (13), Daly and Giertz (49)], we observe that transfer payments are not made through the institutions described in pure economic theory. Charity is almost always paid through nonprofit institutions, either private or governmental. The central task of this paper is to identify the sources of efficiency of nonprofit institutions as producers of charity.

Most economists who have written on charity think they know why

Economics of Nonproprietary Organizations
Research in Law and Economics, Supplement 1, pages 125-138
Copyright © 1980 by JAI Press Inc.
ISBN: 0-89232-132-6

the government provides much of observed charity. Charitable contributions often take the form of collective goods, where everyone else gains
when one individual gives charity (as much as if they had given the
charity themselves). With such goods, it is thought, there is a *prima facie*
efficiency of government provision. But an alternative to government
provision is government subsidy to private provision. A correct argument for government provision is that the value of the real resources
devoted to excluding nonpayers by private providers in an attempt to
internalize the benefits of the collective good may exceed the extra costs
involved in government provision. But individuals who do not give
private charity are not observed to be substantially excluded from enjoying the benefits of another's charitable contribution. Hence, there is no
prima facie case for government *provision* of charity as a collective good.

Moreover, there is a difficulty in applying collective goods analysis to
charity in order to rationalize even a subsidy to privately provided charity. The problem is that private charity induces recipients to devote
resources to enhancing their charity revenue. It works, for example, to
set a positive price on contracting lung cancer by paying one's medical
bills at a cancer treatment research center. Thus, given that donors feel
sorry for cancer victims and help pay for their care, people smoke too
much, since they do not pay the full social cost of such behavior. But since
charity here has the attributes of a collective good, everyone else *suffers*
when a particular person gives charity to the cancer victim. For they do
not like seeing someone suffer from cancer and the contribution increases
the incidence of cancer. Hence, the charitable contribution is a collective
bad as well as a collective good. I am better off when you give another dollar of charity in that I free ride on the benefits you create for the recipient,
but I am also worse off in that I suffer from the losses your contribution
inflicts by inducing more people to smoke. Presumably, you would not
give up your dollar in the above scenario if you knew that the incidence
of lung cancer would rise sufficiently to wipe out the net benefits to the
recipients of your subsidy. So, in equilibrium, the external benefit exceeds the external cost of donation. But now suppose you can internalize
some of the benefits of your donation, which appears to be quite preva-
lent based on studies of social pressure to give to charity [Ireland and
Johnson (80)]. Then you may rationally donate your dollar even though
it does more social harm than good.

Hence, we cannot, with any confidence, rationalize government
support—let alone government provision—of charity with standard, collective goods analysis. (A rationalization of the observed U.S. subsidy to
privately supplied charity based on a noncollective goods argument appears in Thompson [167].) This leaves us with the part of our original
question in which we seek to provide an efficiency explanation for the

observation that a large and growing part of observed charity payments are made by the government sector. We begin our analysis with this question, holding our efficiency rationalization of private nonprofit institutions until Part II of this study.

I. CHARITY AND THE GOVERNMENT

First we shall describe an equilibrium with charity in a private property system. To initially abstract away from collective goods problems, we first assume that there are only two individuals, G & R. To avoid notational complexities, we allow only a single, homogeneous, transferable commodity, whose quantity is indexed by the real number, x. For still more simplicity, we endow individual G, the "giver," with all of the goods; the "receiver," R, is endowed with none of the goods. We thus write x_0^G and 0 as the respective endowments for individuals G & R. Also for simplicity, we allow each of our individuals to freely vary a real, continuous behavior variable of his own, given by y^G and y^R, respectively. These can be thought of as variables representing a particular kind of nontransferable leisure activity which is performed *prior to* any social interaction between the individuals. Its significance will soon become clear. Preferences of our giver and receiver are described, respectively, by the differentiable, quasi-concave utility functions, $U^G(y^G, x^G, V^R(x^R;y^R))$ and $U^R(y^R,x^R) = F(y^R, V^R(x^R;y^R))$, where $(U_x^G, U_V^G, U_x^R, -V_y^R)$ $\gg 0$. V is R's "utility," or valuation, function for x after he has consumed y. It is his relevant utility function at the time he receives his transfer. The assumptions on the derivatives imply that increases in y^R always reduce R's subsequent utility for a given x^R. High living in R's youth takes its toll on his later capacity for enjoyment.

Notice that the giver cares about the receiver, but the opposite is not the case. This reflects a presumption that philanthropy does not become a significant argument in one's utility function until he surpasses a certain level of wealth. While the presumption is not immediately confirmed in the empirical literature on charity [cf Schwartz (147)], we believe, based upon a discussion with Professor Tullock, that these studies, which use gross income from income tax returns for their wealth proxies, are severely biased away from our presumption.

To describe an equilibrium, the giver chooses (y^{G*}, x^{G*}), which maximizes $U^G(y^G, x^G, V^R(x^R;y^R))$ subject to a given value of y^R and

$$x^G + x^R = x_0^G. \tag{1}$$

This produces a differentiable function from y^R to x^{G*}, which we write $f(y^R)$. By assumption, $f' < 0$; the more the receiver dissipates by consuming y, the more charity he will receive. The receiver chooses y^R so as to maximize $U^R(y^R, x^R)$, where $x^R = x_0^G - f(y^R)$. Assuming that these maxima exist, the first-order conditions are:

for the giver,

$$U_y^G = 0, \text{ and} \tag{2}$$

$$U_x^G = U_v^G V_x^R \tag{3}$$

and for the receiver,

$$U_x^R f'(y^R) = U_y^R. \tag{4}$$

Equations (1)–(4) determine the four-tuple which characterizes our minigeneral equilibrium, $(y^{G*}, y^{R*}, x^{G*}, x^{R*})$. Note from Eq. (4) that since $U_x^R > 0$ and $f' < 0$, in equilibrium $U_y^R < 0$. That is, in equilibrium, the receiver's y-activity level is extended to the point where he has a negative marginal utility for it. This is so because the receiver will generate a positive transfer from the giver if he lowers his utility level by increasing y. By making himself worse off, he earns a payment from the giver. Is this efficient? Does the giver want the receiver to be worse off, so he can have the opportunity to help? No, not in the above environment; our giver is too benevolent for that. The Pareto nonoptimality of this private charity equilibrium is easily seen by deriving the conditions for Pareto optimality in the above environment. This is done by maximizing U^R for a given U^G, say $U^G = U^1$. To do this, we maximize the Lagrangian,

$$U^R(y^R, x_0^G - x^G) + \gamma(U^1 - U^G(y^G, x^G, V^R(x_0^G - x^G; y^R))),$$

with respect to y^G, x^G, and y^R. The first-order conditions are:

$$U_y^G = 0 \tag{5}$$

$$U_x^R = -\gamma[U_x^G - U_v^G V_x^R], \text{ and} \tag{6}$$

$$U_y^R = \gamma U_v^G V_y^R. \tag{7}$$

We are assuming, of course, that the optimum exists so that γ is finite. Since $U_x^R > 0$ and since Eq. (3) says that $U_x^G - U_v^G V_x^R = 0$ in the private solution, Eq. (6) tells us that the private equilibrium is not a Pareto optimum. Further inspection of Eqs. (3) and (6) indicates that the inefficiency of a competitive equilibrium reflects a failure of the giver to take into account the full external effect that his giving has on the utility of the receiver. But one should not conclude that private charity is undersupplied or that a simple subsidy to private charity is in order. For Eq. (7) is also violated in a private equilibrium. This can be seen as follows: Since $\gamma = \partial U^R / \partial U^1$ and we are at a Pareto optimum, $\gamma < 0$. So, since $V_x^R < 0$ and $U_v^G > 0$, Eq. (7) tells us that $U_y^R > 0$ in a Pareto optimum. But U_x^R was negative in the equilibrium. This indicates that y is overly extended in the private equilibrium as R overly consumes in his youth in order to reduce his later utility and induce larger transfers of wealth from G. This effect, by itself, is a source of increased charity so that there should be no presumption of a net undersupply of private charity in this model. And a subsidy to charity, while working toward the advancement of Eq. (6), will induce more of the already overdone y^R, and therefore increase the degree to which the free market violates Eq. (7).

What has gone wrong? Haven't we asserted that pure economic theory has no difficulty covering the phenomenon of charity, in which case our equilibrium should be a Pareto optimum? The problem that has naturally made its way into our analysis is the classical—no, biblical— problem that the recipient of charity is encouraged to overdevote resources to activities which will make him more pathetic and therefore increase his charity income. This is why y^R is extended in equilibrium to a point at which $U_y^R < 0$. The problem, what Buchanan (30) calls "The Samaritan's Dilemma," is the result of the giver's inability to make his payment contingent on a certain level of y^R.[1] So, presumably, y^R cannot be observed by G. This seems realistic enough and we shall maintain the assumption throughout our analysis. The fact that G (or some private agent working for G in an extended model) cannot observe y^R suggests that neither can some externally imposed government authority. So, even though y^R appears in the formal equilibrium model as a simple externality, we cannot treat it as such for policy purposes. The government cannot tax it if they cannot observe it. So the efficiency loss involved is not, when correctly understood, a standard, Pigouvian externality loss. I usually call such joint efficiency losses—joint losses due to information differences between contracting parties—"transaction costs," and will maintain that terminology here. Elsewhere I have shown, and will show in Part II in a more general charity model, that if real transaction costs cannot be reduced for a given set of transactions by government intervention, implying that government provision at lower real transaction costs is not possible, then a competitive private-goods equilibrium with transaction costs is Pareto optimal [Thompson (166, 168)]. However, an important, to me quite disturbing, characteristic of transaction costs is that, despite the impossibility of applying Pigouvian taxes, a wide variety of government interventions may serve to reduce transaction costs for a given set of transactions.

For the problem at hand, suppose we allow government intervention, where the government dictates a replacement of the private system of giver-selected charity with a system in which the *recipient* is allowed to choose his own level of charity, subject to a certain minimum amount of utility, U, which the giver must maintain. The reason the government is required to make this change should not be immediately apparent.

Nevertheless, the change in the incentive system changes the optimization problem to one in which the receiver chooses x_G as well as y^R so as to maximize the following Lagrangian expression:

$$U^R(y^R, x_0^G - x^G) + \mu(U - U^G(y^G, x^G, V^R(x_0^G - x^G), y^R)).$$

This is the same maximand used above to compute a Pareto optimum (except that U^1 has been replaced by U). But while y^G was a variable in computing the Pareto optimum, it is here chosen by G and taken as given by R in computing his individual optimum. Nevertheless, Eqs. (6) and (7) apply here so that the misallocation which appeared in the private property equilibrium due to overextending y^R and underproviding charity for a given y^R no longer holds. What remains is to examine the effect of this new system on y^G. Of course, G may still choose it so that $U_y^G = 0$. But what incentive does he have to do so if he is guaranteed U? The answer is that G is only guaranteed a potential of U. He must maximize U^G for given values of x^G and y^R in order to actually attain U. Thus, G, taking the optimal choice of R as given, looking at constant values of x^G and y^R, will obviously maximize U^G by setting $U_y^G = 0$. So our problem is finished.

The result, of course, is that in moving to a receiver-determined system, a Pareto-optimal solution is created. By surrendering his power to decide the amount of charity to the recipient, the giver has freed himself from his overly charitable response to the recipient's dissipation. And since the recipient is not responsive to such behavior on the part of the giver, no new inefficiency is created.

The above amounts to a simple paradigm indicating the allocative superiority of receiver-determined charity over giver-determined charity. But does it really suggest government intervention in the private charity market? Since the givers in a private charity market see their dilemma, why do they not privately grant to the receivers the power to determine their own redistributive incomes? The answer lies, we believe, in the relatively high cost of any private charity contract which ties receivers to a specific set of givers and assures the givers a fixed benefit level. Furthermore, when y^R is unobservable, private charity contracts, which are then contracts without consideration, are unenforceable. In any case, private philanthropists are not observed to be legally bound to give, or not give, anything. The only method of commitment open to a giver is to establish an institution which, owing to its particular organizational structure, would be insensitive to the narrow philanthropic interests of the giver. That is, decisions within his charity organization could be made by individuals who do not have the charitable preferences of the founder. But if the decisions in his organization were made by less charitable individuals, including personal reformers, then the founder would find it very difficult to assure that his initial wishes were carried out. He would have little confidence that his contributions would go to R individuals in the desired proportions.

The decision-makers could simplify their jobs by indiscriminant giving, or, as reformers, by giving to people projecting the "right" attitudes. In any case, a good part of those receiving the charity would be undeserving, according to the preference function of the philanthropist. But not all of these costs suffered by the founding giver would be social costs, as rents would accrue to the undeserving who could most easily qualify for aid from the largely indifferent or overly moralistic administrators. So the founder's private costs of such an organization would exceed the social costs of the organization. Apparently, the private costs of these latter organizations are sufficiently high that they are rarely adopted in the real world. Observed private charities are normally run by benevolent representatives of wealthy philanthropists. This means that private charity markets are pretty much as our paradigm characterizes them. In any case, there is an opening for government intervention in the form of "subsidies" to the kinds of charity run by the less charitable and the reformers. These "subsidies"—which represent government support for a particular organization form over another in providing the same product—amount to what we have called government "provision."

In summary, government intervention in the form of the provision of charity may lower the real social transaction costs of charity by avoiding Samaritan's dilemma problems which private givers are unwilling to avoid due to what they perceive to be wastes but which are mere transfers to the undeserving.

Empirical signs of the applicability of this theory are unmistakable. Private charities are observed to be run, by and large, by benevolent, altruistic beings, compassionately aiding the genuinely needy while public welfare agencies are observed to be run, by and large, by personal reformers and ex-altruists who suspiciously, and often begrudgingly, dole out money as well as services—often on the basis of a rigid, relatively cruel formula—to a motley crew of true indigents, undeserving professional welfare dependents demanding their rights under the law, and simple liars [Weinberger (178)]. It is testimony to the power of economic analysis over intuition that the latter may be an efficient institution when the former is an available substitute.

But the government may, at least in principle, achieve this efficiency not by giving the choice of x^G to the receivers but by simply setting up an institution which somehow or another achieves charity levels and anti-dissipation incentives so as to satisfy Eqs. (6) and (7). So a question may arise as to why we are representing the superiority of the system with government provision as one in which the receivers, at least as a group, are given the constrained power to determine their own charity income. To answer this, first note that a government in which decisions are essentially unanimous is not itself completely immune to the Samaritan's dilemma. While such a government is a collective which includes many recipients of public welfare—deserving and otherwise—and therefore internalizes much of the external costs responsible for the inefficiency in the private supply of charity, it also follows the narrow self-interest of the benevolent voters. It therefore will grant overly large subsidies to charities catering to relatively pathetic cases. But the kind of "government" which we consider here is one which is closer to majority rule in that it generates a continual, democratic, political determination of what we have taken to be the endowed distributions of wealth. In achieving an equilibrium redistribution, in any time period, a subgroup of relatively poor, politically enfranchised individuals will maximize the excess of their redistributional wealth gain over their political costs, the latter being strictly determined by the extent of the redistribution. Because many in the benefiting group are undeserving (or many in the giving group are not charitable) the larger the redistribution the greater the political costs of achieving it. Such a system implies a maximum net redistribution to the poor for given final utilities for—and thus for given redistribution from—the relatively wealthy individuals. This is just the efficient, receiver-determined charity system described above except for noncharitable lump-sum transfers and the presence of variable resources devoted to the political system.

When explicitly accounting for the latter—the dead weight losses devoted to distribution fights within the kind of government considered here—the above conclusions remain intact. Moreover, accounting for these losses enables us to explain the growing dominance of government in the welfare field. In examining democratic political systems which determine the endowments of private properties, it is often convenient, due to the nonexistence of permanent equilibria, to perform the theoretical analysis in historical time. The following historical sketch contains our theoretical analysis.

At earlier, lower levels of aggregate wealth, the relatively wealthy were not so charitable. Being a political minority, they fought hard to keep their property and devoted significant resources to the political process in order to maintain their endowments and protect their savings. Proceeding to the present, aggregate wealth has increased, and the amount of charity which the relatively wealthy wish to give has greatly expanded. One way for them to achieve their desired expansion would be to keep up the political fight, earn a high income, and then give much of the spoils of their fight back to the poor in an expensive system of private charity. But a now easier way for the relatively wealthy to proceed, although some set-up cost is no doubt involved, is to yield more political power to the poor and give less private charity than otherwise. The result is the same desired increase in charity with a lower present cost of *their* resources devoted to the political process. Samaritan's dilemma waste does not occur because the recipients would have to fight harder for their redistribution if it were present; all prefer that the government choose—instead of simple subsidies to the poor such as a negative income tax—public assistance and welfare programs with rigid rules and professional social workers, inured to the sufferings of the poor, not themselves wealthy enough to allow their preferences toward the relatively unfortunate to lead them into activities which might significantly bend the rules for the relatively unfortunate, and bound to rules which transfer significant amounts of resources to undeserving types.

Summarizing our historical sketch: As aggregate wealth has increased, the relatively wealthy have found, because of the increase in their own demand for redistribution toward the less fortunate, that the benefits of reducing their normal expenditures on maintaining political power, while allowing more charitable-redistributional bills and broader political representation of the poor, have increased relative to the set-up costs of the change.

Holding this view of the world, we would expect a rapid expansion of public relative to private charity to occur with the expansion of total expenditures on charity. Along with this would be a greater liberalism (in the twentieth-century sense) of the wealthy, a gradual political enfranchisement of the poor, and an observed increase in the use of political power by groups of welfare recipients. The occurrence of these events is almost undeniable [cf. Pryor (137), Weinberger (178)]. Moreover, Demsetz (57a) has recently presented statistical evidence that the abnormal growth of government sectors, which is largely due to the growth of the welfare sectors, has come *pari passu* with the political enfranchisement of the poor.

II. CHARITY AND PRIVATE
NONPROFIT ORGANIZATIONS

Professor Tullock (171) has argued that private charity firms are different from other private suppliers in that the customers of a charity firm, the givers of charity, care what is done with their payments while the customers of noncharity firms do not. While firms providing financial services such as brokerage houses are an observed exception to this argument, another somewhat distinguishing characteristic of charity is that the customers find it relatively costly to find out what is really done with their payments. In contrast, it is relatively easy for a customer of a financial service company to detect a failure of the company to spend his money in the intended fashion. Combining these two characteristics, we offer the following uniquely determining feature of a private charity firm: a private charity firm is different from other private firms in that its customers substantially care what is done with their contributions *and* cannot easily determine what is, in fact, done with these contributions. We are therefore including private hospitals, schools, and research foundations in what we are calling private charity firms because they all have contributors, or charity customers, who substantially care about what is done with their contributions but cannot easily determine what is, in fact, done.

Now if a private charity firm set itself up as an ordinary firm, where the owner-manager captured the excess of created marketable benefits over the corresponding costs of production, he would find some very suspicious customers. For they would have a very difficult time ever knowing whether or not the product which they desire to purchase is actually delivered. Rather than so substantially straining the customers' credulity, and receiving a corresponding low revenue, the owner-manager may make a legal contract with the customers that he will never make more than a fixed "profit"—i.e., a salary—from the operation. Then the customers would, of course, have concrete, legal assurance that the owner-manager was not pocketing most of his contribution and making a token effort at supplying the desired service sufficient to avoid prosecution for outright fraud. The superior organizational form chosen by the owner-manager is called a private, nonprofit organization. (A similar argument can be made for public nonprofit organizations, but proper elaboration of this would take us beyond the scope of this paper.)

All of this seems to be a natural part of an efficient private property system. Moreover, we do observe in the real world that most private charitable organizations—including private hospitals, schools, and research foundations—do in fact take on a nonprofit organizational form.

While—as Alchian has so well impressed upon us—incentives of the managers of nonprofit organizations are more attenuated in these systems than for managers in for-profit firms, apparently the reduced efficiency because of these incentives is often overshadowed by the increased efficiency in satisfying the customers that their contributions are being put to good use. Nevertheless, as we pointed out in Part I, the private contributor realizes that he must appoint managers with preferences similar to his own or else suffer the large *private* costs of having his managers spend the contributions in ways which do not follow the contributor's preferences. This indicates that managers in nonprofit firms do, in fact, follow fairly closely the preferences of the contributors.

In fact, with Samaritan's dilemma problems, they follow the contributor's preferences too closely, so that government intervention is
sometimes called for in order to provide society with managers who are
not so faithful to the contributors.

But our concern in this section is only for the part of the world represented by *private* nonprofit institutions. Our only problem at this point is
understanding why economic theorists regard them to be such peculiar
animals. Apparently, the answer is that there is no formal economic
theory of the firm and industry for nonprofit firms which stays within
the assumptions of perfectly competitive factor markets and full rationality characteristic of the standard theory of production. So let us consider
an industry composed of rational nonprofit charity firms competing for a
large number of customers such as those described above under conditions of perfect factor markets. Our goal here will be to simply compare
and contrast the model with a standard model of perfect competition
between profit-maximizing firms selling to customers who know
whether or not the product they are paying for has been delivered. We
will close the analysis with a discussion of the policy implication of the
model, tying the analysis into the discussion in Part I.

Measuring the output of a charity firm as the total number of dollars,
or x, collected, the "total revenue function" of a charity firm can be

Figure 1 Competitive Equilibrium in the Charity Industry

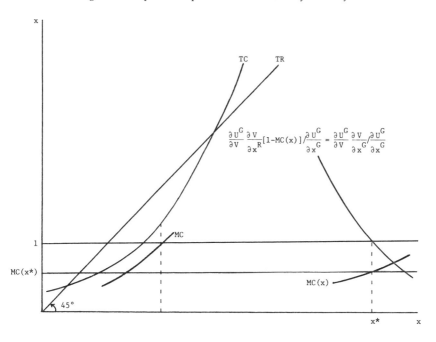

represented by a line coming from the origin at a 45-degree angle, shown in the figure as the TR curve. For every dollar collected, there is a dollar of revenue. The total transaction costs of the firm's collecting and giving are represented by the convex-from-below TC curve. TR − TC is, of course, maximized where marginal revenue equals marginal cost. But TR − TC is not profit. There is no profit. TR − TC is the firm's net charity payment. We could assume that the managers want to maximize their net charity payment, but this would be true only in a special case and not generally descriptive of the actual solution, which generally stays below this level of charity. In general, the managers are competitively paid factors of production and, as such, are indifferent to the firm's possible outputs. If the managers are indifferent and there are no controlling owners, how is the output determined? The answer is that the customers determine the output! A rational giver, in maximizing his net aid to the receivers for a given gross payment, equates his marginal net contributions to all charities. Thus if one charity firm had a lower net marginal transaction cost than the others, it would receive all of the charity business. And if one firm had a higher marginal cost, it would receive no contributions. So the marginal transaction cost of all charities must be equal in a competitive equilibrium. In equilibrium, the level of marginal transaction cost, MC(x), is that for which the supply and demand for charitable contributions are equal, that is, as illustrated in the figure, for which:

$$\frac{\partial U^G}{\partial V} \frac{\partial V}{\partial X^G} \bigg/ \frac{\partial U^G}{\partial X^G} = \frac{\partial U^G}{\partial V} \frac{\partial V}{\partial X^R} [1 - MC(x)] \bigg/ \frac{\partial U^G}{\partial X^G} = 1.$$

This is different than a standard, textbook competitive model in that the customers, not profit-maximizing firms, are making all of the output decisions. And output price is not a variable; only cost is. And customers are attracted to and repelled away from firms according to their marginal production (i.e., transaction) costs rather than market prices.

Since the TR curve is always a line at 45 degrees, the familiar monopoly misallocation is not formally present in the charity industry. More directly, the customers atomistically choose their own contributions to the monopoly charity firm and thereby determine the output of charity to be that point at which their utility of consuming an extra dollar equals their utility from the charity receiver's consuming what is left of the dollar after the marginal charity transaction costs are taken out. This is the same calculation as that which characterizes the competitive solution. So monopolistic charities are, according to this model, no different in welfare terms than competitive charities.

The Pareto optimality of such an equilibrium, given transaction costs, is not immediately apparent. As in Part I, the social value of charity in equilibrium exceeds its private value because the givers only count their own utility for the receiver's gift; the receiver's utility is not an added component of the social value determining the equilibrium. But when we attempt to make everyone better off than they are in a competitive equilibrium by forcing more charity on the system, the only way to compensate the givers is to force the receivers to do less of the y^R activities which decrease the utility of the givers. But y^R is not observable by the givers or the government. So they cannot force such a decrease on the system. On the contrary, were charity to increase, there would be an increase in y^R activities! So the givers cannot be compensated for giving more charity, and the transaction-cost equilibrium is a Pareto optimum for given transaction costs. The only way to improve our private economy then is to reduce transaction costs, as was discussed in Part I.

III. SUMMARY

A. A source of efficiency of government in making charitable payments is its relatively superior ability to solve the Samaritan's dilemma. This occurs for at least one reason: government provision allows a system where social workers are more able to redistribute to undeserving individuals and more able to operate independently of the benefactors that finance the system. Lower social transaction costs for a given amount of charitable redistribution thus result from some government provision of charity. This theory can be used to explain the observed government provision of charity and the observed qualitative differences between private and public charities. An additional reason for lower transaction costs via governmental provision exists when the government is run by simple—rather than Wicksellian (e.g., 80%)—majority rule. Under a simple majority rule government, redistributions continually occur within the political system. With such a government, we can view government-determined charity as receiver-determined charity, where no Samaritan's dilemma exists at all. Using this model of government, an explanation for the rapid increase in public relative to private charity is apparent: as the total demand for giving charity has increased, givers have simply reduced the resources that they devote to the political system in order to maintain their relatively high endowments, thus making it cheaper for the receivers to acquire charity payments through the public sector. The argument also serves to explain the secular trend toward broader political enfranchisement. This argument for the superiority of the government sector in solving the Samaritan's dilemma and for the growth in the political power of the charity recipients can—by thinking of the world as a two-person interaction—be formally supported by a model whose main theorem is that while a charity equilibrium in which givers determine the amount of charity is Pareto nonoptimal, an equilibrium in which the receivers determine their charity incomes subject to a given utility level of the givers *is* Pareto optimal.

B. The concern of the customers of a firm over the distribution of their payments to the firm and the difficulty of discovering what is, in fact, done with their payments, is a distinguishing feature of charity firms relative to other firms. Correspondingly, a source of efficiency of private, nonprofit organizations relative to for-profit organizations in making charitable payments is their relatively superior ability to convince the givers that their contributions will be delivered to their intended beneficiaries. The fact that almost all charity firms are nonprofit firms and almost all nonprofit firms are charity firms (with charity broadly defined) is evidence for the empirical power of this simple, efficiency-oriented theory of nonprofit organizations. A Marshallian type of industry analysis reveals that a charity industry is like others in that its competitive equilibrium is a Pareto optimum, given the costs of private transactions (that is, given the costs of the Samaritan's dilemma). But it is unlike other industries in that the customers rather than the managers determine outputs and that a monopoly equilibrium is equivalent, in welfare terms, to a competitive equilibrium. These optimality results serve to rationalize the absence of governmental tax subsidy intervention (beyond that intervention justified in a general model of optimal taxation and national defense [Thompson (167)]) into private charity markets.

FOOTNOTES

The author is professor of economics, Department of Economics.

Thanks are due numerous social welfare workers and analysts for informative discussions and also to Armen Alchian and Gordon Tullock for very helpful comments on an earlier draft.

1. One might think that the giver need *only* be rigid and commit himself to a given amount of x^G independent of y^R. But this is not the case. To see this, merely note that maximizing $U^R(y^R, x^R)$ with respect to y^R, with x^R considered as a constant by R, yields $U_y^R = 0$, which violates the efficiency condition in Eq. (7), since $\gamma < 0$, $V_y^R < 0$, and $U_y^G > 0$. Intuitively, R's human abstinence in his youth, and resulting health in his later years, benefits G so that he should not be led to ignore the effect. In a more conventional, but less realistic model, in which G benefits from U^R rather than V^R, this would not be the case.

PRIVATE GOODS, COLLECTIVE GOODS: THE ROLE OF THE NONPROFIT SECTOR

Burton A. Weisbrod, UNIVERSITY OF WISCONSIN

There are a wide variety of institutional mechanisms through which the economy's resources are allocated. The decentralized profit-oriented private market and the government are the two institutions on which the bulk of economists' attention has been focused. More recently, the importance of the household as a locus of economic activity has received growing attention. This paper directs attention to yet another economic sector or institutional mechanism: the private (or voluntary) nonprofit sector. Little is known about its size or importance, its role in a pluralistic system of institutions, or its behavior.[1]

"Private market," "government," "household," "private nonprofit" —each of these is itself not a homogeneous institution utilizing a single well-defined instrument, but a versatile, adaptable class of instru-

Economics of Nonproprietary Organizations
Research in Law and Economics, Supplement 1, pages 139-177
Copyright © 1980 by JAI Press Inc.
ISBN: 0-89232-132-6

ments and arrangements interacting with each other and with the ethical-cultural system of the society. Government, for example, is not *an* institution but a complex of legislative, administrative, regulatory, and judicial institutions that sometimes work cooperatively and sometimes at cross purposes, that may correct some private market failures yet exacerbate others and even interfere with efficient allocational decisions in the private market [Niskanen (127), Buchanan and Tullock (31), Downs (59)]. "Government" includes agencies that are ostensibly designed to handle cases of individual citizens, as well as agencies that are designed to correct the "failures" of those very agencies—the ombudsman.

The private market is, similarly, a conglomerate. It has firms producing standardized products under competitive conditions, firms producing differentiated goods under not-so-competitive conditions, firms dealing with strongly organized or with weakly organized factor suppliers, firms producing goods for which the typical consumer is a well-informed buyer, and others producing goods (such as much of medical care and legal representation) for which the typical consumer is poorly informed—often even after the purchase—and so finds himself relying on such private institutional mechanisms as professional ethics codes as guarantors of "quality." In short, (1) every economic sector utilizes a versatile, adaptable class of instruments that vary, however, among sectors, and (2) each of the instruments—and, hence, each of the institutional sectors—has its strengths and limitations as means for achieving policy objectives.

So, too, is the private nonprofit sector a conglomerate, exhibiting a variety of institutional forms, not all behaving in the same manner—a hypothesis to be examined below—and having infirmities while perhaps filling a niche in a pluralistic, multi-institutional system. This paper attempts to sharpen understanding and definitions of the private nonprofit sector, as a step precedent to developing better and more general positive models, and to determining whether "nonprofit" firms—in any specific forms—merit encouragement, discouragement, or neither.

There are, thus, both positive and normative bases for our focus on the nonprofit sector (the term "private" will be dropped henceforth). Whether our interest is in predicting behavior of the firms in the sector, in evaluating their behavior, or in developing public policy toward them, we need to model their responsiveness to various stimuli such as the tax, subsidy, and other regulatory instruments of government, and the competition of the private for-profit and household sectors. This paper is primarily positive, not normative, in orientation. It is not an attempt to judge the usefulness, in either efficiency or equity terms, of the nonprofit forms of institutional organization. Rather, it is an attempt to understand better what the essential characteristics of a "nonprofit" organization's structure are, as one step toward constructing models of behavior.

Before behavior of "the" nonprofit sector and any of its component firms can be understood, we need to decide precisely what we are attempting to explain: what is the nonprofit sector and what is the nonprofit firm? To begin with, the perspective of this paper should be made clear: Our concern is with nonprofit organizations as potential mechanisms for correcting some of the efficiency failures of other forms of institutions. If we recognize the sources of private market failures and simultaneously recognize the factors that limit governmental institutions' abilities to correct them—in short, if we realize that there are also systematic "governmental failures" [Weisbrod (182)]—the *possibility* that some other institutional arrangement may be capable of correcting some of the residual failures can be explored. There is no necessary presumption that organizations called "private nonprofit" have any such capability. Our first task is to *define* this institutional form; the second task is to *understand* (model) *its* behavior, so as then to *judge* (normatively) the likelihood that its behavior, when juxtaposed with the behavior of the for-profit, governmental, and household sectors, will contribute to allocative efficiency and distributional equity goals of society.

In an earlier paper I posited a potential role for a nonprofit sector in the context of collective good problems [Weisbrod (180)]. Given the allocative-efficiency failures of the private for-profit sector, resulting from the difficulty and, at least as important, the inefficiency of exclusion when the marginal cost of supplying output to an incremental consumer is approximately zero, and given the problems that governments have in correcting those failures, some other institutional mechanism may play a useful corrective role. Whether the private nonprofit mechanism is or is not such a corrective is a matter to be determined. What is implied, however, is that we seek to define a subset of all nonprofit organizations (firms) that might be termed "collective good nonprofits," for this paper is directed to a clearer understanding of an institutional form that is a kind of hybrid—it is a private organization but it provides collective goods, generally identified with governments. Systematic thinking by economists about private nonprofit institutional mechanisms is in its infancy; this paper is intended to help the infant crawl a bit forward.

I. HETEROGENEITY OF NONPROFIT FIRMS AND THE PROBLEM OF MODELING

An enormous variety of firms are nonprofit, tax-exempt organizations. The heterogeneity is shown in Table 1, which lists hundreds of purposes, activities, operations or types of nonprofit, tax-exempt organiza-

Table 1. A Partial Sample of Nonprofit, Tax-Exempt Organizations.

Activity Code Numbers of Exempt Organizations (select up to three codes which best describe or most accurately identify your purposes, activities, operations or type of organization and enter in block 7, page 1 of the application. Enter first the code which most accurately identifies you.)

Code

Religious Activities
001 Church, synagogue, etc.
002 Association or convention of churches
003 Religious order
004 Church auxiliary
005 Mission
006 Missionary activities
007 Evangelism
008 Religious publishing activities
    Book store (use 918)
    Genealogical activities (use 094)
029 Other religious activities

Schools, Colleges and Related Activities
030 School, college, trade school, etc.
031 Special school for the blind, handicapped, etc.
032 Nursery school
    Day care center (use 574)
033 Faculty group
034 Alumni association or group
035 Parent or parent-teachers association
036 Fraternity or sorority
    Key club (use 323)
037 Other student society or group
038 School or college athletic association
039 Scholarships for children of employees
040 Scholarships (other)
041 Student loans
042 Student housing activities
043 Other student aid
044 Student exchange with foreign country
045 Financial support of schools, colleges, etc. (use 602)
    Achievement prizes or awards (use 914)
    Student book store (use 918)
    Student travel (use 299)
    Scientific research (see Scientific Research Activities)
046 Private school
059 Other school related activities

Cultural, Historical or Other Educational Activities
060 Museum, zoo, planetarium, etc.
061 Library
062 Historical site, records or reenactment
063 Monument

Code

Scientific Research Activities
180 Contract or sponsored scientific research for industry
181 Scientific research (diseases) (use 161)
199 Other scientific research activities

Business and Professional Organizations
200 Business promotion (chamber of commerce, business league, etc.)
201 Real-estate association
202 Board of trade
203 Regulating business
204 Better Business Bureau
205 Professional association
206 Professional association auxiliary
207 Industry trade shows
208 Convention displays
    Testing products for public safety (use 905)
209 Research, development and testing
210 Professional athletic league
    Attracting new industry (use 403)
    Publishing activities (use 120)
    Insurance or other benefits for members (see Employee or Membership Benefit Organizations)
211 Underwriting municipal insurance
212 Assigned risk insurance activities
213 Tourist bureau
229 Other business or professional group

Farming and Related Activities
230 Farming
231 Farm bureau
232 Agricultural group
233 Horticultural group
234 Farmers' cooperative marketing or purchasing
235 Financing crop operations
    FFA, FHA, 4-H club, etc. (use 322)
    Fair (use 065)
236 Dairy herd improvement association
237 Breeders association
249 Other farming and related activities

Mutual Organizations
250 Mutual ditch, irrigation, telephone, electric company or like organization

Code

Youth Activities
320 Boy Scouts, Girl Scouts, etc.
321 Boys Club, Little League, etc.
322 FFA, FHA, 4-H club, etc.
323 Key club
324 YMCA, YWCA, YMHA, etc.
325 Camp
326 Care and housing of children (orphanage, etc.)
327 Prevention of cruelty to children
328 Combat juvenile delinquency
349 Other youth organization or activities

Conservation, Environmental and Beautification Activities
350 Preservation of natural resources (conservation)
351 Combatting or preventing pollution (air, water, etc.)
352 Land acquisition for preservation
353 Soil or water conservation
354 Preservation of scenic beauty
    Litigation (see Litigation and Legal Aid Activities)
    Combat community deterioration (use 402)
355 Wildlife sanctuary or refuge
356 Garden club
379 Other conservation, environmental or beautification activities

Housing Activities
380 Low-income housing
381 Low and moderate income housing
382 Housing for the aged (see also 153)
    Nursing or convalescent home (use 152)
    Student housing (use 042)
    Orphanage (use 326)
398 Instruction and guidance on housing
399 Other housing activities

Inner City or Community Activities
400 Area development, re-development or renewal
    Housing (see Housing Activities)
401 Homeowners association
402 Other activity aimed at combatting community deterioration

Code

510 Firearms control
511 Selective Service System
512 National defense policy
513 Weapons systems
514 Government spending
515 Taxes or tax exemption
516 Separation of church and state
517 Government aid to parochial schools
518 U.S. foreign policy
519 U.S. military involvement
520 Pacifism and peace
521 Economic-political system of U.S.
522 Anti-communism
523 Right to work
524 Zoning or rezoning
525 Location of highway or transportation system
526 Rights of criminal defendants
527 Capital punishment
528 Stricter law enforcement
529 Ecology or conservation
530 Protection of consumer interests
531 Medical care system
532 Welfare system
533 Urban renewal
534 Busing students to achieve racial balance
535 Racial integration
536 Use of intoxicating beverage
537 Use of drugs or narcotics
538 Use of tobacco
539 Prohibition of erotica
540 Sex education in public schools
541 Population control
542 Birth control methods
543 Legalized abortion
559 Other matters

Other Activities Directed to Individuals
560 Supplying money, goods or services to the poor
561 Gifts or grants to individuals (other than scholarships)
    Scholarships for children of employees (use 039)
    Scholarships (other) (use 040)
    Student loans (use 041)
562 Other loans to individuals

142

064 Commemorative event (centennial, festival, pageant, etc.)	251 Credit Union
065 Fair	252 Reserve funds or insurance for domestic building and loan association, cooperative bank, or mutual savings bank
088 Community theatrical group	253 Mutual insurance company
089 Singing society or group	254 Corporation organized under an Act of Congress (see also 904)
090 Cultural performances	259 Farmers' cooperative marketing or purchasing (use 234)

064 Commemorative event (centennial, festival, pageant, etc.)
065 Fair
088 Community theatrical group
089 Singing society or group
090 Cultural performances
091 Art exhibit
092 Literary activities
093 Cultural exchanges with foreign country
094 Genealogical activities
　Achievement prizes or awards (use 914)
　Gifts or grants to individuals (use 561)
　Financial support of cultural organizations (use 602)
119 Other cultural or historical activities

Other Instruction and Training Activities
120 Publishing activities
121 Radio or television broadcasting
122 Producing films
123 Discussion groups, forums, panels, lectures, etc.
124 Study and research (non-scientific)
125 Giving information or opinion (see also Advocacy)
126 Apprentice training
149 Other instruction and training

Health Services and Related Activities
150 Hospital
151 Hospital auxiliary
152 Nursing or convalescent home
153 Care and housing for the aged (see also 382)
154 Health clinic
155 Rural medical facility
156 Blood bank
157 Cooperative hospital service organization
158 Rescue and emergency service
159 Nurses' register or bureau
160 Aid to the handicapped (see also 031)
161 Scientific research (diseases)
162 Other medical research
163 Health insurance (medical, dental, optical, etc.)
164 Prepaid group health plan
165 Community health planning
166 Mental health care
167 Group medical practice association
168 In-faculty group practice association
169 Hospital pharmacy, parking facility, food services, etc.
179 Other health services

251 Credit Union
252 Reserve funds or insurance for domestic building and loan association, cooperative bank, or mutual savings bank
253 Mutual insurance company
254 Corporation organized under an Act of Congress (see also 904)
259 Farmers' cooperative marketing or purchasing (use 234)
　Cooperative hospital service organization (use 157)
　Other mutual organization

Employee or Membership Benefit Organizations
260 Fraternal beneficiary society, order, or association
261 Improvement of conditions of workers
262 Association of municipal employees
263 Association of employees
264 Employee or member welfare association
265 Sick, accident, death, or similar benefits
266 Strike benefits
267 Unemployment benefits
268 Pension or retirement benefits
269 Vacation benefits
279 Other services or benefits to members or employees

Sports, Athletic, Recreational and Social Activities
280 Country club
281 Hobby club
282 Dinner club
283 Variety club
284 Dog club
285 Women's club
286 Hunting or fishing club
287 Swimming or tennis club
288 Other sports club
　Boys Club, Little League, etc. (use 321)
296 Community center
297 Community recreational facilities (park, playground, etc.)
299 Travel tours
300 Training in sports
　Amateur athletic association
　School or college athletic association (use 038)
301 Fund raising athletic or sports event
317 Other sports or athletic activities
318 Other recreational activities
319 Other social activities

403 Attracting new industry or retaining industry in an area
404 Community promotion
　Community recreational facility (use 297)
405 Loans or grants for minority businesses
　Job training, counseling, or assistance (use 566)
　Day care center (use 574)
　Civil rights activity (see Civil Rights Activities)
　Referral service (social agencies) (use 569)
　Legal aid to indigents (use 462)
406 Crime prevention
407 Volunteer firemen's organization or auxiliary
　Rescue squad (use 158)
408 Community service organization
429 Other inner city or community benefit activities

Civil Rights Activities
430 Defense of human and civil rights
431 Elimination of prejudice and discrimination, race, religion, sex, national origin, etc.)
432 Lessen neighborhood tensions
　Litigation (see Litigation and Legal Aid Activities)
　Legislative and political activities (see that caption)
449 Other civil rights activities

Litigation and Legal Aid Activities
460 Public interest litigation activities
461 Other litigation or support of litigation
462 Legal aid to indigents
463 Providing bail

Legislative and Political Activities
480 Propose, support, or oppose legislation
481 Voter information on issues or candidates
482 Voter education (mechanics of registering, voting, etc.)
483 Support, oppose, or rate political candidates
484 Provide facilities or services for political campaign activities
509 Other legislative and political activities

Advocacy
Attempt to influence public opinion concerning:

563 Marriage counseling
564 Family planning
565 Credit counseling and assistance
566 Job training, counseling, or assistance
567 Draft counseling
568 Vocational counseling
569 Referral service (social agencies)
572 Rehabilitating convicts or ex-convicts
573 Rehabilitating alcoholics, drug abusers, compulsive gamblers, etc.
574 Day care center
575 Services for the aged (see also 153 and 382)
　Training of or aid to the handicapped (see 031 and 160)

Activities Directed to Other Organizations
600 Community Chest, United Givers Fund, etc.
601 Booster club
602 Gifts, grants, or loans to other organizations
603 Non-financial services or facilities to other organizations

Other Purposes and Activities
900 Cemetery or burial activities
901 Perpetual care fund (cemetery, columbarium, etc.)
902 Emergency or disaster aid fund
903 Community trust or component
904 Government instrumentality or agency (see also 254)
905 Testing products for public safety
906 Consumer interest group
907 Veterans activities
908 Patriotic activities
909 Non-exempt trust
910 Domestic organization with activities outside U.S.
911 Foreign organization
912 Title holding corporation
913 Prevention of cruelty to animals
914 Achievement prizes or awards
915 Erection or maintenance of public building or works
916 Cafeteria, restaurant, snack bar, food services, etc.
917 Thrift shop, retail outlet, etc.
918 Book, gift or supply store
919 Advertising
920 Association of employees
921 Loans or credit reporting
922 Endowment fund or financial services
923 Indians (tribes, cultures, etc.)
924 Traffic or tariff bureau

Page 8

Source: IRS Form 990, "Exempt Organizations."

☆U.S. GOVERNMENT PRINTING OFFICE: 1977-O-575-270-87-0321919

tions. While many differences exist among the nonprofits, however, correspondingly great differences exist among firms in the private for-profit sector. Economists have found that despite the vast differences between a private steel producer and a shoe producer, between a retailer and a manufacturer, and between a vertically integrated oil company and a nonintegrated printer, all have in common the pursuit of profit. Thus, a unified theory can predict the behavior of any private for-profit firm, once its production function and prices of inputs and outputs are known.

Just as the differences among for-profit firms have been submerged by the similarities of objective functions, so we should seek to find the essential similarities among nonprofit firms. It is notable that, to date, attempts to model behavior of nonprofit firms have dealt almost exclusively with a single "type" of firm in a single "industry," generally hospitals.[2] In the for-profit sector we do not have a separate theory of behavior for each industry. Why should there be one for each industry in the nonprofit sector?

Why has the modeling of nonprofit behavior been so narrow and industry oriented, in such sharp contrast with the familiar, broad microeconomic theory of the decentralized private market sector? There may well be a number of answers, but one, I believe, is that so little attention has been paid to the similarities and differences among nonprofit organizations that researchers have sought more "homogeneous" groupings, and "industry" has had an obvious appeal. The contrast between the breadth of our economic models of the private for-profit sector and the narrowness of our few models of nonprofit organizations reflects the corresponding contrast in the depth of research on the two sectors.

Given the emphasis in this paper on collective good problems, I pursue the implications of distinguishing among nonprofit firms according to the "degree of collectiveness" of their activities. This term will be defined shortly, but for now the point to be emphasized is that the legally nonprofit organizations (as portrayed in Table 1) may well cover a wide range in terms of how collective their activities are—that is, how much they act like governments, providing collective consumption goods. If we could measure the degree of collectiveness we might well be able to develop a general model for all the nonprofits that are "heavily" engaged in collective goods activities, while some other model might be appropriate for nonprofits that are engaged virtually entirely in private goods provision. "Industry" per se—for example, hospitals—would not be a distinguishing characteristic. Even within an industry, nonprofit firms might vary in the balance between their private goods and collective goods activities and hence might vary in their behavior.

But firms engaged in a similar relative degree of collective behavior might have much in common—that is, might share an objective function—regardless of their industry, just as conventional for-profit firms have behavioral characteristics in common despite the differences in their particular private goods outputs. Thus, we turn now, in Sections II, III, and IV to a measure of the degree of collectiveness (or its converse, a measure of the degree of privateness) of a firm's activities. Subsequently, Section V sketches some elements of behavioral models of nonprofit organizations of the collective good and of the private good types.

II. UNTANGLING THE KNOT: NONPROFIT FIRMS, TAX-EXEMPT ORGANIZATIONS, AND MEASUREMENT OF COLLECTIVENESS: CONCEPTS

To begin with, the degree of collective-goodness of an organization's activities should not be confused conceptually with tax status considerations. It is true that the income tax deductibility of contributions to some but not to other nonprofit organizations alters the relative prices (costs) of giving to each. It is also true, however, that if there were no differences among organizations in the character of their outputs, there would be no reason to expect any gifts to be given to any organization, regardless of tax deductibility, provided the marginal income tax rates were less than 100 percent. That is, if, but only if, individuals perceive benefits (in any form) from gifts in the *absence* of tax deductibility, would the introduction of deductibility be expected to affect the level of giving. It is noteworthy that voluntary nonprofit organizations provided collective goods long before income taxation. As I have pointed out elsewhere, such organizations provided hospitals, schools, roads, and numerous other collective goods and services centuries ago [Weisbrod (180)]. In short, the nature of the firm's output should be our focal point, not its tax status per se, although, of course, the two need not be independent; favorable tax treatment might well be bestowed on firms providing particular types of outputs.

In thinking about an ideal measure of a firm's collective *vis-à-vis* its private goods activity, it is useful to consider a spectrum of all nongovernmental firms arrayed according to the degree of privateness (or collectiveness) of their outputs. Many firms—those that are traditionally thought of as in the private for-profit sector—will be at the pure-private pole of the array. So, too, I suggest, would be organizations that, while often termed "nonprofit," are captives of for-profit firms and hence are essentially instrumentalities for enhancing the profits of those firms. A business trade association, for example, may be thought of as a mechanism through which profit-maximizing firms cooperate in the promotion of profitability. Thus, to treat such an "organization of firms" as if it were an independent firm would be similar to treating the shipping department of a manufacturing firm as a separate organization. The shipping department or the trade association may or may not produce a profit for itself, and may or may not be termed a nonprofit organization, but each may nonetheless contribute to the profitability of the firm or firms with which it is associated. Thus, we seek an ideal measure of degree of collectiveness that treats "captive" nonprofit firms just like for-profit firms. Such organizations may be termed "nonprofit privates."

By contrast with nonprofit privates—nonprofit firms or organizations that are understandable as mechanisms for maximizing the private profitability of the firm or firms with which they are "associated" financially—at the other end of the spectrum are "nonprofit collectives," pure providers of collective goods, goods that simultaneously enter (positively) the utility or production functions of many, even nonassociated, persons and firms. Firms in the for-profit sector are not likely to be found at this collective pole since the necessity of exclusionary practices to overcome free-rider behavior serves both to limit the private profitability of providing collective goods and to limit the actual collectiveness of the form in which the goods are provided (as distinguished from their potential collectiveness).

If nongovernmental firms that are substantial providers of collective goods exist, it is at least arguable—if not even presumptively true—that they do not behave as profit maximizers behave. Insofar as they actually provide "pure" collective consumption goods or, more generally, goods from which beneficiaries are not excluded by price, they are dependent on sources of revenue other than *quid pro quo* sales. These other sources are varied; they may include governmental grants, private gifts, court-awarded fees, or other types of donations, contributions or transfers, but whatever the precise form may be, the result is a set of pressures, rules, restrictions, and reward structures—in short, incentives and constraints—that influence the ability of the firm to earn profits and the mechanisms by which it can seek those profits. The existence of constraints, of course, does not necessarily preclude maximization of profits subject to those constraints, but the point is that the behavior of these nonprofit collective organizations is not likely to mirror the behavior of firms in the for-profit sector.

This is true, *a fortiori*, if the preferences of entrepreneurs and managers of the nonprofit collective-goods firms differ systematically from the preferences of their for-profit sector counterparts. If, for example, those entrepreneurs and managers who gravitate to the nonprofit collectives are more willing to trade off money income for the opportunity to engage in such collective goods activity, then utility maximization will imply different behavior in the private goods and in the collective goods parts of the private sector. Profit maximization may be a far better proxy for utility maximization for private goods producers—whether "nonprofit" or for-profit—than it is for nonprofit collective-goods producers.

The question next arises, can we distinguish among private firms in the degree to which they are private or collective goods producers? Perhaps the baker, the shoemaker, the automobile producer are nearly polar cases of private sector providers of private goods, but which private firms, if any, are close to the collective goods pole? We will turn below to an operational measure of "privateness" or "collectiveness."

To summarize, this discussion of private and collective goods production in the private sector has been motivated by the goal of defining and understanding a "nonprofit" sector for which predictive models and welfare analysis can be pursued. The assertion is that it would be useful to focus attention on the role and behavior of those organizations that, while private, provide collective goods; we term these "nonprofit collective" firms, and suggest that this class of organizations is important and merits our attention. Combining an attribute traditionally identified with governmental activity—provision of collective goods—with an attribute of private activity, the absence of legal compulsion to pay for benefits, nonprofit collective-goods firms may be thought of as hybrids.

In an idealized textbook model, in which any failures of the private (for-profit) market that can be corrected efficiently by governmental intervention are actually corrected, hybrid organizational structures would serve no function. In a world, however, in which governmental failures also occur, other institutional mechanisms may evolve to fill niches in the arsenal of devices for achieving society's allocative efficiency and equity objectives.[3]

III. THE DEGREE OF COLLECTIVENESS OF A FIRM'S ACTIVITIES: NONPROFIT TAX-EXEMPT ORGANIZATIONS

Being interested in policy measure for correcting failures of private markets and governments, we are interested in the extent to which a firm's activities generate (external) benefits at the margin that the firm does not capture or internalize. Thus, when we refer to "external benefits" (calling them benefits does not preclude their being negative) we mean those social benefits that are not internalized. Our references to "collective" goods thus reflect the difficulty that a producer of such goods has in internalizing the social benefits it generates and, thus, the external benefits that would result if those goods were provided.

Every organization or firm may be thought of as providing some combination of private and collective goods, ranging potentially from pure private to pure collective. By collective goods is meant simply those goods that provide a high degree of external (uncaptured) marginal benefits.[4] There is still a lack of uniformity in economics regarding definitions of "collective goods," whether in technological or utility-function terms, and regarding the relationship between collective goods, however defined, and goods that provide important external benefits. In this paper the essential characteristic of collective output, in terms of which I distinguish among nonprofit firms, is the degree to which the firm provides goods that would not be provided in optimal quantities in the private for-profit sector because the goods benefit many consumers simultaneously. An idealized textbook version of a conventional private sector competitive firm provides social benefits that are fully internalized (at the margin) in the firm's sales revenue. Such a firm would be a pure private goods producer, and the measure of collectiveness we seek to develop should give such a firm a measure zero. Similarly, a *non*profit organization of the private type should be characterized by a zero. By contrast, a nonprofit *collective* organization, one that provides only pure collective goods from which many people benefit substantially without paying—there being no significant "congestion" problems and no exclusionary actions—should be found to have the highest measure of collectiveness, say (arbitrarily), one hundred. Between these limits would lie nonprofit organizations combining various degrees of privateness and collectiveness of outputs.

In this market failure context, the proposed theoretic measure of collectiveness—that is, the proposed measure of the "degree" of collectiveness of firm i—C_i^*, is

$$C_i^* \equiv \frac{E_i}{E_i + I_i} \times 100, \tag{1}$$

where E_i and I_i are, respectively, the external (noncaptured) and internal (captured) benefits from a marginal unit of output by firm i.[5] C_i^* ranges from zero, for a nonprofit private organization or a perfectly competitive firm in equilibrium, to one hundred for a pure collective good provider, for which I_i approaches zero.[6]

The operationalization of the C^* index is not simple. One simplifying assumption that will prove useful is that marginal and average ratios of external to internal benefits are equal.

The confusing array of organizations that are deemed to be nonprofit in terms of U.S. tax law was shown by Table 1, which is a list of "codes" by which organizations identify their activities on the tax return (Form 990). There is little doubt that the activities range widely in terms of their degree of privateness and collectiveness. Recognition of this variation in the degree of privateness and collectiveness seems to be reflected in the tax law. All organizations filing Form 990 returns, for "Exempt Organizations," are not treated alike. In particular, some, but actually a minority, are permitted to accept gifts and grants that are deductible on the federal tax return of the giver. These organizations include primarily those listed in Section 501(C)(3) of the Internal Revenue Code. From an allocative-efficiency perspective we might hypothesize—and, perhaps, hope—that these are the organizations that have the greatest degree of collectiveness at the margin, the highest C^* values. Since tax deductibility of contributions reduces the private cost to the giver, it encourages contributions and thereby expands output by the recipient organizations. The presumption that certain kinds of activities deserve expansion relative to others would seem to flow from a determination that the former activities generate more external, uncaptured marginal benefits than do the latter.

Although the tax laws encourage contributions to some organizations relative to others, the magnitude of the encouragement should be kept in perspective. The cost to the giver is never zero; even for a donor in the 70 percent marginal tax bracket, a dollar of giving still costs 30 cents. At the same time, an individual is not precluded from making a contribution that is not deductible and, as we will see, many such contributions are given. Thus, whereas ordinary consideration of price elasticity would suggest that contributions will be greater the lower the cost of giving, *ceteris paribus*, other explanations are needed for (1) the total absence of contributions to the vast majority of private organizations in the economy, (2) the giving of gifts to some organizations even though the contributions are not tax deductible, and for (3) the presence of any contributions even when gifts are tax deductible, since there is some private cost and no "apparent" private benefit. We will return to these questions briefly later in this paper. Now we turn to our principal goal, development of a means for distinguishing among organizations according to their degree of collectiveness.

Consider three potential sources of revenue for any private nongovernmental firm or organization—*sales* of goods and services, membership *dues*, and *gifts*. Each source of revenue may be associated with a different set of characteristics of the organization's activities. (a) Some firms (nonprofit and for-profit) are of the type normally identified with the private market sector—that is, engaged in the provision of private goods for which exclusion is easily, and efficiently practiced—and so we can expect such firms' revenue to be in the form of sales. (b) Some organizations are engaged in provision of goods or services that are somewhat collective—in the sense that the marginal cost of permitting an additional consumer is approximately zero, at least over some range beyond which congestion costs appear—but exclusion is practiced easily (that is, at low cost). For such organizations—for example, country clubs—benefits are essentially limited to members, there are no substantial external benefits, and the principal source of revenue is likely to be dues from the limited membership. (c) Other organizations, however, provide collective goods of types for which exclusion is costly, impossible, or for whatever the reason, is not practiced, so that benefits are not limited to "members" or other financial supporters. Such organizations—as in medical research or charity—may not be able, technically, to restrict their output to contributors, or if the technical capability exists, the organization may not wish to exclude, perhaps because an objective of the organization is to provide certain collective goods—that is, the organization is a nonprofit collective. The result, however, is the familiar problem of private finance for collective goods. Neither sales revenue nor dues is a promising revenue source. The organization is likely to be dependent for its survival on non-*quid pro quo* sources of revenue—contributions, gifts, and grants—from either private or governmental sources.

Direct measurement of the magnitude of external benefits of a firm's activities is costly; a proxy would, therefore, be useful, even if it were imperfect. The preceding discussion, which related the form of a firm's *revenue* to the character of its *output*, can serve as the basis for such a proxy measure. In the next section we make use of a proxy—admittedly imperfect—based on revenue sources to distinguish among nonprofit organizations and thereby to move closer to the point at which we can identify and then model the behavior of nonprofit-private and nonprofit-collective organizations.

The distinction among sales, dues, and gifts should not be drawn too sharply. That is, any observed data on these three revenue sources may not correspond precisely to the theoretic concepts presented above. "Dues," for example, may combine an element of payment for an excludable collective good with an element of sales—as when membership includes receipt of a magazine, journal, newsletter, and so forth. Similarly, "sales" (or even dues) may include an element of "gift"—as when the buyer knowingly pays more than he or she would pay for the private good alone, the buyer regarding the additional sum as a contribution to the organization. Despite the imperfections in revenue sources as proxies for outputs, the usefulness of developing a measure of the degree of collectiveness of a firm's activities suggests that such a measure be explored more fully.

In addition to the fact that reported sales revenue may include a gift component, there is another reason for regarding sales as an imperfect measure of private goods output across firms. For some firms, sales are also an indicator of collective good output; for example, insofar as givers of "gifts" are motivated by the desire to disseminate specific outputs, sales will represent benefits to givers as well as to purchasers.[7] The point is that while for some firms sales are only revenues from private goods, for other firms they are *both* revenues from private goods and measures of benefits from collective goods. Gifts and grants to a nonprofit economic research organization, for example, may indeed be intended to finance activities that will bring benefits to others, via the provision and circulation of articles and books. Insofar as such publications are sold rather than given away, the revenues, while reflecting private benefits to the purchasers, also constitute a measure of benefits to the givers.

Another conceptual issue relating to the interpretation of sales revenue as private goods output involves the uses of any "profit" made on those sales. If a firm that is providing some collective goods (that is, generating external benefits) were also selling private goods, then profit on private good sales could be a source of finance for the firm's collective goods. Competitive forces would tend to limit such profits, however, as any abnormal profit on the private goods attracted competitors. There are two reasons, however, for believing that economic profits might not be competed away: (1) the nonprofit firm may have some monopoly power, for example, in the form of its logo that is sold on tee-shirts, umbrellas, or other consumer goods; and (2) as noted above, some consumers may be willing to pay more than a competitive market price for a private good purchased from an organization that is engaged in collective good activities—that is, the consumer may combine, in effect, a purchase with a gift. (Consumers in sufficiently high income tax classes may also find it profitable, albeit not legal, to take income-tax charitable deductions for "gifts" to exempt organizations when the gifts are actually payments for private goods. In such cases the tax system is subsidizing provision of private goods by "nonprofit" firms *vis-à-vis* for-profit firms.)

IV. AN EMPIRICAL MEASURE OF COLLECTIVENESS

This section presents and utilizes an operational form of expression (1) presented earlier. The measure, termed a Collectiveness Index, C, is seen as an index, a means of ranking organizations. Those ranked lower (closer to zero) are held to be closer to the pure private-goods pole, and those ranked higher (closer to unity) are held to be closer to the pure collective-goods pole. Such an indexing is seen as a step toward eventual modeling of the behavior of nonprofit organizations of the private and of the collective types. The collectiveness index could be applied to for-profit firms, which, as pointed out earlier, would generally receive a value of zero. Since the focus of this paper is on nonprofit firms, however, only data from them will be used.

In the earlier discussion that linked sales, dues, and gifts to private and collective goods, a major distinction was drawn between gifts, which were associated with the financing of goods that provide significant external benefits, and the other forms of revenue, which were not. Gifts were identified with the financing of goods having the greatest uncaptured external benefits.

The fact that an organization is a recipient of gifts does not imply that the giver receives no private benefits. To the contrary, the presumption is that the giver, being rational, does benefit in some direct or indirect manner.[8] Our assumption is simply that gifts are employed to finance provision of goods that bring more external relative to internal benefits than do other types of revenue. Our operational collectiveness index is:

$$C_i \equiv \frac{\text{Gifts}_i}{\text{Total Revenue}_i} \times 100. \tag{2}$$

The index ranges from zero, for firms receiving no gifts, to 100 for firms receiving no revenue other than gifts.

As an initial basis for examining the variation among nonprofit organizations, I turned to Gale's Encyclopedia of Associations (71), which includes listings of thousands of nonprofit organizations. I took a random sample of organizations listed in each of the seventeen categories (Table 2 lists the categories, which I term "industries"), and the tax return for that organization was requested from the Internal Revenue Service for those organizations that file the Form 990 "Exempt Organization" return. The Collectiveness Index, C, was calculated for the organizations in each category, the expectation being that we would find not only variation among classes but a ranking of index values that would be positively correlated with our "prescientific" judgments about the collective-good ordering of organizations engaged in different types of activities. That is, at this stage in the research process, we are simple proposing a measure—in effect, a definition. As such, it cannot be right or wrong: it can only be "more useful" or "less useful." For now, its usefulness can be judged by whether it ranks organizations in accord with subjective judgments about the relative "public interest" or external benefits component of its activities. Ultimately its usefulness will be

Table 2. Types of Nonprofit Organizations

Trade, Business, Commercial
Agricultural; Commodity Exchanges
Legal, Governmental, Public Administration, Military
Scientific, Engineering, Technical
Educational
Cultural
Social Welfare
Health, Medical
Public Affairs
Fraternal, Foreign Interest, Nationality, Ethnic
Religious
Veteran, Hereditary, Patriotic
Hobby, Avocational
Athletic, Sports
Labor Unions, Associations and Federations
Chambers of Commerce
Greek Letter Societies

Source: Gale's Encyclopedia of Associations (71).

determined by the insights it offers and the testable predictions that flow from them. The reason for seeking a measure of collectiveness for non-profit organizations is the hypothesis that to understand the behavior of organizations that are called "nonprofit," either in common parlance or in the sense defined as "exempt organizations" by the tax code in the United States, it is necessary first to distinguish between "private" and "collective" nonprofit organizations. Later, distinct models of behavior must be developed and tested. In sum, nonprofit organizations are too heterogeneous to be examined as a single class, whether the examination is for the purpose of predicting behavior or making normative judgments about their contribution to social objectives. But only when behavioral models that distinguish between private and collective non-profit organizations are developed will the usefulness of our collective-ness index be resolvable. Section V, below, contains some notes on the kind of models that would appear to be useful for each polar type of nonprofit organization.

Table 3 presents estimates of collectiveness index values for seventeen "industries" in which nonprofit firms function, and Table 4 summarizes those values. Although I believe the principal use of the index is to rank, the index may be useful as a cardinal measure, in which case the varia-tion in degree of collectiveness is impressive. The seventeen industries range from zero to 90, and nearly half (8 of 17) of the "nonprofit" indus-tries receive collectiveness indices of under 10.

The operational version of the Collectiveness Index, C, is a function of

Table 3. Index of Collectiveness, Seventeen Classes of Nonprofit Organizations, 1973–1975

Type of Organization	Collectiveness Index (C)[1]	Sample Size[2]
1. Cultural	90	28
2. Religious	71	32
3. Public Affairs	47	29
4. Social Welfare	41	40
5. Agricultural	41	50
6. Educational	34	33
7. Legal, Public Administration, and Military	20	50
8. Veteran, Hereditary, and Patriotic	12	45
9. Athletic and Sports	11	28
10. Honor Societies	9	51
11. Scientific, Engineering, and Technical	6	51
12. Ethnic	3	37
13. Labor Associations and Federations	3	70
14. Trade, Business, and Commercial	2	58
15. Health[3]	2	35
16. Hobby and Avocational	1	20
17. Chambers of Commerce	0	27
Total	20	684

[1]Gifts as percentage of total revenue.

[2]Excludes organizations for which tax returns were incomplete and those for which photocopies of the tax returns were illegible.

[3]The collectiveness index for this group is affected in a major way by three organizations, each of which has at least 10 times the total revenue of any other organization in the group, and each of which has a collectiveness index of 1 or less. Excluding those three, the index for the group would be 12.

Source: Gale's Encyclopedia of Associations (71).

monetary receipts only. By omitting in-kind receipts it introduces a bias, but the nature of the bias is to some extent known. While a measure of "full revenue"—monetary revenue plus the market value of nonmonetary, in-kind receipts—would surely disclose some cases of understatements of full *sales* and full *dues* because of payments made in-kind, the major effect would be on *gifts*. This is so primarily because of volunteer labor, which amounts annually to billions of dollars of donations.[9] Hard information about the distribution of these in-kind gifts among organizations is, I believe, nonexistent, but there seems to be little doubt that volunteer labor (as well as transfers of other resource inputs at below-market prices) is concentrated among those nonprofit organizations that engaged in activities that are commonly held to be "charitable," "philanthropic," or "public interest."[10] Rarely, if ever, does one hear of people donating services to ordinary private sector firms such as General Motors, Exxon, or Macy's, or even to such "nonprofit" organizations as

Table 4. Frequency Distribution of Collectiveness
Indices, Seventeen Types of Organizations

Collectiveness Index	Number of Classes
0–10	8
11–20	3
21–30	0
31–40	1
41–50	3
51–60	0
61–70	0
71–80	1
81–90	1
91–100	0
	17

chambers of commerce or country clubs. Without additional data we might guess that in-kind donations are positively correlated with monetary donations (gifts).

The result of limiting our collectiveness index to monetary flows is, therefore, to understate both the numerator and the denominator of C, for any given organization, by the same absolute quantity. At both the lower and upper limits of C, where the firm receives either no monetary gifts or receives all of its monetary revenue as gifts, the C index is unbiased.

Generally, however, the C index is a biased estimate of C^*. If, to consider one plausible case, in-kind gifts were assumed to be a fixed percentage of monetary gifts, then the absolute downward bias of C would be maximum for organizations with C values around 50 (percent). If, for example, the full value of gifts to an organization were uniformly 20 percent greater than the value of its gifts in monetary form, then the following table shows the relationship between the C values as calculated from monetary data and the values as calculated from full-gift data ($\hat{C}$), for hypothetical firms having various C values:

C	$\hat{C}$
0	0
10	12
50	55
90	92
100	100

Since the estimated C values vary systematically by industry (Table 3), the omission of in-kind giving might conceivably lead to changes in rankings. More likely, however, the inclusion of full-giving data, if available, would have virtually no effect on the index values for the "low-value" and "high-value" industries while increasing the index values for the "middle-value" industries, leaving the rankings little changed. But this will remain conjecture until data on industry-specific nonmonetary receipts can be obtained.[11] The balance of this paper utilizes the C index based on monetary values alone.

In a heuristic effort to examine the validity of the proposed collectiveness index, the following set of organizational vignettes is presented. The descriptions of real organizations were prepared by the organizations themselves. The organizations described in Table 5—together with their respective collectiveness indices—were not selected randomly. They were selected on the basis of the quality of the descriptions—how easy it is for the reader to judge the extent to which the organization is essentially a private or collective good provider—or, in some cases, on the basis of the well-known character of the organization.

The variety of organizations that are nonprofit in both the IRS and the *Gale's Encyclopedia* sense is highlighted by Table 5. A trade association and an association of professional tennis players have a collectiveness index of zero. A professional fraternity that sponsors awards for scientific achievement, and that has a committee concerned with the Boy Scouts, gets an index of 10. An economic research organization has an index of 32. An organization that operates a library and museum has a collectiveness index of 68. A Ralph Nader organization gets an index score of 86, and an educational television station, 95. The C index does seem capable of distinguishing among nonprofit organizations, doing so in a manner that appears (to me) to correlate positively with a ranking of organizations by the degree to which they bring benefits to persons other than those who support the organization financially. I invite the reader to decide whether his or her subjective judgment as to the relative external-benefit (or "public interest") character of these organizations would correspond to the rankings in Table 5 (or even the cardinal measure, if the indices were so interpreted).

The activity-code information, gleaned from the Form 990 tax returns, permits us to classify organizations more finely than the seventeen classes in Table 3. Each tax-exempt (nonprofit) organization was asked to "select up to three codes which best or most accurately identify [its] purposes, activities, operations or types of organization..." (Table 1 shows the activity codes that could be listed on the tax return.) Some organizations did not list any code, but a considerable majority did comply. Table 6 utilizes the activity-code information to show that many industry groupings mask considerable variation in degree of collectiveness within industries. For example, while the "Public Affairs" industry

Table 5. Selected Nonprofit Organizations, Descriptions and Collectiveness Indices, 1973–1975

Organization and Description	*Collectiveness Index (C)*
General Aviation Manufacturers Association	
Members: 33. Manufacturers of general aviation airframes, engines, avionics, and components. To create a better climate for the growth of general aviation.	0
United States Professional Tennis Association	
Members: 1,900. Professional tennis instructors and college coaches; membership also includes sporting goods salesmen and producers and wholesalers of tennis equipment. Seeks to improve tennis instruction in the United States. Maintains placement bureau.	0
Alpha Chi Sigma	
Members: 33,500. Professional fraternity, chemistry. Sponsors awards in chemistry, chemical engineering, and service to the fraternity. Committees: Boy Scout Activity.	10
Descendants of the Signers of the Declaration of Independence	
Members: 810. Lineal descendants of a signer of the Declaration of Independence; includes seniors (627 adults over 18 years of age) and juniors (267). Places tablets at birthplaces, homes, and graves of signers; contributes toward restoration and preservation of Independence Hall and other historic monuments. Awards annual scholarship to a boy or girl descendant.	22
National Planning Association	
"Independent, nonpolitical, nonprofit organization to encourage joint economic planning and cooperation by leaders from agriculture, business, labor, and the professions." Committees: Agriculture; America's Goals and Resources; British North American (sponsored with C. D. Howe Research Institute of Canada and British North American Research Association); Business; Canadian-American (sponsored with the C. D. Howe Research Institute); International; Labor.	32
Aerospace Education Foundation	
"For the education of the public at large to a greater understanding of aerospace development, and the dissemination of information concerning new accomplishments in the field of aerospace development and aerospace education."	51

Note: Descriptions were provided by each organization.

Table 6. Collectiveness Indices, By Subtype of Organization, 1973–1975

Organization Type	Activity Code[1] (1)	Collectiveness Index (2)	Sample Size (3)
Public Affairs	all	47	29
a. Other instruction and training activities	120–149	75	10
b. Advocacy	510–559	18	5
Social Welfare	all	41	40
a. Other instruction and training activities	120–149	58	6
b. Activities directed to other organizations	600–603	4	5
Agricultural	all	41	50
a. Breeders associations	237	0	12
b. Business and professional organizations	200–229	36	9
c. Conservation, environmental and beautification activities	350–379	49	6
Legal, Governmental, Public Administration, and Military	all	20	50
a. Business and professional organizations	205	1	11
b. Employee or membership benefit organizations	260–279	1	7
c. Other instruction and training activities	120–149	20	12
Veteran, Hereditary, and Patriotic[2]	all	12	45
a. Patriotic activities	908	23	14
b. Veterans activities	907	23	8
c. Cultural, historical or other educational activities	60–119	18	18
d. Historical site, records, or reenactment	062	12	6

as a whole averages 47 on the collectiveness index, one subsector, Instruction and Training (other than schools and colleges), has an index of 75, and another subsector, Advocacy, has an index of 18. Table 6 includes all industries, as defined in Table 3, that had at least two subsectors, as defined by activity codes, containing five or more organizations. The eight industries excluded from Table 6 were, in general, more homogeneous than the nine included.

A few additional illustrations from Table 6 highlight the differences in degree of collectiveness within industry classes. Among agricultural organizations we find that "Breeders Associations"—which a priori I would characterize as adjuncts of profit-maximizing firms and, hence, would expect to have a low collectiveness measure—do have a C index of zero. By contrast, "Conservation, Environmental, and Beautification

Table 6. (Continued)

Organization Type	Activity Code[1] (1)	Collectiveness Index (2)	Sample Size (3)
Athletic and Sports	all	11	28
a. Sports, athletic, recreational and social activities	280–319	12	10
b. Business and professional organizations	200–229	0	6
Honor Societies	all	9	51
a. Schools, colleges, and related activities: Fraternity or sorority	36	7	31
b. Schools, colleges, and related activities: scholarships	40	42	8
Scientific, Engineering, and Technical	all	6	51
a. Other instruction and training activities: publishing activities	120	9	14
b. Professional association	205	12	13
c. Scientific research activities	180–199	4	19
Ethnic	all	3	37
a. Employee or membership benefit organization: fraternal beneficiary, society, order, or association	260	1	12
b. Cultural, historical, or other educational activities	60–119	26	5

Note: Each of these tax-exempt organizations was asked to select up to three codes most accurately identifying its activities.

[1]See Table 1.

[2]One large organization, The Colonial Dames of America, dominates this class. It has a collectiveness index of 5 (percent), and is not included in any of the subclasses because it listed no activity code.

Activities" have an index of 49, among the higher values observed. Similarly, those "Honor Societies" that provide scholarships have a collectiveness index of 42, while those that do not, and that characterize themselves as "Fraternity or Sorority," have an index of only 7.

"Industry," in the sense described in Table 3, may or may not be a useful way of thinking about organizations, given our goal of identifying organizations by their degree of collectiveness. We turn next to the question of whether the IRS activity codes or the *Gale's Encyclopedia* have captured more homogeneity of collectiveness in their "industry" classifications. Table 7 shows the index values for organizations that are in the same class of IRS activity codes even though they are in different industry groupings in the *Gale's Encyclopedia* groupings that are used in Table 2. Table 7 also discloses considerable variance, as did Table 3. It is

Table 7. Collectiveness Index Values: Different "Industry" Groups, Same "Activity Code" Classes, 1973–1975

Activity Code Class	Number of Organizations	Industry Group	Collectiveness Index
Cultural, Historical, or Other			
Educational Activities	18	12	18
(Codes 060–119)	3	13	3
	10	4	63
Business and Professional			
Organizations			
(Codes 220–229)	12	8	32
	18	9	36
	6	14	0
	21	16	0
Employee or Membership Benefit			
Organizations	7	9	1
(Codes 260–279)	54	15	1
Sports, Athletic, Recreational, and			
Social Activities			
(Codes 280–319)	6	13	0
	10	14	12
Advocacy			
(Codes 510–559)	5	5	18
	5	6	4

Note: For list of "Activity Codes," see Table 1. For list of "Industry Groups," see Table 2.
Source: Calculations from U.S. tax returns, Form 990.

not surprising, perhaps, that "Business and Professional Organizations," for example, should vary considerably in their collectiveness indices, depending on the nature of the business or profession.

The variance in the degree of collectiveness of organizations that are nonprofit in a tax sense is shown even more sharply by the chart, which shows the distribution, by the C index, of organizations *all* of which can accept tax deductible gifts. (While some organizations not included in Section 501(C)(3) of the Internal Revenue Code can also accept gifts that are deductible on the donor's federal income tax, all 501(C)(3) organizations are able to accept tax deductible gifts.) Nonetheless, the chart shows that more than a third (38%) of those organizations actually receive no gifts at all. The median organization receives 25 percent of its total revenue as gifts.

A. A Modified Collectiveness Index

It might be argued that "sales" of private goods by nonprofit organizations are means by which the objectives of the organizations are financed, and that those objectives are of two types: (a) the interests of members of the group, and (b) the interests of a wider group, of which members may be a part, but a small part. The distinction between (a) and (b) corresponds to the difference, discussed earlier, between the uses of revenues from "dues" and from "gifts." If we continue to identify dues and gifts with these internal and external benefits, but now

Chart 1

Gifts as a Percentage of Total Revenue,
for 501 (c) (3) Organizations, 1973-1975

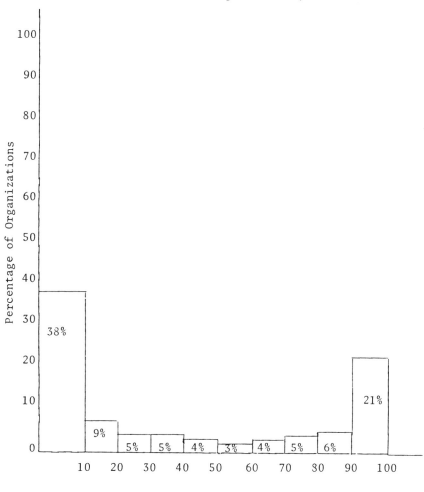

Gifts as Percentage of Total Revenue

Source: Random sample of 274 Form 990 tax returns

identify "sales" with fund raising to support those activities, then
another measure of collectiveness is suggested, one that regards all
nonprofit organizations as devices for supporting activities of type (a) or
(b) in varying degree. One such modified index is

$$M_i \equiv \frac{\text{Gifts}_i}{\text{Gifts}_i + \text{Dues}_i} \times 100. \tag{3}$$

Gifts revenue is used again to proxy collective-goods output, and dues
revenue is used to proxy outputs that are collective only for members.
The M index would give a value of zero to an organization that collected
"dues" but received no gifts, and a value of 100 to an organization that
received no dues revenue but some gifts. Because the index disregards
sales revenue it is undefined for the limiting case of a firm—rare among
nonprofits—that has revenue only from sales, and none from either
dues or gifts. It is useful, however, in concentrating attention on the two
sources of revenue that distinguish the organizations that are conven-
tionally termed nonprofit from ordinary private sector profit-oriented
firms, which have revenue only from sales of private-type goods.

One undesirable property of the M index is that it gives the same
collectiveness score to an organization for which private good sales constitute an overwhelming proportion of the firm's total revenue, and
another organization, with the same ratio of gifts to dues, that has no
sales revenue at all. Consider, for example, the following two hypothetical organizations (revenues are stated in thousands):

Organization	Sales	Dues	Gifts	Total	Gifts/ Total (C)	Gifts/Gifts and Dues (M)
1	$950	$ 5	$ 45	$1000	4	90
2	0	100	900	1000	90	90

The two organizations have the same M index but vastly different C
indices. Firm 1 receives 95 percent of its revenue from sales; firm 2 gets
none from sales and 90 percent from gifts. Organizations that differ so
much in their relative dependence on sales and gifts are not likely to be
describable by the same behavioral model. This observation explains
both my preference for the more comprehensive measure of collectiveness, C, and the difficulty that economists are likely to have in modeling
"nonprofit" firm behavior until the degree of collectiveness of the entire
organization's activities is recognized. "Nonprofit" hospitals, for example, now receive only some 2 percent of their total revenues from gifts,
while nonprofit educational organizations receive about 40 percent of
their total revenues as gifts. Corresponding differences in behavior can
be expected.

Table 8 arrays the seventeen types (industries) of nonprofits according to the M index. The higher the score the greater the degree to which the organization's activities are deemed to bring external benefits. It is noteworthy that the industry rankings using the M and the C indices (Tables 8 and 3) are quite similar. Indeed, the Spearman coefficient of rank correlation indicates that the rankings are not statistically different from one another. The only industry changing by more than three ranks is Scientific, Engineering, and Technical, which moved from position 11 on the C index to position 4 on the M index.

Whichever index, C or M, is used, a firm's revenue from gifts is held to be a useful index of the external benefits generated by its activities—that is, of its collective good output. It would be useful, however, to go beyond the measurement of the volume of gifts, to inquire into their source. The point is that gifts (grants) from governmental sources may have a different influence on behavior than grants from private sources, and, indeed, different sources of grants even within the overall governmental or private categories may well imply different incentives and constraints, and, hence, different degrees of external benefits.

Our analysis of the Form 990 tax returns points up the fact that an

Table 8. Modified Collective Indices, Seventeen Types of Nonprofit Organizations, 1973–1975

Type of Organization	Modified Collectiveness Index
1. Cultural	99
2. Religious	95
3. Public Affairs	92
4. Scientific, Engineering, and Technical	74
5. Social Welfare	73
6. Educational	61
7. Agricultural	56
8. Legal, Governmental, Public Administration, and Military	37
9. Veterans, Hereditary, and Patriotic	22
10. Honor Societies	18
11. Athletic and Sports	17
12. Ethnic	16
13. Health	9**
14. Hobby and Avocational	4
15. Labor Associations	4
16. Chamber of Commerce	4
17. Trade, Business, and Commercial	3

*Gifts/Gifts plus Dues.
**If the three large and extreme "outlier" observations are excluded, the M index for the remaining 32 organizations in this group would be 28. See also Note 3 to Table 3, above.

organization's tax status and either of the measures of collective good-
ness are by no means perfectly (rank) correlated. There are only two
statuses that an organization can have with respect to the income tax
deductibility of donor's gifts to it. Either the gifts are deductible or they
are not (although there are upper limits on individual tax-deductible
gifts, and these limits vary somewhat among types of organizations).
Depending on the type of organization as shown in the tables above, tax
status is essentially dichotomous—in general, virtually all organizations
in a given industry are "tax deductible" (that is, gifts are deductible on
the giver's federal income tax return), or virtually all are nontax deductible. Nonetheless, collectiveness indices show considerable variation.
There are, in short, many tax-deductible organizations that receive no
gifts, and there are nontax-deductible organizations that receive substantial gifts. Important examples of the latter are the Sierra Club,
Common Cause, and Ralph Nader's Public Citizen, all of which are
nonprofit organizations that do not have deductible status because of
their lobbying activities. Yet, each receives sizable amounts of nontax-
deductible gifts to finance their collective-good activities.[12]

Further work is necessary to develop measures of collectiveness. The
data utilized here do appear, however, to be promising sources. As
economic research moves on to the development and testing of models
of nonprofit behavior it will be important, I believe, to distinguish more
carefully than has been done in the literature to date among the wide
variety of nonprofit organizations. "Variety" should be judged, this
paper argues, by the criterion of the degree to which the organization is
involved in provision of collective type goods—goods bringing substantial external benefits.[13] The observation of nongovernmental organizations providing collective goods does require further theorizing.

V. MODELING NONPROFIT FIRMS: SOME CONJECTURES

As we seek to model behavior of nonprofit firms, our data suggest that
we should think of those firms as hybrids of private good and collective
good producers. We have found that legally nonprofit firms vary tre-
mendously in their hybrid status. If, to begin with, we think of the firm's
objective function as being separable into private and collective components, then it is likely that the former can be modeled as an ordinary
profit maximizer. The collective component is in need of further
analysis. This section contains some preliminary thoughts on the ingredients of useful predictive models for organizations having "high" and
"low" collectiveness indices.

It may or may not be appropriate to regard the "hybrid's" objective function as separable; decisions on behavior of the private and the collective good "divisions" of the firm's activities may well be interdependent. For example, (1) there may be demand interdependencies between the private and collective goods, as when the price at which the firm can sell private goods is a function of the quantity and quality of its collective good output. This is another way of saying that the purchaser of the firm's private good output may be making a contribution to the firm's collective output in the form of a price greater than that which the purchaser would be willing to pay if he were simply purchasing the private good alone. (2) There may be production interdependencies between the private and collective outputs, as when the collective good information—e.g., about product quality or political candidates—can be embodied as an input to a salable, private-good book.

As research on behavioral models of nonprofit firms proceeds, it may be useful to begin by considering "pure" cases—the pure private-good nonprofit and the pure collective-good nonprofit. Consideration of hybrids will wait.

A. Modeling Nonprofits with High Collectiveness Indices

The behavior of a private firm that provides collective goods would seem to hinge on its struggle for finance. Unable (or unwilling) to exclude consumers, as private firms normally do, and unable to compel payment, as governmental providers of collective goods normally do, how can the private provider of collective goods sustain itself?

Reference to the tax subsidies that are available to some nonprofit organizations—presumably greatest for the producers most likely to use the subsidies to provide collective goods—is at best a partial answer. These subsidies, which reduce costs of operation, and reduce the private cost of donating, do not bring either type of cost down to zero. They do not explain why donors give any money (or goods) at all. Why are there any such gifts, and how is the magnitude of gifts related to the degree of collectiveness of the firm's actual or promised activity?

The donation function for a private provider of collective goods is analogous to the for-profit firm's demand function. What are the key arguments in a donation function? Of particular importance, I hypothesize, is information—in the form of *publicity*—regarding the collective good activities of the firm. The speculation that publicity is an important determinant of donations is discussed somewhat more fully elsewhere [Weisbrod, Handler, and Komesar (183)] and additional study is under way, but the argument may be summarized briefly here by pointing to the benefits of publicity to a private provider of collective goods.

First, unless the collective good is in a form that individual donors can easily (costlessly) detect—which is generally not the case—the prospective donor will be discouraged from giving to finance an activity that may or may not actually be provided in the intended fashion. In the private good case this is not a problem, but it can be when collective goods are involved. If, for example, a firm claims to be a provider of income transfers—in cash or in subsidies, for example, to the indigent for legal assistance or in educational scholarship aid—prospective donors, whether ordinary consumers or wealthy foundations, may welcome evidence that donations to the organization are actually used that way. Publicity can provide that evidence.

Second, publicity for the firm's collective-good activities may have the effect of shifting "outward" its production function, permitting it to increase its output with the same inputs. This would be the case if, for example, the firm were in the business of providing a stronger voice for interests that are "underrepresented" because of group organizational costs; the effectiveness of Ralph Nader—and any funds given to him—is doubtless enhanced by his being widely known. Such publicity-induced productivity enhancement can be expected to strengthen efforts at fund raising.

Third, publicity identifies the managers of the nonprofit firm as "productive," which will tend to increase the managers' marketability if they should contemplate switching jobs (as the publicity from publishing does for an academic scholar).

The hypothesized importance of publicity as an argument in the objective function of a collective nonprofit may also be related to a demand by consumers for "trust," for dealing with a seller in whom they can be more confident of being treated "honestly." Such a demand is important for a subset of commodities for which the consumer is ill-equipped to judge for himself or herself the quality of what is being purchased. "Charity" and "research" are but two illustrations of activities of this sort in which nonprofit organizations engage. In general, the role of the collective nonprofit firm as an agent providing trust, when information is costly to obtain, is worthy of further attention.

Thus, a firm having a high index of collectiveness is, I believe, *not* a *private* goods producer that chooses a higher or lower rate of output than would maximize profit, thereby eliminating profits. Rather, it is a *collective* goods producer that sells the collective good at a price less than average cost (or gives it away), financing the privately unprofitable sales out of gifts. The gifts may be in the form of an explicit gift, in cash or in kind, or in the form of a "sales" or "dues" payment that is "above market" in the sense that the payment exceeds what the consumer would be willing to pay were it not for the desire to contribute to the organization's collective-good activities. The ability of the firm to obtain gifts may be a function of the collective benefits of the organization's activities, presumably at the margin, and of the information that the organization can convey regarding the collective benefits. A collective nonprofit thus may be thought of as confronting a market demand that is a function of both "ordinary" demands by "consumers" of its outputs and "donation-demands," willingness of donors to pay for the provision of particular collective goods, the bulk of benefits from which would accrue to third parties.

One other element in a collective nonprofit's behavioral model appears to be the preferences of its manager-enterpreneurs to accept lower-than-market returns in exchange for the utility from engaging personally in "public interest," external-benefit-generating activities. In effect, the manager-entrepreneurs of collective nonprofits may be giving in-kind gifts.[14]

B. Modeling Nonprofits with Low Collectiveness Indices

"Nonprofit" organizations with *low* collectiveness index values, posited to be providers of essentially pure private goods, would appear to be of one of the following two types: (1) adjuncts or "captives" of profit-maximizing firms, or (2) profit maximizers in disguise. In the type 1 case—illustrated by trade associations of for-profit firms—my presumption is that the nonprofit firm behaves precisely as a profit maximizer, spending funds obtained (from its members, the demanders of its output) up to the point where the profits of members are maximized. These captives may appear to be different from the standard profit-maximizing firms; the captive maximizes not its own profits but the profits of its "captors." But there is another way to view the behavior of the captive firm. It may be thought of as maximizing its own profits (as well as its captors) or, in this case, minimizing its own losses. The captive may be seen as undertaking activities that produce profits for its captors, up to the point at which the marginal loss to the captive is equated with the marginal profit to the captors; the resulting loss for the captive is then made up by contributions ("gifts," "grants," "subsidies," and so forth) from the captor, so that the captive breaks even. Thus, its profit is maximized at zero *after* the "owners," the captors, earn at least a normal profit on their investment (including subsidy) in the captive. Subsidies from the captors are, in effect, variables in the firm's donation-demand function.

In the type 2 case, observed profits would be zero only by virtue of the organization's paying above-market prices to the factor suppliers who "own" it—managers or partners, suppliers of capital, suppliers of land. The above-market rewards they obtain are simply profits paid out as wages, land rents, and so forth.

VI. CONCLUSION

Interest in the "nonprofit" sector has grown as its importance has come to be recognized and—although little firm evidence of this exists over time—as its importance has increased. Special tax treatment of nonprofit organizations has raised questions about the efficiency of those organizations as mechanisms for achieving social goals. Economists have only recently begun to pay attention to the role and behavior of the nonprofit organizations that the U.S. Congress has addressed itself to for a number of years.

Fundamental to any normative assessment of the nonprofit form of institution is the development of a positive theory of its behavior; armed with such a theory it would be possible to predict the responses of the firms in this sector to a given stimulus—set of incentives—with given constraints. But a satisfactory positive theory of behavior by nonprofit firms is not enough.

Equally fundamental to a normative assessment is a theory of what society would regard as "desirable" behavior. This requires a more general theory of "institutional failures" than we now have. If the private nonprofit mechanism has even a potentially useful role to play in the economic system, it must be because it is superior, in a benefit-cost analytic sense, to the other institutional mechanisms with which it competes. These include the private for-profit sector, the government sector, and the household sector.

The present paper has set out to sharpen thinking about precisely what organizations we should have in mind when we think about the nonprofit sector from either a positive or a normative perspective. It has noted that the handful of attempts to model the behavior of nonprofit firms has each examined a particular, rather specific type of firm; thus, we have models of nonprofit hospital behavior and of nonprofit college behavior. These output-specific models are in sharp contrast with our model of the profit-maximizing private market economy, which embraces the steel industry and the baking industry, the retailer and the manufacturer, the farmer and the industrialist, the importer and the exporter.

The development of a comprehensive behavioral theory of the nonprofit firm and sector does require the drawing of distinctions among the wide variety of organizations that have come to be termed nonprofit, but the useful distinctions do not seem to be based on "industry." This paper has suggested that:

1. All nongovernmental organizations can be thought of as combinations of private and collective good providers.

2. The typical private sector firm is a polar case, being a pure private-good producer.

3. Some firms, however, provide goods with a significant collective-good component, performing a role more traditionally identified with government.

The paper has proceeded to present and apply an operational measure of the degree of collectiveness of any firm's activities, ranging from zero for a pure private-good producer to one hundred for a pure collective-good producer. An underlying axiom is that the direction required for research is to model the behavior of the private producer of *collective* goods. Such firms do exist, in varying degree, and they are, presumptively, not describable as profit maximizers. By focusing attention on the degree of collectiveness, we have set forth a dimension in which firms providing otherwise heterogeneous outputs are comparable. Indeed, in these terms our traditional theory of the private market sector is a special case: whereas the firms in that sector produce goods and services of enormous diversity, the firms are homogeneous in their "degree of collectiveness"—zero.

FOOTNOTES

The author is professor of economics and fellow of the Institute for Research on Poverty, University of Wisconsin, and visiting professor, ISPS and Economics, Yale University (1976–77).

I have benefited greatly from discussions with Kenneth Wolpin as this paper evolved. Helpful comments have been made by Susan Rose-Ackerman and by faculty and students at Harvard University and the University of Virginia, where I presented earlier versions of the paper.

1. On hospital behavior see Pauly and Redisch (130), Lee (95), and Newhouse (124). On the university see Levy (99) and James (82). On the nonprofit sector in general see James (81), Weisbrod (180), and Niskanen (127).

2. See citations in note 1 above.

3. For an elaboration of this theme see Weisbrod in collaboration with Handler and Komesar (183).

4. An alternative to the term "collective" goods might be "corrective" goods. The latter term, while unconventional, would highlight the degree to which a firm's activities served to *correct* failures of the profit-maximizing and governmental sectors. The failures that might potentially be corrected would include those resulting from collective consumption goods but also from other sources such as monopoly. A profit-maximizing nondiscriminating monopolist would be in equilibrium when the firm captured only part of the marginal social benefit of its output; that is, the monopolist provides marginal benefits that it does not capture (in the amount of the difference between price and marginal revenue). The

efficiency case for subsidizing or otherwise bringing the monopoly to expand output is, thus, in essence the same as the efficiency case for subsidizing private providers of collective goods—the difference between private and social benefits (costs). I use the term collective goods in this paper, for my main interest is in the role of nonprofit organizations as providers of collective-type goods, not in their potential or actual role in correcting other sources of allocative efficiency failures.

5. For a firm producing "bads"—e.g., pollution—E_i and I_i may be interpreted as the marginal external and internal costs or negative benefits, in which case the C^* measure would be negative.

6. It is interesting to note that a profit-maximizing monopolist seller of pure private goods would have a C^* index greater than zero, by virtue of the deviation between marginal revenue (internal marginal benefits) and demand price. The difference would represent marginal external benefits. In short, the C^* index may be thought of as a market failure index.

7. I am indebted to Kenneth Wolpin for a stimulating conversation in which this point evolved.

8. The benefits may, for example, have been derivative of the benefits to the eventual recipient. See Hochman and Rodgers (78).

9. For a summary of recent estimates of the magnitude of volunteer labor see Weisbrod and Long (184). The latest publication reporting on a new survey of volunteer labor appeared after the present paper was completed. See Morgan, Dye, and Hybels (121).

10. The new paper by Morgan et al., cited in the preceding note, does provide new data on volunteer hours given, by type of organization (religious, health, education, etc.). See especially their table 13, p. 171.

11. The number of hours worked by "volunteers," classified by "subsector," has been estimated by the U.S. Department of Labor for 1965. See *Americans Volunteer* (11).

12. Their C index values are: Sierra Club, 19; Common Cause, 31; Public Citizen, 86. The affiliates of Common Cause provide most of its national revenue, shown as "gross dues and assessments, from members and affiliates." To some extent such dues are actually gifts.

13. It is clear that to some people the activities of these groups are collective *bads*—that is, the activities enter negatively into the individuals' utility functions.

14. Data for lawyers in private practice and in collective nonprofit "Public Interest Law" work suggest strongly that this is the case. See chap. 5 in *Public Interest Law, op. cit.* (181). This theme is being developed in another paper now in preparation.

DELIVERED COMMENTS

Mark Pauly (Northwestern University). Weisbrod has made a useful suggestion here in terms of classifying heterogeneous nonprofit industry into more homogeneous groups. My comments are really of two kinds. First, I raise some questions about what the collectiveness index really is supposed to mean, and second, I argue that although it is an improvement to classify organizations on the basis of this collectiveness index, there are still a number of other characteristics of nominally nonprofit firms that would need to be taken into account before we could be sure that we have arranged them into homogeneous groups that are consistent enough to use a single model for each group. What is the collectiveness index supposed to measure? One important thing to recognize is that the collectiveness notion of Weisbrod is not the usual Samuelsonian collective good notion which is based on nonrivalry in consumption. Weisbrod's definition is based on whether or not exclusion is possible, something which is sufficient but not necessary for Samuelsonian collective goods status. That leads, I think, to some perverse results. For example, Weisbrod defines trade associations as noncollective, yet it is reasonable to argue that most such organizations do provide goods which are collective. Some goods are collective for firms in a given industry, such as advertising for the citrus growers. All collective firms presumably cater to their donors to a greater or lesser extent and I'm not sure what the rationale is for distinguishing between, say, the TV manufacturers' trade association and a public interest law firm, since the activities of both can impose costs and benefits on nondonors.

Let us turn to the collectiveness index itself. The general point I want to make is that if we think of dividing up the index into quartiles, those organizations which have a very high value or are in the top quartile might reasonably be thought to be relatively homogeneous. So for those organizations with index values around 80 to 100, it might be reasonable to use a single model to describe their behavior; although exactly what that model is, is not yet known. On the other hand, if we take the organizations who are in the bottom quartile, zero to 25 percent, I think we have a very heterogeneous group. Let me suggest some reasons why firms could be in the bottom quartile, yet not be similar types of firms at all. First, there are obviously private firms in disguise in the bottom quartile. We'd still need a model for them because we'd like to know why they're private firms in disguise rather than coming out of the closet. A second reason for locating in the bottom quartile is based on the distinction between provision and production of the collective good. A firm can be involved with a collective good in at least two ways. It can collect money and disburse it in some earmarked ways so that it could get more of that good produced, or it can collect money and actually produce the good. The distinction would be between collecting money and using it to give, let's say, vouchers for food to the poor, and actually running a soup kitchen. There would be a substantial difference in the collectiveness index depending on which strategy the organization follows, so you could have a firm with a very low collectiveness index just because it happened to choose, for reasons we don't know and for reasons we'd like to model, to produce the good as well as provide it.

If we turn now to the general question of collectiveness, it is possible to think of three kinds of ways of doing things. Consider a group of people who have some collective goal in mind. They wish to get some migrant workers' children immunized. That will cost $2,000, of which the workers are willing to pay $1,000. There are three ways the initiating group could raise this sum. First, they could conduct a fund-raising campaign, hiring solicitors, buying circulars (although that might cost more than $1,000), then use the funds to compensate some group of physicians or nurses to do the inoculating. Second, they could sell candy door to door and use the profits to pay the medical group. Third, they could hire the physicians and nurses themselves, pay them $2,000, charge $1,000 to the workers, and raise the extra $1,000 by selling other medical services to people in the population who are willing to permit them to generate the profit. So, under Plan 1 the organization would have a collectiveness index of 100, and under Plans 2 and 3 the index would be zero. Yet, so far as some underlying notion of collective activity is concerned, I would argue that the firm is doing the same thing for the same group of people. At least one can argue, I think, that what ought to be meant by collectiveness should not be based on *how* firms get their money, which is what Weisbrod's index does, but rather *what* they do with it. We need to know how much of the subsidy is provided to some ostensibly collective good, or good with collectiveness aspects, not the particular technology that is chosen to get around the free-rider problem.

Even within the category of the group with a high collectiveness index, which is likely to be relatively homogeneous, there is still a possible distinction one might wish to make between those firms which raise most of their money from donations and then give most of it away to the people for whom the donations are intended, and those firms which raise money from donations almost exclusively but use almost all of the donations to pay the solicitors or the people who are actually running the firm. One might expect behavior to be different and expect and need a somewhat different model for those two cases. To summarize my comments on Weisbrod, I think the collectiveness index is certainly one aspect of classifying nonprofit firms. But I think one needs to look at a lot more characteristics, especially for firms with low collectiveness indices, to be sure that the organizations are homogeneous enough so that a single model would apply.

I will now talk about Thompson's paper, which really deals with two separable questions. First, why charity should be governmental, and second, why private charity firms when they exist are nonprofit. As usual with Earl's papers, this one requires and rewards effort to understand, and so some of my comments will be in the nature of questions about some things that I still don't understand. Let me take the last question first. Why should firms, whose business it is to accept and disburse donations, be organized in a nonprofit form? The basic answer here is that since donors cannot monitor output (that is, what is actually done with the donation), it would be easy for a for-profit firm to divert some contributions to dividends instead of to largess. In order to avoid that, the reward for the owner-manager is fixed in advance by a contract, thus defining a nonprofit firm. Contributors can be satisfied not that their contributions are put to the use that they prefer, but that there is nothing else that would be worthwhile for the manager to do with them. In connection with this, it seems that the manager would have to get a little bit of utility from doing what contributors want, so he would not just distribute the money randomly on random activities. I think I agree with this explanation and I think it is a good one. It is an important one because it addresses a question which has not really come up yet at the conference. If property rights are suppressed in nonprofit firms and this reduces economic efficiency, why do such firms exist? This argument is an attempt to answer that question. I do have some qualifications, however. First, for-profit firms clearly could agree to some limitations on profits in order to reassure potential benefactors if they wanted to get into the business of collecting and disbursing charitable funds. The second qualification is based on noting that the nonprofit owner-manager, or at least the manager, will in practice have a good bit of control over the perquisites he receives and presumably over his own salary. Donors are not well informed about output—that is where we start—but if they are also not well informed about compensation to the manager, the manager can arrange ways of transferring surplus revenues to himself in cash or in kind. We talked about some examples of that yesterday. Put another way, fixing compensation by contract will not prevent the owner-manager from appropriating some surplus from donors who monitor neither output nor the contract, and the form in which he extracts this surplus, in this case, will be different from what would happen in a for-profit arrangement, but the substance would be the same.

Let me raise another and more speculative point that is related to the last one. In Thompson's paper consumers cannot monitor output very well, but they can monitor contracts. In the real world both are likely to be costly to monitor and so one thinks of extremes. If consumers could not monitor output at all but could monitor contracts then you might expect to find a firm in which property rights are very attenuated, but what if they could monitor output but not contracts?

We spoke yesterday about a kind of spectrum or degree of property rights, or degree of appropriability of surplus. My observation here is that where a firm will end up on that spectrum could be reasonably determined, at least intuitively, based on casual observation, by some thought about the relative cost of monitoring output versus the relative cost of monitoring compensation. So where it is somewhat costly to monitor output and cheap to monitor compensation we might suppose that there would be many nonprofit firms. As we move away from very high costs of monitoring output, and permit the cost of monitoring compensation to increase, we would find nonprofit firms, ostensibly nonprofit firms, permitting managers to extract more and more of the surplus for themselves, and so might expect to find fewer such firms.

A final comment: the role of profit in Thompson's model is unclear since there is no risk, no risk capital, and the role of incentives is explicitly ignored. In a more general model, the ideal compensation for an owner-manager (I'll call him that) whose actions cannot be monitored perfectly is likely to be neither wholly salary nor wholly residual, but some combination of salary and incentive payments. The incentive payments would not be termed profit because there is no equity over which the owner-manager has property rights, but functionally they would be the same as profit. Since equity capital or physical capital in general is probably of relatively minor importance to firms whose business is taking money and giving it out again, and since labor and human capital, especially in terms of the skill of the owner-managers is likely to be important, it would probably not be surprising if the residual income shows up as returns to labor rather that profits on capital investment.

The second part of Thompson's paper is an attempt to show why collective action is needed to deal with the Samaritan's dilemma. I accept two of the propositions that are argued here. I accept the proposition that private charity in which the amount of payment to the recipient depends on his perceived misery is inefficient compared to the theoretical optimum, for reasons given. And I also accept the point that a donor strategy (this is in a footnote, but I think it is important), in which the amount of the donation is fixed, independent of the recipient's behavior, will still fall short of the theoretical optimum because it does not sufficiently encourage what he calls nondissipation performance.

But I have two problems with this section. The first is one of understanding the model. How can the government achieve the theoretical optimum, given that it wanted to? The optimum involves fixing donor utility at some level and permitting the recipient to choose the mix of dissipation and goods transfer that maximizes his utility. As I understand the argument, this would require that someone measure the level of both the goods transfer and the level of dissipation. In effect, the donor's indifference curve becomes the opportunity set for the recipient. So, in order to fix the donor's curve, we have to be sure that what the recipient is doing or what we are giving him is moving us around the donor's indifference curve and not pushing the donor to a lower indifference curve. But Thompson specifically forbids the government or anyone, for that matter, from observing the level of dissipation, so how can the bureaucrats and government design policies which guarantee the level of donor utility? Thompson argues that this can be done if government charity sets up an institution which somehow or other achieves appropriate charity levels and antidissipation incentives. Well, if the government cannot monitor dissipation I don't know how it can set up incentives to reduce it beyond the point that the recipient would choose if he simply received a fixed donation. In Thompson's remarks I got a partial answer to that. It really depends on a two-time-period status of the dissipation activity, something which is not in the formal model at all. In other words, if one cannot observe whether somebody is drinking in his youth, one can at least observe if he is a drunk in later life. The arrangement would then be one in which if he becomes a drunk he gets less from the government if he is unemployed, say, than if he is not a drunk. That is not how government organizational rules are really set up. Government rules do not distinguish between those people who are poor because of things that they could have done differently in their youth, and those people who are poor for external reasons.

Even if you grant that the government may be able to do this, there remains the question of why private donors cannot do it. There is an attempt to answer this question following the final solution to the problems after Eqs. (1)–(7), which I just do not understand.

My second question is somewhat related to that point. Even supposing the government could do the optimal thing, why should we expect it to do so? Why should we expect it to try to achieve the theoretical optimum? This really sounds—I hate to say it—like the "grass is always greener" fallacy. For example, think of a community of homogeneous philanthropists who solve the free-rider problem and set up a United Fund. Thompson tells us that what this private charity will do will not be efficient. But then, suppose they simply switch to raising the money through taxes. They vote as citizens rather than as trustees and they pay taxes rather than donations or pledges. We are supposed to believe that the outcome will be different, but I don't see why. This seems to me to be a relatively minor change in how things are paid and who makes choices. Wearing a different jacket should not make any difference in the outcome. Finally, Thompson gives a kind of quasi-history of why the government got involved in this business. He seems to be saying that people have chosen the government to redistribute wealth rather than private charity, because the government was there at least in embryonic form to begin with. Well, he said he was not sure he believed it and I guess I am not sure I do either.

Armen A. Alchian (University of California—Los Angeles). I would like to disagree with everything said so far but I can't. There are a few things that I agree with, but I will not specify what they are, since we are not here to tell each other what we know in common but to try to see what we don't know in common. I don't know what market failures mean nor do I know what government failures mean. In fact, I don't know what failure means in this world. If I were a biologist or a chemist I wouldn't go around saying chemistry or the chemical world has failed because hydrogen is lighter than lead. And I don't want to be understood to say that the government has failed in something, it just behaves in certain ways. Tigers go out and eat deer and I don't call that a failure of the deer, it's just the way the world is. Having said that much about that subject let me dismiss it.

I can give little weight to the importance of the classification that has been proposed by Weisbrod, either empirically or theoretically. The idea that the nonprofits are more varied than private so-called for-profit firms I find a little strange. When I think of what private firms do, I find a great variety—from massage parlors to teaching golf to making golf balls, to making tea, to running ships, to providing education, to running hospitals, to running charity drives. Their variety is greater than a so-called nonprofit, so I'm a little hard-pressed to know what to make of the idea that somehow private firms are narrower in their activities. But, more fundamentally, the reason for having looked at hospitals and savings-and-loan institutions is not because that is the only kind of activity performed by charities or by nonprofits, but because that kind of activity is conducted by *both* private and by nonprofit. The trick is to try to see what difference in behavior can be explained in these two. I think we are looking at the problem incorrectly when we think there are certain activities that nonprofits do that privates do not do. Even in this matter of charity, there are for-profit firms that raise money, there are for-profit firms that distribute the money. For example, if you go to a golf tournament to raise funds for some hospital, you will find the hospital is the profit end of that line. That is, you put your money in, you pay to see these golf players play, and then the residual goes to the hospital. If that is not making profit as a profit enterprise, I do not know what is. It is called nonprofit because there is less tax. If it were taxed, they would call the hospital a profit enterprise.

It's difficult to believe that Thompson's paper was written by the same man who wrote a paper on government a year or two ago, in which government was looked upon as the agency which took from you all it could get, to speak crudely, and left you with just enough for you to survive. I have a great deal of sympathy for this theory. Although he is using this theory in this paper, somehow it turns out now these takers are people to whom we are giving charity rather than having them take our wealth away from us. I do not see any difference between the two characterizations, nor does Earl, because he clearly says earlier in his paper that whatever these transfer payments are "let me call them charity." That is a neat trick but I do not know what to say about that kind of charity. I can assure you that I am one of those customers who is out there deciding how much charity I am going to give. The family is a private firm and it engages in a lot of charity. It is not a government institution, it's probably in a sense not a for-profit institution, but it's a hell of a good charitable arrangement. I came from a large family clan with about five uncles and two sets of grandparents. We took care of each other. We knew who the bums were, the guys who would get drunk most of the time or who would spend their money rather unprofitably or just did not care for themselves properly and we gave them charity. They survived but we know what we thought they deserved. We had no problem with how much charity to give these people, or to those who had sickness or illness or what we called an unfortunate event from which they could recover; we thought we were very generous. That was a great institution. It is disappearing now. The question I find interesting is why that institution has disappeared or what it is that's destroyed the family clan as a charitable arrangement for caring for people you know something about. If you think that caring for your kin is somehow not as appropriate as caring for those you do not know—well, you have a lot to learn about the nature of the human beast.

Another point that Earl talks about is Pareto optimality. For me that is a criterion I would just as soon let stay in the garbage can, however elegant it may look. No one ever uses it for any policy purpose except economists who draw diagrams and like to think they know what the world should be like. Another point is on the issue of receivers versus givers of gifts. Who are these givers going to be? How are you going to determine who they are to be in advance?

CHARITABLE ORGANIZATIONS: DISCUSSION

Thompson.   With regard to my remarks about the history of charity, I don't see what is wrong with saying that people are much more generous than they were two hundred years ago and that they are giving up more political power to the poor, which is a form of charity. Charity is given now by giving up political power to the poor. The nonpoor have been enfranchising the poor for the last one hundred or two hundred years. I don't see any reason why they should give that power away [give women and southern blacks the vote] except to give more charity through the political process. I don't think I'm contradicting anything in the history of charity with this very general view of people getting wealthier, becoming more liberal, giving up political power to the poor, and having the poor take much more redistribution rather than having it granted them by people who have political power. The most striking observation to social welfare historians is the dramatic change in the twentieth century from charity bestowed on the poor by wealthy benefactors to demands for charity by a politically active poor. But whether

Economics of Nonproprietary Organizations
Research in Law and Economics, Supplement 1, pages 179-188
Copyright © 1980 by JAI Press Inc.
All rights of reproduction in any form reserved.
ISBN: 0-89232-132-6

that history is accurate or not, the main purpose of my paper is to develop a model, one that has not been available before, that integrates charity into economic theory in a realistic way.

Regarding Alchian's comments about my use of Pareto optimality, I consider Pareto optimality not just a goal, but a highly predictive tool. Its use is little different from what Armen Alchian does when he employs joint wealth maximization for a group and says that it is a very powerful predictor of what that group will do. But wealth is a proxy for something more basic that we associate with utility. Therefore, Alchian is really saying that there is joint utility maximization when there is joint wealth maximization by a small group of producers. He claims that notion has very powerful predictive value. Why not apply that notion to the whole population? I don't know why utility maximization is such a disaster at the population level and so terrific at a small group level. I don't know why one would want to jettison Pareto optimality. In all the work I have done, I have found it an extremely powerful predictive tool in figuring out what the government is going to do.

I will move on to Alchian's comments about the breakup of the family. I would guess that the main reason for family breakups is the social security system. It takes care of the aged and they no longer need the young as much to help them. The reciprocal gain there is not as large as it used to be. As a result, the parents do not train their kids as much, they rely more on public schooling. Public schooling and social security have replaced a traditional system of relatively private schooling and no social security. Unlike Armen Alchian, I don't think it is a particularly unfortunate evolution because there were family misallocations of the same kind that I have talked about with respect to private charity. Families will find people that have overconsumed or dissipated because of the familial subsidy for doing so. They are going to be helped by the family and this will give rise to the same Samaritan's dilemma problem that arises in my paper. Following the general argument of the paper, one way to solve that problem is to introduce incentives such as government welfare and social security that break up the family. Family members are then induced to tell each other that they must seek help from a less sympathetic source. I suggest that this results in the individual having better incentives to improve his character instead of dissipating or overconsuming and then relying on more sympathetic, familial redistributions.

I now turn to Mark Pauly's comments concerning the operational notion of dissipation. I assume that no one can observe the dissipation activities of the recipient except the recipient himself. This suggests that monitoring recipients is too costly. So only if wealth transfers are disassociated with activities that dissipate resources can the social waste of resources at the hand of the recipient be avoided. One way to accomplish this is to give the recipient the power to acquire charity *independent* of his "need." He won't dissipate his potential talents in this model because his payment is not going to be based on his level of dissipation but on the basis of his political power. Therefore, Pauly's concern that the recipient's dissipation level is unobservable is not a problem for my model. Indeed, it is the problem overcome by the model.

A most interesting question remains. Why can't an informed benefactor set up institutions that will do essentially what the government is doing? My answer is that the benefactor has a psychological problem in that he cannot deny charity to those in need, even though that need might have been the result of dissipation. The only way he can avoid encouraging dissipators is to use an institution, a nonprofit institution, that hires people that do not suffer from the benefactor's particular psychological problem when giving out charity. The price he must pay for this is that people he doesn't care about will also be the recipients of institutional charity. But this is only a private cost of the benefactor. It is not a social cost because it is largely a transfer.

If you go to the government, you use an agency that includes the nondeserving person in its calculus. This is significant, because the political distribution that results can be much different than the private distribution. This follows because, in the political distribution, some of the people that are voting are the welfare recipients themselves, including the people that get welfare that are not really deserving. As a result the allocation of transfer payments will be different. I think that is what we observe.

Weisbrod.   Mark Pauly asked what my collectiveness index was supposed to measure. I intended to measure the extent to which an organization provided uncaptured benefits. That is simply what I had in mind. The reason that I would prefer a measure that gave a trade association— to use an example that Pauly selected—a low value on the index is that it seems to me that there are few, if any, of the benefits from a trade association's advertising or lobbying activities that go uncaptured by its owners, the members of the trade association.

Pauly's other main point was that one should discover how organizations spend their revenues and not the sources of those revenues. That is exactly what I think is important also. However, as I discussed in my paper, the problem of finding out what organizations do with their revenues is a difficult task and hence I proposed a proxy for the uses to which an organization puts its revenues. The proxy is the *sources* of its revenues. I don't believe that Pauly's example exposing a weakness of the proxy was convincing.

My observation is that, in general, people do not give donations to organizations that spend a lot of their money on administrative expenses, but rather to organizations that spend it on the purposes for which the donor gave the money. Therefore, although Pauly's example of the two organizations may be a good counter example—that is, a good example of a case in which the collectiveness index for two organizations would be the same even though they would be using their money in very different ways—my judgment is that it is not a very typical example. It represents a *deviation* from equilibrium. Although it may occur occasionally, I think it does not deny the overall correlation between the sources of revenue and the uses to which the revenue is put.

Kenneth Clarkson (University of Miami). I think Thompson raises a very interesting point, but I believe the results go in exactly the opposite direction from the one he has suggested. One could actually replace public with private government. This is because most of these problems are very heterogeneous, which often implies that there will be differences in the rules or institutional arrangements used to solve these problems. If we continue Alchian's earlier example, but go beyond the family to the local communities, where there are churches, community chests, and other kinds of organizations, we find different institutional forms for providing charity. For example, if a house burned down, it is not unheard of for the whole community to get together and rebuild it. Next, we compare these forms of charity with government forms where charity by statutory law must be provided equally to all potential recipients with similar characteristics. In this comparison you find that private organizations are far more efficient in the distribution of charity. For example, we have had a food stamp program for approximately a decade and a half to solve the problem of poor nutrition in the United States. The way that the program is carried out, however, has created precisely the opposite result—nutrition has probably worsened rather than improved as a result of that program. The program gives participants relatively more food-purchasing power for items that taste better, but are not necessarily more nutritious. On the other hand, earlier methods for improving nutrition were often carried out at the local level, through churches and other institutions that were able to focus on the problem more directly. Solving the nutrition problem in Appalachia is very different than solving it in the Southwest. For a much smaller amount of money, these private organizations were able to more effectively alter the behavior of the recipients and to mitigate nutritional problems. One of the reasons that we don't see more of this form of organization is that mobility costs have been substantially lowered so that people are not in the same location for long periods of time. This implies that systems of informal exchange, where individuals would help each other (such as rebuild a burned-down house), are more costly to enforce. This is also true for exchanges that occur in the family since families today are more spread throughout the country making it more difficult to monitor their behavior.

John Moore (University of Miami). Clarkson has just made, in a more general way, a point that I was going to raise in connection with the family. The extension of the social security system, as we know, has led to a considerable decline in the rate of personal savings. What has it done to private giving? Data on private giving and private charities reveal that between 1929 to 1959 there is no clear trend in the proportion of private domestic charity as a percent of total charity in the United States. It follows, instead, a kind of cyclical path. It falls in the early part of the thirties, reaches a trough in 1935, and then rises again. Omitting the war years, it falls again immediately after the war and then rises again. The trend, if it's there, is rather small.

I think one could better explain what's happened to private charity in another way. For example, the wave of New Deal programs in the thirties is a prime candidate for investigation of charitable behavior. Similarly, if the private charity data were extended beyond 1959, I expect one would probably see another decline that resulted from the Great Society programs. I don't think the initiation of these programs is very well explained by the kind of theory that Earl has suggested.

Donald O'Hara (University of Rochester). With respect to Earl's paper, I thought that he was attributing different behavior to individuals, or associations of individuals, when they were operating privately and through the government. As private individuals or associations, they weren't willing to tolerate callous administrators who would distribute charity according to rules which were in conflict with their own preferences. When it came to government organization, however, that was somehow tolerable and sustainable. The reason for this, I believe, is that the welfare beneficiaries are also a part of the decision-making apparatus in government but are excluded from that role in private associations. I also think there is another side to this. The government is supposed to be able to avoid the Samaritan's dilemma. That is, a situation in which the availability of benefits induces people to use real resources to become eligible for those benefits. This problem exists with government welfare programs. Where eligibility criteria are arbitrary, you may get people devoting real resources to becoming eligible according to those arbitrary criteria; at the same time people who would have been eligible according to criteria used by taxpayers as private benefactors are excluded. One example is the provision of a special bonus for buying new furniture if you happen to have had a fire in your tenement. In New York City there were alleged to be a substantial number of probable arsonist-initiated fires in order to get that bonus. It's not clear, therefore, if the Samaritan's dilemma is more efficiently dealt with by government provision of charity.

H. E. Frech (University of California—Santa Barbara).   Thompson's argument is that donors will not voluntarily set up an impersonal redistribution system. They won't voluntarily do it because it results in private costs to them that are not necessarily social costs. This is so because money is given to the wrong people, from the private benefactor's point of view. They are just giving it away to everybody, rather than targeted individuals so they won't do it privately. But Thompson then argues that donors will voluntarily agree to transfer wealth through the government which does exactly the same thing. That is, government also gives away wealth indiscriminately. Once again, private costs which are not social costs would be imposed on the donors. Why, then, would donors agree to do charity through this other mechanism, one that has the same excessive private cost for them?

Thompson.   Because it is cheaper. There is a certain difference in providing a given amount of benefits to the recipients through a political process. The point is that in the political process the welfare cheaters have a way to make their preferences count even if the benefactors prefer an alternative system. Alternatively, the benefactors could be compensated by the welfare cheaters (lump sum), before the process starts. In that way you can say it's just cheaper for the benefactors to run a government system than a private system. Either system would work. Privately you are not going to get the welfare cheaters to agree to compensate the benefactors. But socially you will. A government process will cause welfare cheaters to compensate the benefactors.

Frech.   I don't see the mechanism for that.

Thompson.   I don't really have a model of the political process. But that is a characteristic of it which, I would presume, would be present. I just haven't constructed that model yet. I don't think it's necessary for me to do so. The point is that the solution of the government is going to be like a Paretian optimum. Everybody's preferences are accounted for and they are going to get to a Paretian optimum. It's not difficult to construct political models that have that characteristic whereas the private market doesn't guarantee it.

Andrew Whinston (Purdue University).   I just wanted to raise perhaps a somewhat far-fetched explanation of the growth of charity. There is an analogy with insurance in that individuals pay premiums to receive, let us say, automobile insurance and then when, and if, their car has an accident, they get a payment which in some sense is a payment from the society that constitutes the membership or customers of that insurance company. In a way you could think of it as a kind of contracted charitable contribution. Assume that over the last century or two life has become less predictable. That is, maybe two hundred years ago people were born rich and stayed rich or people were born poor and stayed poor. Now there exists a more fluid society. People can start from a rich family, yet have their assets dissipated in speculative, risky ventures, ending up in a state that would require transfer payments. This has caused a growth in the demand for "insurance," except that we call it charity. We are paying premiums when we can and since, as individuals, we are not really that sure that we are going to be in states in the future which would preclude us from having to ask for charity, we generally will support it, pay for it, and have it there if we need it.

William Meckling (University of Rochester). I really wanted to ask two questions about the political model which I think Thompson is using. Although he denies having one, I think that unless he has a political model he is guilty of the "grass is greener" fallacy. I was shocked at the statement he made which was to the effect that you could easily get models which produced Pareto-optimal results, especially in the government sector but not in the private sector. I know of not one single model, by anyone, which has been able to start with politicians as utility maximizers and derived Pareto-optimal results in the government sector. Consequently, I would like to know what model Professor Thompson has in mind for that optimization. I would also like to ask him what he means when he says that somehow we have given this political power to the poor in recent years. Does he believe that if we had a referendum on the level of welfare benefits they would be anything like what they are now? Is he saying that we have had a democratic majority decision to have welfare benefits at the level they are now? I, for one, believe you could never pass welfare benefit programs at the level they are now by a truly democratic process.

Thompson. There are some very poor models that generate Pareto optimality from the political process. The most elementary theorem is that any majority rule equilibrium is a Pareto optimum because if you are in political equilibrium that means that there is no other bill that can get a majority.

Meckling. You mean that all those bills are subjected to general referendum?

Thompson. Yes. There are very unrealistic assumptions in that kind of model. I'm not particularly happy with that kind of model. But I think that you shouldn't be so unsympathetic to the conclusion based on the literature.

Evsey Domar (M.I.T.). I disagree with Thompson's statement that the extension of the franchise is an act of charity on the part of the rich to the poor. I would rather say it was an act of self-preservation. If you examine, for instance, the British Parliamentary Act of 1832, you find that this was preceded by a great deal of strife. The Duke of Wellington, who opposed the bill thoroughly, and who, by the way, predicted all the developments that would follow, nevertheless acquiesced because he wanted to avoid civil strife. That was the real reason. At the same time, as the poor became more educated, giving them the franchise appeared somewhat less dangerous than giving it to illiterate and ignorant people.

On to the other question. Why have we such a great development of what you might call institutional charity? I think there are several problems here. On the one hand, it's difficult for the donor to decide whom to give and how to give. It's one thing helping a member of your family whom you know well. It's quite different to help the member of the family who lives far away, or the person you don't know personally. Helping people is an extremely difficult task and this has been substantiated by various comments here. So I think that a donor prefers to give the money to some organization so as to avoid the search cost to find out whom to give and how to give. At the same time I have a feeling that the recipients of charity, who have acquired political power, may prefer to receive it from some organization according to some rules rather than as a personal donation from a particular individual. If I fall on bad times after my retirement, which with the present inflation is very likely, I think I'd be very offended if I were given help, say, by a member of our department. I would rather not have it. But if government suddenly decides that they want to increase the pensions of retired professors, that would be quite acceptable. If the federal government decides that retired professors should get twice as much social security as ordinary people, that would be acceptable. You see, I don't think that the recipient would feel himself put in the power of the donor.

O'Hara. My comments are relevant to Weisbrod's paper but were provoked by Alchian's remarks about bimodal distributions and whether it's appropriate to study savings-and-loans institutions to discover differences in the behavior of nonprofits. We study savings and loans because they are organized as both profit and nonprofit firms. The same is true for hospitals. I wonder if the very fact that both forms of organizations survive is not an indication that in those industries it doesn't make so much difference and you cannot discern anything much more than different rates of growth or survivorship. That is, if you find a measure of collectiveness and apply it only to hospitals and it gives you a bimodal distribution, then there is something wrong with the measure, because both kinds of firms survive. But if you apply it to a wider range of industries or firms, bimodality is not necessarily objectionable. That is, the distribution may be bimodal because certain industries are primarily nonprofit and other industries are primarily for-profit. The interesting problem is, and this is the kind of problem that Thompson tries to deal with, to discover why it is that some things are done primarily one way and other things primarily the other way.

Frech. It seems that Weisbrod's theoretical collectiveness index is very defective. It does not identify anything with the degree of nonprofitness of institutions. This is so because it is just an index of uncaptured benefits. Suppose, for example, that you had a beekeeper who was not charging for the services that his bees were performing for all the neighboring trees. Steve Cheung has shown us otherwise, but let us assume the contrary. According to Weisbrod's theoretical index, this profit-seeking beekeeper (he might supply a tremendous amount of external benefits) would register a very high index number. He would look like a great nonprofit firm. But we wouldn't want to call him a nonprofit firm. On the other hand, Weisbrod's proxy measure for his index relates to how firms are financed, whether they get contributions from donors, or whether they get money from selling things. It seems to me that this latter measure is more than a proxy. It is what we really want. This follows because a nonprofit structure avoids the problem of donating money and having it go into the pocket of a profit-seeking owner. That seems to be the argument of the second part of Thompson's paper. So I think Weisbrod's so-called proxy "inaccurate" measure is the one we should be interested in theoretically and his theoretical index is the one we do not want.

Roland McKean (University of Virginia). Weisbrod pointed out that there seemed to be a considerable heterogeneity among nonprofit organizations according to his collectiveness index. At the same time, I believe, he said that we ought to have a general theory of the nonprofit organization, the counterpart of the theory of the profit-making firm. In one sense the situation doesn't seem to me to be all that different from our theory of the conventional firm. We do have modified theories for different constraint situations, such as regulated profit-seeking firms or, according to demand conditions, pure monopoly, competition, and so on. On the other hand, I would really expect there to be more heterogeneity, and in a different sense from the collectiveness index, among the nonprofit organizations. I would not expect, in either case, to have a theory for each industry, or anything like that, but one does need some kind of a theory to give one implications according to the differences in constraints or perhaps differences in demand conditions. In the nonprofit organizations, I would really expect a wider variety of constraints than I would expect to find variety worth considering among the profit-seeking firms. If I had two categories, for example, baseball games and nonbaseball games, I would expect a lot more heterogeneity within the category called nonbaseball games and so I sympathize with the idea of having a general theory of the nonprofit organization. Indeed, we do have, I think, a theory that gives you at least some sort of implications about nonprofits, thanks to Alchian and others, but to develop more precise or more numerous implications I think you have to do what's been stressed a number of times here: look at a wider variety of constraints on them.

GOVERNMENTAL
ORGANIZATIONS

IS THERE A THEORY OF PUBLIC ORGANIZATIONS?

Cotton M. Lindsay, UNIVERSITY OF

CALIFORNIA—LOS ANGELES

It is widely believed among economists that there exists an a priori efficiency argument for government intervention in the provision of collective-consumption (hence, public) goods. That is, it has come to be regarded as sufficient reason to invoke government involvement in some sector by demonstrating public good type characteristics of the output of that sector. In view of the fervor with which this view is entrenched,[1] it is surprising that nowhere do we find a straightforward demonstration of the source of the government's advantages in organizing economic activity in this area.

Instances abound of demonstrations of "market failure" where public goods are concerned, though even these are often flawed by an overly circumscribed view of the options available for voluntary organization of

Economics of Nonproprietary Organizations
Research in Law and Economics, Supplement 1, pages 191-207
Copyright © 1980 by JAI Press Inc.
All rights of reproduction in any form reserved.
ISBN: 0-89232-132-6

collective goods provision. Furthermore, there is a large literature containing similar demonstrations of corresponding failures of the government to produce efficient levels of anything; see Hayek (73), von Mises (118), Alchian and Kessel (10), McKean (113), Niskanen (127), and Lindsay (102). Indeed, the literature on the problems of economic organization by government was quite well developed even before the nature of public goods was understood and the phrase "market failure" was coined.

The question, after all, is not whether there is a public goods *problem*. What we are seeking is the best public good *solution*. Missing in all of this discussion is a clear-cut operational distinction between government organization on the one hand and market organization on the other. Only when such concepts are concretely established does it make sense to attempt to demonstrate the advantages of one form of organization over the other.

In many of these treatments the representative legislative process is singled out for analysis as if this process itself identified government.

A moment's reflection should convince the reader that voting, representation, legislating, and all the activities analyzed within this framework are neither sufficient nor even necessary conditions for government. Most of the governments in existence today function without any of these activities (a nontrivial proportion came into existence by disbanding such apparatus), while at the same time numerous institutions that are clearly not governments exhibit all of them. Indeed, corporations, country clubs, professional organizations, unions, and universities all possess bodies with functions which correspond identically with similar bodies in the government.

This collective decision-making machinery is that and nothing more. It gets its form from the fact that those governments which have them allow many people to participate in the making of some of the decisions of the government, just as many participate in the decision-making process of those other institutions named. As it thus may be true that both democratic governments *and* voluntary private agencies which organize the provision of public goods will adopt some sort of parliamentary process for the making of decisions, it is not useful to focus attention on properties of such a process to discover which one is likely to reach more efficient decisions. If the processes adopted are identical, the decisions will be also.

It is the purpose of this paper to attack this issue systematically by (1) defining government in a useful way, (2) developing explicit transaction cost "problems" involved in the organization of public good provision, (3) attempting to develop realistic models of private sector institutions which could emerge to do this organizing, and (4) using the analytical framework thus produced to attempt to derive empirical propositions about both governmental and private organization of the provision of these goods. We conclude that there is no a priori theoretical argument connecting public goods and government intervention.

In order to develop the "role" of any institution convincingly, one must be able at a minimum to identify properties of that institution which render it suitable to perform the activities assigned. Convincing arguments for government organization of an activity must demonstrate that the outcome predicted to result from such a policy will be preferred to the outcome which is predicted to result from voluntary market organization. Such a demonstration must rely in turn on identifiable differences between private institutions and government which form the basis for such comparative advantage. The first step in the proposed analysis is therefore to operationalize government.

I. GOVERNMENT AS AN ECONOMIC ENTITY

Having already eliminated the collective decision-making machinery which fills most discussions of the behavior of government, we find little in the form of antecedent discussion to illuminate this concept. Except for the acknowledgedly empty discussion of the "social welfare function" by Samuelson, there is nothing else. Governments do have at least one attribute, however, which differentiates them from that set of institutions regarded as private. They have the undisputed power to redistribute rights (hence, wealth in the broadest sense) among their citizens. The use of this power (force, coercion) is unavailable to private institutions in their normal dealings; hence transactions with and among them may not result in decreased wealth for anyone.

This coercive power of government has a profound influence on the behavior of its citizens, not only in the government's relations with the citizenry but also in connection with their relations with each other. It may assign property rights to the output of economic activity which differ from those which would prevail in the absence of such coercion, and these assignments themselves will influence the character and level of output. Government's crucial role here in creating an environment conducive to commerce is often taken for granted. Thus we frequently see an orderly and functioning market system referred to as a "no government economy." Recognition of the importance of the government's role in this "no government economy" would have prevented a great deal of confusion concerning the issues we confront here. For though it is taken for granted in discussion of the organization of the provision of private goods, it is almost universally assumed away in the case of public goods provision.

II. THE MEANING AND IMPORTANCE OF EXCLUSION

By public goods we mean here those "which all enjoy in common in the sense that each individual's consumption . . . leads to no subtraction from any other individual's consumption of that good" [Samuelson (144)]. This embraces both those goods for which "exclusion" is economically feasible and those for which it is not. As it has long been recognized that the feasibility of "exclusion" itself has important effects on the manner and level of the provisions of public goods, it is essential that the meaning of this concept be understood as well as its implications for both public and private organization. By exclusion we mean here the provider's ability to regulate other people's use of these goods, that is, his property rights over these goods.

Recognition that exclusion describes qualities of property rights over goods makes immediately apparent the generality of this concept and its direct applicability to private goods as well as public goods. Just as without at least the threat of government intervention to make them "excludable" there might be underprovision of many private goods, a lack of exclusive rights to the use and/or resale of the goods produced will make engaging in the supply of *public* goods unattractive as well. Indeed, one of the yet unexplored but highly promising topics to which property rights analysis might be applied is the connection between the technology of property rights enforcement in the output of an industry, and the way in which that production is organized and distributed.

For evidence that this subject has been given insufficient attention, we need only look to the way in which the topic of exclusion is treated in connection with public goods. This inability to exclude users of such goods is perceived to represent a crucial "market failure" because it seems to be this very ability to exclude which prevents "free riding" (that is, using without paying) in the provision of private goods. Individuals may not use private goods unless they gain possession of (use rights to) them, and they are excluded from obtaining possession of them until they have satisfied the producer-owner. Thus, it is argued that producers of private goods use their ability to exclude in order to *command reimbursement* from the ultimate beneficiaries of their production.

Consider the following quotation from a leading text in public finance [Musgrave and Musgrave (122)]:

> The market can function only in a situation where the "exclusion principle" applies, i.e., where A's consumption is made contingent on his paying the price, while B, who does not pay, is excluded. Exchange cannot occur without property rights and property rights require exclusion. . . . A hamburger eaten by A cannot be eaten by B.

At the same time, the nature of the goods is such that exclusion is readily feasible. The goods are handed over when the price is paid, but not before. But budgetary provision is needed if consumption is nonrival and/or if exclusion cannot be applied.

While such a convenient arrangement works well for hamburgers, it clearly works less well for many other private goods. McDonald's may do business this way but Chasen's does not. In the latter establishment the bill is presented and paid after the meal is eaten. Nor is it likely that such transactions would take place as described in either place if some agency weren't looking over the shoulder of the customer to protect the rights of the supplier. Protection of the rights of suppliers is a private good, but one with almost indisputable claim to some involvement by government, whether the output of that supplier is a public good or a private good.

The single novelty which publicness in a good adds to this general exclusion problem is that collectiveness vitiates this simple process by which free riding appears to be prevented in the hamburger case above. In that case suppliers are able to command payment by withholding delivery of the goods until payment is received. This simultaneous exchange of goods and payments prevents free riding by either customers or the suppliers.[2] One may not withhold delivery of a concert in the park to exclude nonpayers without depriving willing supporters as well. Interruption of the transmission of radio beams to discipline would-be nonpayers affects contributors, too.

The importance of this novelty is easily exaggerated, however. For, though it is true that suppliers may not enforce their own rights to the services of public goods they produce via "withholding delivery," this is also true for many private goods. For services and goods with high storage costs, individual exclusion in the sense of insisting on hamburger/money type exchanges is just as technically infeasible as it is for collective goods, though for different reasons. We do not observe widespread free riding in the provision of gourmet meals or of elementary school teaching because ultimately the government protects the rights of vulnerable suppliers and demanders in these transactions.

We may conclude our discussion of exclusion with three comments: First, exclusion as a "principle" or problem applies with equal force to both private goods and public goods. Unless suppliers can expect to command some sort of compensation in the market, they are unlikely to engage in production. Second, for many goods, both public and private, individual exclusion in the form of "withholding delivery" will prove inadequate, and government involvement in the protection of suppliers' rights will be required to elicit desired levels of supply. Third, unlike the case with private goods, perfect exclusion rights on the part of suppliers does not, in the conventional one-on-one market environment, result in the provision of the efficient level of public goods. As Thompson (165) has shown, such a situation results in a bilateral monopoly relationship between each user and each provider of the public good, the outcome of which depends on the power of individual bargainers.

Our analysis does not end there, however. For the important feature of exclusion as it applies to public goods provision is *not* its effect on the interface between supplier and individual user, where attention is typically focused. Rather its importance follows from its implications concerning the form of the implied relationship between co-users of public goods. For though private organization of the provision of public goods may not yield optimal levels of these goods (at least in conventional presentations of this problem), there does seem to be consensus that some (perhaps tolerably efficient) level of these goods will be produced in this setting. Where exclusion is not feasible, on the other hand, private provision is universally regarded as impracticable. We argue in the next section that this conclusion is invalid, and that in such circumstances private production is no more likely to be nonoptimal than public provision.

III. TRANSACTION COSTS OF PUBLIC GOODS PROVISION

Unfortunately, most of the literature considering private provision of public goods has analyzed the special case of these goods where exclusion is feasible, hence the analysis has borrowed, perhaps inappropriately, both the point of view and the analytical hardware of standard private-good price theory. The one implication that emerges unequivocally from the welfare analytics of public goods is that, for voluntary public or private arrangements to yield efficient levels of public goods, procurement plans must be coordinated; see Olson (129) and Buchanan (29), chap. 2. Yet analytical treatments of the transaction costs problems of private coordination are virtually nonexistent. In this section we shall therefore consider the economic problems posed for voluntary organization of the provision of public goods and how these problems themselves shape the character of the organizations which have emerged to engage in this provision. We shall also consider the advantages (or lack thereof) in dealing with these problems of attaching such organizations to governments.

There are three sorts of transaction costs which shape the character of organizations seeking to arrange the efficient provision of public goods. First, there is the "free-rider" problem, related to exclusion in which individuals fail to contribute to public good provision since they perceive no connection between their contribution and the level of public good made available for their use. Second, there is the problem of dissipation of the surplus from public good provision in wasteful bargaining. Finally, there is the problem of assembling, communicating, and using the large amounts of information required to determine the efficient level of public good supply. We shall consider each of these three problems in turn. It will facilitate our focus on these individual problems to assume away for the purposes of analysis the remaining two transaction cost problems. Thus, in connection with "free riding" we assume that users of public goods voluntarily share the surplus resulting from provision of these goods, and further, that economic organization in connection with these goods is costless.

A. Free Riding as a Transaction Cost

By "free riding" we mean here specifically the transaction cost problem created by the absence of exclusion rights to the services of public goods. Once such a good is produced, the rights of suppliers are by definition not enforced. Thus, although such goods are valuable to users, their supply will appear unattractive to producers (at least for *quid pro quo* exchange) and undersupply is predicted.

Recognize, however, that there is a group of potential users in this market who by assumption may communicate costlessly and will not conceal their valuations of the good in question. Under these circumstances users need only contract among themselves to finance the optimal amount of the public good, then collectively engage a supplier to produce this amount. In short, the infeasibility of collecting from each lighthouse user once the light is produced does not suggest that no lighthouse services will be provided without government intervention to arrange this financing. Rather it simply suggests that voluntary organization of the provision of lighthouse services must occur prior to the light's production. Potential users of these services must make arrangements among themselves for their provision in advance.

One predicted characteristic of voluntary organization for the provision of public goods is, therefore, that users themselves will organize *together* to provide a public good. Results of analysis which stops at the level of the individual cannot be generalized to society at large. It has long been recognized that, for voluntary public or private arrangements to yield efficient levels of public goods, group procurement plans must be coordinated, and that individual arrangements would be nonoptimal; see, for example, Olson (129), and Buchanan (29), chap. 2. What has been imperfectly understood is that individuals may and do operate collectively in the private sector.

The government role emerging from this sort of free-rider possibility falls far short of nationalization of the industry. Willingness to enforce such user financing arrangements is all that is implied. As is pointed out at length above, a similar function is required for efficiency in the private provision of many private goods. Thus far, therefore, the theory of public goods has not expanded the role of government beyond that implicit in a world containing only private goods, that is, enforcement of rights and contracts.

B. Dissipation of Surplus through Bargaining

The second problem associated with the voluntary provision of public goods arises out of the absence of any arbitrary mechanism to determine the distribution of the costs of these goods. The consumer surplus associated with the provision of private goods is distributed arbitrarily by the market. Prices (or at least supply curves) may not be influenced by demanders; hence the level of surplus is fixed for each. Bargaining for more surplus, that is, for a lower price, avails nothing since sellers of private goods invariably equalize marginal revenue to each purchaser.

A certain amount of consumer surplus inheres in each arrangement for the provision of public goods, however, and the share of the cost paid by each, hence the share of the surplus, is negotiable. Members of contracting groups will be influenced to devote resources to capturing larger amounts of this surplus. The value of this surplus—that is, the rent from public good provision—may thus be dissipated by bargaining users in this purely redistributional activity.[3]

In our analysis of this bargaining problem, we will assume that financing arrangements are made prior to the production of the good. Complications arising from potential free riding of the sort just described are therefore minimized. We also assume that the cost of communicating terms of offers and agreements concerned with such arrangements among potential users is negligible. These assumptions permit us to focus our attention here on the essence of the public goods bargaining problem: that is, that competitive market conditions do not eliminate scope for increasing one's share of the surplus arising from the provision of these goods.

One method frequently depicted as an example of wasteful bargaining activity is declining to acknowledge true valuations of public goods. Samuelson (144) and others subsequently have focused on deception—"giving false signals," "unwillingness to reveal preferences,"—as constituting the principal manifestation of bargaining behavior. It is easy to see, however, that the availability of this information does not necessarily reduce the incentive to behave strategically, though, of course, the form of this activity will necessarily change. In order to give credence to this point, we will begin our analysis by adding to the list of assumptions the postulate that all individual preferences for public goods are public knowledge.[4]

Under these assumptions, the way in which bargaining rents will be dissipated depends on the nature of the public good as well as the existing property rights structure. In many cases, however, scope for such bargaining exists in one form or another, and economic waste will be the result. Consider the case of flood control projects whose benefits to downstream communities may realistically be calculated with some precision. Awareness of these benefits does not eliminate the incentive of each beneficiary to increase his surplus by bearing a smaller share of the cost of these projects. The net surplus (over and above the costs of the projects) may in principle be captured by anyone.

If everyone comes to the bargaining table with the same information, then the first to execute a Schelling-type gambit gets the surplus, and the extent of waste is minimized.[5] In the more typical case, however, all do not have the same information. The first to discover and propose such a project may simultaneously make a bargaining commitment which secures for himself all the bargaining surplus. The law may even foster such dissipation by granting to the originator property rights to such proposals. Under such circumstances excessive resources will be devoted to discovering potential projects. As originators may capture the full surplus of each downstream property owner, the latter are not benefited by provision of the flood control project. Originators, on the other hand, dissipate the expected rents in developing such projects.[6]

This case presents a potentially wasteful situation. In the introduction, however, it was promised that this paper would seek to do more than simply identify potential inefficiencies. Here we seek to explore such situations for evidence that government has some transaction cost advantage in organizing behavior in these instances. This must be done by examining the institutions in the private and government sectors with an eye toward assessing their performance at reducing such inefficiency.

Superficially, it seems that government is ideally suited to eliminate this type of waste. According to one scenario, it might establish a reimbursement scheme which awarded prizes of optimal value to inventors and project originators. It might then levy arbitrary taxes to finance the provision of public good projects which distributed the surplus in any way it saw fit. In so doing, it would eliminate any scope for affecting the level of surplus obtainable through bargaining and thus remove the incentive to engage in bargaining.

By definition, democratic governments do not behave in arbitrary ways, however. Indeed, "taxation without representation" may be economically efficient, but it is typically unpopular. Decisions concerning the adoption of government projects as well as taxing arrangements for their finance are reserved in the U.S. government for the legislative branch. Democratic government legislative apparatus, as was pointed out earlier, merely duplicates institutions which proliferate in the private sector. Any sort of technique likely to evolve in a government collective decision-making environment should also evolve in a private collective decision process. Only one distinction is noteworthy: membership in a private "club" producing public goods is voluntary. One may opt out of the government process only by leaving the jurisdiction.

It is widely believed that this option to decline to join or participate in private voluntary efforts to organize public good provision is a crippling defect, that such an option will lead to wholesale avoidance and under-provision of the public good. This argument is defective for two reasons. First, it fails to deal realistically with the apparent economic function of such private organizations which, in spite of economists' predictions, continue to prosper. Second, it overlooks the overwhelming bargaining advantage which such organizations will have in dealing with nonmembers. Recognition of these two points makes clear that private organization of the provision of public goods will *not* be impeded by avoidance of club membership. On the contrary, we predict spontaneous joining by potential beneficiaries to public good projects.

To see this, we must return to the problem posed by bargaining itself and practices which groups of beneficiaries might introduce to eliminate such an inefficiency. For groups likely to be presented repeatedly with new proposals for public good projects, it will be worthwhile to maintain a standing organization to serve as a forum for the presentation of such proposals. Civic groups, Chambers of Commerce, and trade organizations are examples of standing organizations of the type we have in mind. Such groups will form permanent rules for the sharing of the cost of any public goods secured by the group which mitigate the extent of bargaining by reducing the range for cost shares to vary. It may be decided, for example, that costs will be shared equally, or in proportion to benefits, or whatever parameter is deemed to be reasonable. They may also adopt rules for "cost plus" type reimbursement to outside suppliers to give them bargaining power in these negotiations.

It will always be in the interest of persons likely to be affected similarly to those within an organization to seek membership in these organizations. Failure to join the group does not (as it may superficially appear to) ensure use of the group-provided public good at no cost. On the contrary, it means that nonmembers must bargain with the group over the available public good surplus. In such situations, since proposals are far more likely to originate within the organization than with the individual, the group will have a significant bargaining advantage. It will therefore pay each individual to join such groups where membership, through the sharing rules adopted, guarantees to each some portion of the surplus associated with such projects.

Consider the following example. A civil engineer develops a flood control project which he perceives will benefit each member of a community in the flood plain. He carries his project before the Chamber of Commerce which recognizes its value and elects unanimously to support such a project *contingent upon* the participation of beneficiaries who currently are not members of the organization. A standing rule for such projects provides that all members who remain members (anyone may resign at any time) will share the costs of such projects in proportion to their benefits (or equally, or in proportion to the value of their real property, etc.).

No such standing rule determines the relative contributions of members *vis-à-vis* nonmembers, however. As the Chamber of Commerce is the effective originator in negotiations with nonmembers, it is in the position of making a Schelling-type offer which may not be refused—and which captures the full surplus of nonmembers. As an extreme and unnecessarily ostentatious example, it may contract with some third party to turn over all organization assets in the event that it accepts a less favorable counter offer by any nonmember. Confronted by such an offer, nonmembers must logically surrender all surplus from the flood control project to the organization. It is therefore in the interest of all potential beneficiaries to join and remain in such organizations. Indeed, the principal function of such a standing organization is to distribute surplus from recurring public good projects in a way which minimizes the dissipation of such surplus through bargaining.[7]

So far the theory has suggested three characteristics of organization for the provision of nonexcludable public goods. First we predict that organizations of individuals expecting to be joint users of public good projects in the future will form to make arrangements for the provision of these goods. We should not expect to observe bilateral exchange between producers and individual users of these goods. Second, such organizations for the provision of public goods will adopt standing rules for the sharing of the costs of such projects. When projects are proposed, in other words, the cost of sharing arrangements will not be determined on a project by project basis. Third, membership in such organizations will be sought—not avoided—by all potential users.

These implications hold for the provision of public goods whether they are organized privately or under the auspices of government. We also observe large numbers of such organizations in both sectors. The various levels of legislative government, from municipal and county government to the U.S. Congress, correspond more or less to the model suggested by the discussion above, but so do the American Automobile Association, the Downtown Merchants Association, and the PTA. Let us therefore consider the extent to which the behavior of the public and private organizations may be predicted to differ.

The principal *way* in which these organizations differ is that government legislative bodies are invariably geographically based. Their membership is *determined* by geographical boundaries exclusively.[8] Private interest groups may and do form on the basis of both geography and many other varied special interests that transcend geography. The American Cancer Society is an organization which serves those with an effective demand for research and treatment of cancer. The Metropolitan Opera Guild brings together opera buffs from all over the world in the promotion and enjoyment of opera, produced in New York but transmitted (via privately sponsored broadcasts) to members everywhere.

This difference in government and private organization suggests two implications for government organization. First, to the extent that standing rules for the distribution of surplus are insufficiently refined (and this will be a real problem in a world of imperfect information), scope for bargaining will remain. Indeed, realistic decision rules for governments constituted in this way must allow more scope for bargaining than will rules for more interest-specific organizations. Governments must tax according to conventional bases such as income or land value which may be correlated in general with benefits received from government, but will in most specific cases be a very crude proxy. In order to get such programs passed, deals are made via explicit and implicit logrolling and combining bills with others. Where such a process is permitted, the advantages of permanent cost-sharing arrangements for preventing excessive bargaining in the provision of public goods is vitiated. Surplus from the provision of collective goods will be dissipated in this bargaining process.

Second, advantageous proposals providing benefits to a small and specialized group which is not heavily represented at any level of government will not be adopted. Such projects will cost more than they are worth to most of the constituents of such governments, and unless they can be attached to other bills providing offsetting benefits to others, they will not be adopted. In short, the standing rules adopted to prevent bargaining over the sharing of the cost of public good projects will themselves frequently interfere with the transacting of these contracts. The same measures, if brought before a private organization more appropriately constituted, will pass with less difficulty.

Consider a high-income neighborhood which desires more intensive police patrolling than does the rest of the municipality. Proposals to increase the level of such patrols in that neighborhood will be defeated (since they must be financed by taxes on property all over the city) unless such proposals are tied to municipal parks or schools which provide differential benefits to citizens outside this neighborhood. If such a proposal were made before a *private* citizens' group made up exclusively of members of this neighborhood, it should pass with little difficulty. As benefits inherent in this proposal itself exceed the cost to each person whose consent must be obtained, passage is ensured.

C. Public Goods and Imperfect Information

The foregoing implications depend on the assumption made in the last section that individual valuations of collective goods are known. When they are not known, additional problems are confronted by both government and private organizations in their attempts to organize the provision of these goods. Even when we abstract from the problem of users' disclosure of their valuation of these goods, the communication problem associated with their provision is of a higher order of magnitude than that concerning private goods, regardless of setting. Users must not only agree on the level and the nature of the items provided; they must decide on the cost share of each user as well. Each of these decision variables is interdependent. Much of the institutional character of the scheme adopted—whether public or private—will be shaped by the objective of economizing on communication costs.

One of the most obvious ways of reducing these communication costs is the process of representation. Allocative decisions are rarely made in either public or private processes by all members affected. Governments almost uniformly employ representation, but so do private organizations. Stockholders of corporations elect directors, private universities have trustees, churches, their vestrymen. In each case these ruling boards act *in the name of* all members of the larger body.

Representation also suggests problems for government organization which may be avoided by private organizations. For government representatives are almost exclusively representative of geographical areas, while economic interests may correspond very imperfectly to the boundaries determined in such a process. Indeed, in the case of *gerrymandering* the process of defining representative areas itself is used to suppress any such correspondence. Private organizations are not bound by such geographical imperatives and frequently are constituted with the explicit objective to include among members of such boards representatives of minority interests in the organization. Such interests might never be voiced in negotiations over government provision of public goods, since majority interests may be more heavily represented in any sort of geographically based representation.

But let us reconsider the problem of spontaneous participation in voluntary private organizations when information is imperfect. It may seem that individuals whose preferences are *not* known have an unambiguous incentive to avoid such participation, since, in so doing, they may "free ride" on whatever amount of collective good is eventually provided by participants. This is simply not true. For if the group *believes* that such individuals outside the group have nonnegligible demands for public goods being considered, they may still force them to participate on very unfavorable terms. They may, for example, make effectively the same offer to such nonparticipants when the demands of these persons is only suspected as that discussed where demands were known. Contemplation of such adverse developments may influence potential beneficiaries into the permanent organizations discussed above.

Such groups are predicted to adopt standing rules for cost sharing, hence preference revelation within the organization should not typically be a problem. Elaborate procedures to elicit members to reveal preferences have recently been developed and discussed by Clarke (39, 40), Tideman and Tullock (169), and others. These processes are not "immune to strategic maneuvering" as advertised, but rather assume away (in the context of a very implausible set of institutions) any avenues by which bargaining gains may be achieved.[9] A question frequently posed by readers of these schemes is why, if they effectively eliminate the scope for strategic maneuvering, do we not see them employed. One explanation for the absence of such processes is that, in the context in which most group decisions are made in both government and private organizations, there is no incentive to conceal preferences.

Understating preferences for public goods is an intelligent strategy, as we pointed out above, only if shares of the cost of financing these goods depend on the valuations revealed. This will be true only if the decision on the financing in each case is linked to the revealed demand. Where such linkage is broken, as it would be in the case discussed here in which standing rules for cost sharing are adopted, such preference-revealing schemes are not required. Individuals will voluntarily reveal their true preferences. It has long been recognized that it does not pay to conceal preferences for public goods indefinitely unless institutional decision rules constrain the sorts of offers and acceptances of arrangements in implausible ways.[10]

IV. CONCLUSION

This paper has examined the age-old question of government versus private organization of economic activity for cases involving public goods for which exclusion is infeasible. This has been done by attempting to differentiate as clearly as possible between useful concepts of government and private organization. The analysis then sought to identify transaction cost problems encountered in this organization process and attempted to determine how the government and private entities defined here would respond to these difficulties.

The transaction costs with which we were concerned here were: (1) free riding, that is, the problem that nondelivery could not be used to secure payment for use of the public good; (2) the indeterminacy of the shares of the cost in voluntary arrangements for public good provision which may lead to the dissipation of surplus; and, finally, (3) the large information requirements which public good provision makes on any organization.

No advantages for voluntary (that is, democratic) government organization were perceived over voluntary private organization. On the contrary, because of unexplained anomalies in the structure of democratic government in which legislative bodies and representation within legislative bodies are tied to geography rather than to characteristics more likely to correspond to interests in our society, certain advantages to private organization were identified. These would, of course, disappear should these idiosyncrasies in government organization be eliminated. In essence, economic theory offers little a priori advice on this issue because the theoretical constructs with which we were dealing here themselves differ so little. It has frequently been remarked that there is little to distinguish modern private organizations such as corporations from governments—see, for example, Tullock (172), pp. 52–53—and this similarity itself belies attempts to contrast sharply the implied behavior of the two. Both are processes in which the behavior of many is coordinated in pursuit of private objectives. One is attached to government. The other is not but depends upon government sanction of its processes to function effectively.

We should not exaggerate this dependence, however, for private organizing of economic activity concerning purely *private* goods is equally dependent upon the willingness of government-proper, the wielder of dominant force in society, to enforce the contracts and agreements made by these private good transactors.

While voluntary representative government possesses no discernible advantages in the organizing of public goods arrangements, dictatorial government does. It was pointed out in our discussion of bargaining that a pure dictatorship which was unresponsive to bribes or any other material advantages offered by disputing public goods bargainers could, by making arbitrary assignments of the surplus arising from these arrangements, avoid the problem of the dissipation of public good surplus. The principal difficulty with this solution is to motivate such a dictator to concern himself with efficiency in arrangements in which he takes no part. If the advantages of government involvement in the provision of public goods arise from its undisputed and arbitrary use of power, we must address ourselves to another, even more unsettling set of questions. Rather than asking what sort of goods governments should engage in producing and in what quantities, we must ask whether and why such governments provide anything. We must answer in other words why they do not simply take.

Reassuring results are generally obtained in analyses which assume at the outset that governments always do the right thing. More interesting and informative results are likely to be produced, however, by postulating that government—like the other economic agents we deal with—serves our interest only incidentally as it serves its own. The cataloging and analysis of the influences toward and away from this convergence of interests comprise a rich agenda for future research in the positive analysis of government behavior.

FOOTNOTES

The author is associate professor of economics, Department of Economics.

1. Casual demonstrations of the "public goods problem" and its government "solution" are now universally found in textbooks for public finance, and frequently in price theory textbooks as well.

2. Vulnerability to free riding depends on the timing of such an uncoordinated exchange. If the hamburger is delivered before payment, the hamburger may be eaten and then the debt revoked. On the other hand, advance payment exposes the payer to chiseling (i.e., accepting payment without providing the good), a form of free riding by the supplier.

3. The analysis of public goods is held to be essentially identical to that of standard bilateral monopoly by Shibata (153). Arrow (12), p. 58, downplays exclusion as the source of difficulty in voluntary provision of public goods. He observes: "Each commodity has precisely one buyer and one seller. Even if the competitive equilibrium could be defined, there would be no force driving the system to it; we are in the realm of imperfectly competitive equilibrium. . . . If in addition the costs of bargaining are high, then it may be most efficient to offer the service free."

4. Concealing preferences as a bargaining strategy will be employed whenever the "benefit principle" is intended to operate in determining individual cost shares for the public good, that is, when the financing scheme seeks to relate individual payments to individual valuations of the good as in a Lindahl process. If it is known that the cost of a project is to be shared equally, for example, and all have the same preferences, each will freely volunteer his own preferences. If preferences differ, even though costs will be shared equally, it will pay to give false signals in an attempt to influence the level of public good provided. This is a conceptually distinct problem, however, from giving false signals to obtain a *larger share* of a fixed surplus.

5. In Schelling's (145) analysis, bargaining gains are captured by making a commitment to give up property of value equal to or greater than the potential gain, if the gain is not won. A salesman might, for example, make a wager with one of his colleagues that he would turn over his full year's earnings if he ever cut his price below his initial offer. In so

doing, such a bargainer makes it irrational for him to yield any of the surplus to other bargainers.

6. It is important to note that the practice of granting patents in this country is merely a special case arrangement for this type of transaction involving the public good, technical innovation. "Originators" are reimbursed by being given a monopoly on the sale of the private good which embodies the public good innovation. Such private goods exchange at a single price in the market, however, and originators are thus prevented from perfectly discriminating, allowing consumers to retain some surplus. The efficiency of this arrangement is impossible to judge (even if the patent period is optimally calculated to provide just the correct incentive to innovate) since the price charged for the private good is not marginal cost. Alternative methods which do not introduce such price distortion are available (see below).

7. The counterstrategy for the individual, i.e., taking a Schelling-type position of refusing to cooperate in projects with anyone at any time under any circumstances, is dismissed as self-destructive.

8. There seems to be no reason for government to limit its legislative bodies to those concerned with geographically based legislation. Its administrative departments certainly recognize other interest groupings.

9. Potential participants in such a process are given one option. They must reveal a demand function for the public good under consideration which will be used to determine both the level of provision of the public good and marginal adjustments in their tax liabilities. The decisions are implicitly assumed to be inflexible and immutable over time, so that it does not pay to sit out one accounting period to discover everyone's demand function, then make a Schelling offer which captures all of the marginal potential surplus for the person engaging in such a maneuver. Even more implausible, it assumes that people will allow themselves to be committed, via the large lump sum elements of the scheme, to taxes which for any given program may exceed the worth of the public good project to them.

10. See Shibata (153) and Lindsay (101). One way that such arrangements have been excessively constrained has been to assume that participants must invariably pay a Lindahl tax in which their average tax per unit must equal their marginal demand price for the good. If such is the case, it frequently pays to decline to acknowledge true preferences for public goods indefinitely, even though offers in which the marginal tax price exceeds the average will lead to efficient levels being adopted.

PRODUCING KNOWLEDGE IN NONPROPRIETARY ORGANIZATIONS

Roland N. McKean, UNIVERSITY OF VIRGINIA

One of the least satisfactory aspects of a market economy is its performance in producing information. At best, the market for information is a peculiar one, since by definition the buyer does not know the value of the unknown items he is bidding for, and the seller does not know what value of output his efforts can produce. In other words, this market is an extreme example of decision-making under uncertainty. For this and other reasons, the profit incentive leads to questionable results pertaining to the generation and dissemination of knowledge.

First, there is the well-known difficulty with externalities. For example, profit-seeking firms cannot capture many of the benefits from basic research or from developing and disseminating information about product or workplace hazards. Profit-seekers can be expected, therefore, to

Economics of Nonproprietary Organizations
Research in Law and Economics, Supplement 1, pages 209-237
Copyright © 1980 by JAI Press Inc.
All rights of reproduction in any form reserved.
ISBN: 0-89232-132-6

produce "too little" of these kinds of information—and to suppress information whenever it is *genuinely* profitable to do so.

Second, consumers' tastes for knowledge are vulnerable to criticism. The nonfiction bestseller lists do not reflect a burning desire for accurate or profound knowledge. Because thinking and choosing among alternatives are hard work, people often prefer distorted oversimplification to honest descriptions of uncertainty. Occasionally they would rather be left unaware of potential disasters having low or unknown probabilities of occurrence. ("None loves the messenger who brings bad news.") Serious external costs may result from these preferences or from viewers' demands for newscasts to be attention-getting (televised executions?) rather than helpful to their decision-making. Do consumers even know what bits of information, unknowable in advance, are good for them individually? Their appraisals of expert or scientific information are particularly precarious; since they cannot evaluate the substance, they adopt crude rules of thumb, such as "whatever Ralph Nader or Edward Teller advocates is probably correct." Their final judgments and choices often depend, therefore, on the sequence of events. Hence, there is no unique optimum regarding information production or use, and the optimality of any particular outcome has rather weak appeal.

Not surprisingly we turn to government and not-for-profit organizations for much research, investigation, data collection, evaluation, and regulation (which ought to be based on a good deal of information and in any event affects information production). The nonmarket or nonprofit sectors, however, are plagued by the same problems— externalities and questionable preferences. We have in the nonprofit sector a more tenuous linkage between consumers' tastes, decisions at the top, and the behavior of subordinates. Public producers of information too will produce whatever promises to bring *them* gains in excess of costs, and as in the private sector, there are gaps in managers' abilities to capture gains from beneficial actions. Nonprofit producers, including government officials, often have understandable incentives to suppress information, to produce too little *or too much or too low-quality* information, or to disseminate misleading reports. In this paper I will review some theory about information production by nonprofit (including governmental) organizations and some of the results that one can observe.

I. THEORY OF INFORMATION PRODUCTION BY NONPROFITS

Nonprofit organizations, such as universities and foundations, undertake research, surveys, policy analyses, and publications to disseminate knowledge. Government personnel perform basic research, investigations, evaluations such as cost-benefit analyses, and data collection, for example, by the Census or the Disease Control Center. What, if anything, can economic theory say about the performance that we should expect?

By and large, the familiar propositions about profit-seeking versus nonprofit enterprises apply to information production and dissemination.[1] For example, the proposition that requires the fewest auxiliary assumptions is that, in producing the same product, a set of independent nonprofit enterprises will employ more variable input-mixes than a set of independent profit-seeking firms. Unless managers have identical utility functions, the nonprofits will not converge as much as the profit-seekers on the cost-minimizing (or any other single) set of input ratios.[2] This hypothesis should apply to publicly and privately owned newspapers, television programs, research projects, information processing systems, opinion surveys, schools, and so on—*if* one could find public and private ventures producing identical outputs. Locating comparable producers of *new* information would presumably be difficult, though, since new information is unknown in advance and the outputs are unlikely to be identical. Furthermore, since many government and nonprofit undertakings are unique, all one can say is that the possible performance in any one venture covers a wide range. In other words, each has to be regarded as a relatively uncertain enterprise, though we have no testable propositions about how erratic the performance may be.

Propositions about *average* behavior in a set of public or nonprofit enterprises require additional assumptions. For instance, to the extent that the following items could be measured on a comparable basis, one might predict that government research units would have longer coffee breaks or larger staffs per unit of output or more pages of output not valued by recipients (as percentages of total information output) than would profit-seeking research units. To derive such predictions, one has to assume that certain goods, such as breaks from work and larger staffs, are arguments in managers' utility functions (or are correlated with such arguments). One also has to assume that constraints prohibiting long coffee breaks or requiring valuable information outputs do not exist or are not effective. In those circumstances, it should be relatively less costly *to nonprofit managers* to permit long coffee breaks, hire excessive staff, and tolerate worthless output.

The constraints imposed by bargaining pressures on nonprofit and government entrepreneurs are hard to unravel. Nonetheless, they are crucial, for the fear of reactions by alumni or voters makes certain actions too costly to administrators—actions to which utility maximization would otherwise lead. The impact of such constraints is hard to unravel also because their effectiveness depends on the monitorability of the behavior in question. It is not easy, for example, to police the length of coffee breaks in a research organization, yet it is much easier than monitoring the value of research output or the quality of information on which an OSHA regulatory decision is based.

To see some of the major factors that shape opportunity sets in non-profit units, we should keep in mind the groups that have leverage over personnel and those groups' abilities to police personnel behavior. In government, for example, agency officials have leverage over subordinates, though Civil Service rules attenuate this influence in several respects. Congress, in turn, has a good deal of leverage over each administration official, as do fellow bureaucrats and the president. At the "top" of the heap, voters and those who can influence voters (including campaign contributors) can put pressure on congressmen. Now voters are free riders with respect to informing themselves, voting, responding to surveys, writing their senators, joining a lobby organization, or otherwise monitoring government. Nonetheless, quite a few voters do these things if they have been indoctrinated with a sense of duty to participate or if they become emotionally involved. Citizens often become emotionally involved when they have large personal stakes or when they are aroused by a "cause" or when an election promises to be close; such factors can make the game exciting, even though the voter may realize that his individual action will not affect anything. (After all, if voters behaved completely as free riders, campaign contributions, and indeed campaigns, would be futile and nonexistent.) Hence congressmen and thence bureaucrats are sensitive to what they think *those voters who participate* will do. Special interests that have high stakes per member and that can be aroused en masse, such as farmers, occupational groups, and groups that can directly influence voters, such as unions, or that can contribute campaign funds, have special leverage.

Thus there is a network of pressures on Congress and a network-and-chain of pressures on the agency personnel who produce information. Keep in mind, however, the crucial role of monitorability. The pressures may result in a good deal of environmental research effort by EPA, for it is comparatively easy to verify the number of dollars and man-years allotted to a general topic. The pressures may not elicit very careful or complete research, however, for that is much more difficult to police, even if top officials desire it. On balance, moreover, the pressures sometimes call for low quality (e.g., biased) inquiry or data compilation, which is often relatively easy to police. For example, if the Corps of Engineers finds net pressures for (that is, net rewards from) expanding its operations, there is a derived demand for biased project evaluations, and supporters can easily tell whether or not the Corps keeps coming up with benefit-cost ratios in excess of one.

In general, as we proceed, we should keep the fundamental utility-maximizing model in mind. Information-producing personnel will have various arguments in their utility functions. In the light of the pressures and monitoring possibilities, each official or employee will in effect seek to equate the marginal productivity *to him* (summing up the gains from any sources of utility affected by each action) of each type of action or input: working harder, modifying the data collected, designing analyses differently, changing the direction of investigations, shifting research effort, modifying regulations that affect or require information production, designing surveys differently, disseminating knowledge in a different manner, monitoring contracts for research differently, and so on. The marginal gain *to that employee* from increasing each source of utility (prestige, convenience) should end up approximately equal to its marginal cost *to that employee*.[3]

This does not mean that poor government performance must always be expected. In some information programs, the effective constraints will permit or encourage good performance, such as in Census data collection, where most pressures push officials to carry out a relatively unambiguous task and where achievement of the task is fairly easy to monitor. In some information programs, such as the Public Broadcasting System or selected basic research programs, the mix of constraints on, and sources of utility to, the personnel involved may at times produce relatively good results. In many programs, or at other times, however, we can expect poor results.

Throughout the discussion, I shall assume that the utility functions of nonprofit and government personnel include such arguments as convenience, leisure, prestige, job security, promotion, larger staffs of subordinates, control, freedom from conflict and painful decisions, satisfaction from doing a good job, and progress toward their individual conceptions of the "public interest." It seems most unlikely that the network of bargaining pressures somehow forces nonprofit administrators to pursue Pareto optimality or the social equivalent of profit maximization. Hence, nonprofit administrators will find it relatively inexpensive to themselves to pursue these other utility-yielding items. As for the specific constraints that are generated, I shall in each part of the discussion assume some of the points mentioned above (such as monitorability) and/or indicate selected major constraints that seemingly apply in the organizational units concerned. The differential constraints will stem from different laws or directives, from different wishes by groups that can harm or help the decision-maker, or from differential monitoring costs to organization managers and to those groups who try to influence the decisions. With appropriate auxiliary assumptions, utility maximization in the light of these constraints will then imply certain kinds of behavior affecting information production and dissemination.

I shall not test any hypotheses because we have no set of profit-seeking ventures producing the same outputs. Hence the implications as derived merely point to *unspecified* amounts of inefficiency or worthless information. The examples presented are, I believe, consistent with these unspecific implications—that is, they can be explained by the theory—but the analysis does not deal with the expected magnitude of these phenomena, with alternative explanations, or with the possibilities that the behavior comes about by chance. My procedure, then, will be simply to examine the constraints on selected information-affecting activities of nonprofit organizations, to ask what kind of behavior one would expect, and to indicate what kind of behavior one observes. The paper will prove nothing, but I hope it will help one sharpen his intuition and judgments about the issues.

II. PRODUCTION OF INFORMATION: PRIVATE NONPROFITS

What kind of constraints shape the utility-maximization process in universities,[4] foundations, and other private nonprofits?

First, government regulates foundations in an effort to prevent abuses (mainly avoidance of taxes) and regulates universities to increase "affirmative action," alleviate sex discrimination, and so on. Federal control of many grants and state control of portions of budgets for many universities provide great leverage. The resulting regulatory measures can influence the direction and amount of research, for example, by subsidizing work on energy and the environment. They may reduce its efficiency, in comparison with independent research, through inevitably crude monitoring efforts to prevent the misuse of funds. In colleges and universities that get part or all of their budgets from state governments, the teaching loads required by legislatures help determine how much time can be devoted to research. These constraints that emanate from government are shaped by the utility-maximization process within governmental units. In some eras and countries these constraints on information production and transmission have been capricious or oppressive, but in the United States thus far they may not be as pertinent (except for research grants) as the other operative forces.

Who else can help or harm university officials? Donors, boards of trustees, and alumni all have considerable leverage. Also, faculty, staff, and students can significantly influence the opportunity sets of administrators and thence researchers. Given the prevailing sentiments or traditions in this country (which are also powerful influences on opportunity sets), the outsiders usually do not interfere much with teaching (i.e., dissemination) or research. The trustees and alumni will push a few causes ("We're with you, Coach, win or tie!"), but, at least in the current atmosphere, these causes rarely have direct impact on research or curriculum.

Note the importance of policing costs in the process. Boards of trustees, as well as government officials and other concerned groups, can tell whether or not beautiful buildings are constructed, but the vast majority of us cannot begin to judge whether research in someone else's field is worthwhile. To a certain extent, one tends to adopt crude rules of thumb: "If the buildings are splendid, the teaching and research must be good." The effective constraints may quite understandably give rise to an "edifice complex." Other items that are easily monitored are whether or not one's nephew is admitted to the university, whether or not any publicized scandals are occurring. Consider the cost to a well-meaning trustee, however, of acquiring accurate information about the teaching, research, left-wing emphasis, or right-wing emphasis in a university or department. Even if someone wanted to monitor such matters, it would ordinarily be too difficult. If the nonprofits became politicized and officials were determined to control academic activities, the impact on information production could be tremendous, but monitoring rules would have to be crude and undiscriminating.

In good times, the constraints on faculties from above pertaining to information production may be minimal. Within academia, however, opportunities and monitoring costs result in powerful influences on research. Officials value having national or international reputations in order to attract endowments, students, and faculty members. It is too costly for any of the participants to monitor the quality of the curriculum and teaching in various universities. As a consequence, donors, administrators, and faculty begin to rank the larger universities to a considerable extent on the basis of a proxy—the renown of its faculty because of publications. Promotions and salary increments within such universities become based mainly on publications, partly because they bring the desired eminence, partly because it is so costly to measure and monitor the quality of the educational program, and partly because, to reduce conflict and accusations of favoritism, administrators and faculty accept a *relatively* unambiguous criterion for promotion and salary increases.

The resulting "publish or perish" policy has enormous influence on the volume and type of research and on the teaching program, yet this mechanism is a bit like gasoline taxes being earmarked for highway construction: it appears to divorce subsequent decisions about the output from concern about its social value.

Monitoring costs are extremely important in another way. Without any direct market for research output, how do researchers decide what they will work on? Their own intellectual curiosity plays a role, naturally, and the urgency of current issues channels grants in certain directions. The major payoff from university research, though, is acceptance in a refereed journal,[5] and peer opinion constitutes the main shaper of opportunity sets. In some physical sciences, where the quality of research can be appraised in a comparatively objective manner, the process probably weeds out much of the incorrect, trivial, and duplicate articles. Even there, the constraints may generate inefficient "fashions" in research. (The importance of peer approval brings about a situation somewhat like Keynes' description of the stock market: researchers write what they expect other researchers to think that other researchers . . . would approve.) In some disciplines, however, such as the social sciences, the quality and significance of research outputs are more difficult to appraise. At the same time it becomes costly to faculty members (including journal editors) to spend time on critical appraisal and to keep up with new literature, let alone past literature, even in increasingly narrow fields of specialization. If a piece of work is neatly typed, it is hard to be sure that it is nonsense or trivial, and opportunity sets often reflect a live-and-let-live atmosphere.[6] There is a good deal of hasty refereeing, reinventing the wheel, proving rigorously that the sun rises in the East, or showing that with some models the sun rises in the West.[7]

The fashion problem becomes relatively acute in the "soft sciences." In addition, in the frenzied push for publications, researchers can gain—given the monitoring difficulties already described—by concentrating on work that yields the most articles per man-year. In economics, for instance, it pays to proliferate mathematical or verbal models[8] without regard to testing them. Also, as someone has observed, our work is often like figuring out the optimal arrangement of deck chairs—on the Titanic. Next best is to retest a hypothesis "under the lamppost where the light is good"—that is, find a large collection of data (which will already have been used to test several variations on one hypothesis) and test the hypothesis again, using a slightly different model.

Foundations that perform or sponsor research face somewhat different opportunity sets. Unless heavily endowed already,[9] they must impress donors, which partially guides them regarding the general subjects and thrusts of their work. They must compete for personnel and therefore seek at least a respectable image in the academic community, so they will typically stress publications and will usually be fairly responsive to fashion. Again the differential monitorability of research in the physical sciences and in other fields helps shape the output. Administrators will usually, however, be more anxious than university officials to communicate with the public, and less reluctant to guide their researchers; as a result, their output may be less arid and more frequently aimed at businessmen and nonspecialists. As for their efficiency in producing these outputs, the input mixes are no doubt rather variable, but on the average I conjecture that foundation luncheons and conferences are more lavish than those in academia—partly because tradition does not call for as much austerity and officials have greater discretion, partly because envious peers have fewer opportunities and incentives to criticize foundation activities. One sees examples of some of these points in Kwitny's (92, p. 22) description of a 1976 research-planning conference organized by the Ford Foundation.

One of the most desirable features of foundation research is that it does sometimes yield comparatively independent views on issues or criticisms of public policies. Within any one foundation, natural selection in the evolution of its staff may result in something like a "party line," but because donors have diverse views, foundations in the aggregate reflect a diversity of views, and they are relatively independent of the government. Even if their research output is not always profound, they do often summarize pros and cons or diverse points of view in ways that *may* reach a nonspecialist audience.

It is impossible to demonstrate how much of this academic and foundation research is worthwhile (though in the "Conclusions" of this paper I shall offer a few comments on its marginal worth). It is fairly clear, however, that in nonprofit organizations the decisions about the nature and amount of research to be undertaken are not closely linked with even guesses about its social worth.[10] I am persuaded that without nonprofits our system would undertake too little basic research. With our present institutions, though, it is possible that we are undertaking far too much of the wrong kinds. Certainly there is abundant reason to believe that we have "nonmarket failures."

III. PRODUCTION OF INFORMATION: GOVERNMENT

A. In-House Production

The constraints and decision-making processes in government can hardly lead to identity between social costs and individual costs or between social benefits and benefits to decision-makers. What is good for the Corps of Engineers is not necessarily good for the country. Externalities, the government counterpart of market failures, will plague us.

1. *Basic research.* We would not expect municipal governments to tackle much basic research, for essentially the same reason that we cannot, except in special circumstances, count on private enterprise for such work. Similarly, however, individual *federal* agencies or officials

have a parochial viewpoint unless carefully constrained by institutional arrangements. Federal personnel are often unable to capture sufficient gains from basic research to induce them to produce it. For example, Pentagon officials have tended to shift research funds toward applied or engineering developments.[11] And, according to one critic, "The most massive [R&D] programs appear to be sound choices only if evaluated on the basis of the perpetuation of the agencies involved" [O'Leary (128), p. 11]. Needless to say, opportunity sets in government are not always unfavorable to basic research, and important contributions in the physical sciences have come from in-house laboratories. As in other cases, what is actually done depends on the arguments in decision-makers' utility functions, on the costs to those decision-makers of monitoring subordinates, on the wishes of those groups who have leverage over the decision-makers, on the monitoring costs to those who have leverage, and on the incentives of each to monitor performance.

Monitorability of basic research is poor in any setting. In government, however, misguided attempts to monitor such work are prompted by understandable pressures on administrators to keep track of what their shops are doing and be ready to defend their activities. Such policing in government focuses on indicators that are not very relevant but that economize on administrators' time and effort—pages written,[12] man-hours of input, progress reports—and should make research in government inefficient and unattractive. One would expect natural selection to yield comparatively ineffective research teams and atmospheres, and he should on the average have modest expectations from this nonprofit basic research.

2. *Policy evaluations.* Much has been written about the limitations of policy analysis, particularly if prepared within government; see, for example, De Alessi (53), McKean (114), Hanke and Walker (72), Strauch (163), Wildavsky (186), and Alchian (5). Public choices are inherently political decisions, shaped mainly by the network of voter-political pressures [Hanke and Walker (*op. cit.*), pp. 410–411]. When choices are thrown into the political arena, to expect the criterion to be economic efficiency is like saying, "Here's a jug of whiskey, and we're going to decide whether to drink it by majority rule, except that the decision should be not to drink it." Wherever and however prepared, therefore, economic analyses will have limited relevance to the decisions (past or present) being considered. But government evaluations are especially handicapped in providing economic analyses or unbiased information about policies. First, as mentioned earlier, the constraints placed on legislators and officials by the political process do not cause those officials to demand objective analyses in terms of economic efficiency (or *any* widely accepted criterion). Hence, these higher officials do not have

incentives to enforce the preparation of such information. In other words, their ability to capture net gains from having or using careful analysis is quite limited. Second, whatever those in the higher echelons want, the details, though not the conclusions, of policy evaluations are costly to monitor. In the policy analyses that emerge from government, therefore, surely one should expect information that is on the average of low quality (though variable around that average). I would expect government policy analyses to be less useful for social-profit maximization (or for achieving any one particular objective) than I would expect corporate analyses to contribute to profit-maximization—though I see no way to test this proposition. This does not say that government analyses have zero usefulness or that they are never high quality. Also when agencies are competing for budget—for example, Bureau of Reclamation vs. Department of Agriculture or Army vs. Navy—their rival analyses and mutual criticisms taken together may have a wholesome influence even if each agency's evaluations are biased. Furthermore, the General Accounting Office seems to have enough independence so that its analyses, even if not always of high quality, play a useful role in a sort of adversary process.

Examples of public behavior can prove nothing but can perhaps make the point more vivid. First of all, in its grant-in-aid programs, and probably in most programs, the government seldom evaluates its own operations after they have been launched, unless they are sensational successes or explicit pressures for postproject evaluation exist.[13] Second, when preproject evaluations are prepared, the information is often of dubious value. For instance, the Corps of Engineers recently came up with an 8,000-page, $2.4 million report favoring the resumption of work on the barge canal across north central Florida; as a rough clue to the quality of the analysis, consider its use of a 2⅞ percent interest rate. Another evaluation that illustrates the point is the Bureau of Reclamation's cost-benefit analysis of the Garrison Diversion Unit, an irrigation project in North Dakota. It is estimated (by the Bureau) to cost $380 million and provide benefits to 1,300 farms.[14] Evaluations by the military often reflect parochial viewpoints and perverse incentives.[15] Many of the shortcomings arise because the problems are inherently difficult, but incentives account for additional shortcomings and also appear to favor glossing over rather than candidly stressing the uncertainties [Stockfisch (162)]:

> Although numerous incidents can be recounted to suggest that information failures [such as the Pearl Harbor warning story] have a pathological dimension, emphasis upon the pathological can be misleading if the conclusion is drawn that information failures are exceptional rather than frequent. ... the perspective of pathological information failure overlooks a possibly more pervasive kind of information

problem—that centering around the countless decisions that go on daily with respect to resource allocation and production processes. (p. 19)

. . .

Models and the critical behavior propositions that they contain are not well verified, and usually not validated at all. The input data used in models often have an obscure or unknown empirical foundation, and the relevance of much data (even when it is valid) to the military effectiveness of systems is unknown. (p. 12)

. . .

The expression "quantitative methodology" in this context has a potential to be misleading because its valid quantitative underpinning is necessarily meager. (p. 13)

Nonprofit opportunity sets can also be seen at work in the analysis of proposals for pollution abatement on the Delaware River [Ackerman, Ackerman, Sawyer, and Henderson (1)]. The work in the Delaware Estuary Comprehensive Study shows vividly how cost-reward structures lead (a) to using measurable and policeable proxies (e.g., dissolved oxygen) that will often be misleading, (b) to sophisticated handling of monitorable details, (c) to biased or careless treatment (or shelving) of less monitorable but crucial questions, and (d) to "looking the other way" in connection with gross uncertainties. Inconsistent attitudes toward evaluation also are unlikely to be accidental; government agencies disapprove plans for private nuclear plants such as Seabrook unless risks are reduced by redesign, yet go along with government "plans" for waste storage that apparently consist of optimistic assertions.

3. *Other information-producing activities.* In the last few years, some of the weaknesses of governmental investigations and intelligence gathering have been publicized; see Wilensky (187).[16] Perhaps I ought not hit the CIA and FBI while they are down, but I think their activities do illustrate where nonprofit incentives, with only a few general constraints, are capable of leading. The government's original efforts to investigate Watergate and assassinations also left much to be desired. Utility-maximization models suggest that such outcomes should be expected. They also cause one to expect government inquiries to be less efficient "in the small" than say those of Pinkerton's or investigative reporters. This is not to say, of course, that we could leave such activities to the market, because the benefits of many important investigations are not marketable, and cost-covering ventures could not undertake them. It is to say, however, that the constraints should be thoughtfully designed and our sights kept low.

Statistics collection, like other more easily monitored chores, may turn out better. Unambiguous tasks that are approved by the vast majority of citizens, urgently demanded by some, and opposed by few will often be done effectively *if* bad performance can easily be detected and complained about. I have not reviewed their activities, but I would expect the Bureau of Labor Statistics, the Departments of Agriculture and

Commerce, and the Federal Reserve Board to do good jobs of data collection for their clientele. I would also expect publicizing the swine flu program or erecting highway signs to be effective.

B. Contracting for Information

Many persons believe that government contracting with private nonprofit organizations for basic research or evaluations gives better results than in-house production, because the private nonprofit will have more independence and flexibility than the in-house unit. There is some force to this argument, but the degree of independence may not be great, because the government often has strong incentives and the leverage (through the purse strings) to police the general thrust of the research or the conclusions of the evaluations. Monitoring the details may well be too troublesome and costly to the contracting officers, who will usually be able to capture gains (avoid reprimands) only from policing certain proxies that superiors can observe. To the extent that it does emerge, the greater flexibility about conducting internal activities may increase productivity in basic research, but it also allows more scope for the nonprofit managers to do whatever is rewarding to them. In fact, having nonprofit contracting officers supervise contracts with nonprofit organizations may increase that scope erratically, in many ways other than mere avoidance of civil service rules and federal bureaucratic regulations. It may therefore increase the variability or unpredictability of input-mixes, side-effects, and (in this case[17]) outputs.

Many also believe that fixed-price contracts with profit-seeking firms for various tasks are economical because such firms would at least have incentives to minimize the cost of whatever they do produce. The latter point is correct, but it should be remembered that contracting officers can capture few gains from tough bargaining about the target price or from careful monitoring of the output. Such contracts may result in unnecessarily high prices, that is, large transfers from taxpayers to owners of the firms, or poor quality control even of familiar monitorable outputs. Such contracts would be especially likely to generate wrong or shoddy outputs if the latter are hard to monitor, as in the case of research and development. And, in the case of evaluations, the contracting officer might have an incentive to encourage low-quality—that is, biased—analyses. Thus, as long as one party to the contract is a nonprofit, we still encounter most of the difficulties arising from such incentives.

C. Government Regulation and Information Production

One of the ways in which governments, though not other nonprofits, influence information production is through regulation of the private sector. Some of the effects are intended, and others are unintended spillovers. What kind of impacts on information should one expect from nonprofit incentives in connection with regulations? In this section I have drawn heavily on my paper [McKean (115)].

1. *Private research and development.* One major impact on information comes about through the influence of regulations—for example, on drugs and chemicals—on private research and development. In recent years, considerable attention has been devoted to this kind of impact; see, for example, Peltzman (131), Wardell and Lasagna (177)]. Therefore, I shall comment only on selected issues.

The impact that has attracted most attention is the substitution effect *away* from R&D. The regulatory climate increases the expected cost of developing new products because, for example, of the required tests, the delays in marketability, truncated patent periods, and outlays on more "losers." The result should be to reduce R&D on new chemical products relative to other forms of investment and activity. To the extent that product development is deliberately guided (part of the process is serendipitous), there would be a shift in composition from bolder projects toward those involving less dramatic changes, assuming that innovative products would have lower chances of approval and higher R&D costs.

The impacts might be comparatively heavy for certain categories of chemicals such as prescription drugs or pesticides. The precise effects depend upon expectations for each category regarding required testing, probabilities of delays, chances of approval, and the chances of adverse publicity and consumer reaction. The consequences depend also, of course, on the opportunity costs to inputs (managers, researchers, workers, capital) of staying in their existing employment.

There are numerous detailed substitution effects superimposed on the broader reallocations of R&D. The expectations about the rewards from and costs of alternative R&D efforts will depend upon the specific provisions of the legislation covering different chemicals and situations, on the particular tests required, and on the particular regulatory agency involved. Profitable directions for R&D will depend on the differential costs of partially "avoiding" certain regulations—for example, by hiring more lawyers, bargaining with the agency, or engaging in litigation. The precise substitution effects will depend especially on monitoring and enforcement costs. Most regulations are imperfectly monitored (the Kepone episode occurred despite the months-earlier complaint that should have elicited an OSHA inspection). Some regulations, such as the general duty clause under OSHA or the requirement that only licensed applicators can use certain pesticides, are harder to enforce than others. The less effective a regulation, the less its intended impact and the less also its side effects on R&D.

Despite the decline in total investment (including R&D) and the *general* substitution away from R&D on new products, certain kinds of R&D would be stimulated. For example, if a particular product or process is banned—and the atmosphere does not make the outlook for substitutes similarly bleak—one would expect the prospective profits from substitutes to rise, and R&D on such substitutes to rise. One can see a great deal of this happening currently. Although saccharin, aspartame, and cyclamates are under fire, still-buoyant profit-seekers are developing new sweeteners, such as monellin (derived from the West African serendipity berry!) and an amino acid derivative that is 1300 times sweeter than an equal weight of sucrose. [18] With respect to processes, considerable research is focused on sludge-pyrolysis processes to handle toxic solid wastes (a growing problem with curbs on disposal into the air or water); and Dow Chemical and McGraw-Edison have developed an insulating fluid to replace PCB's in power capacitors—"betting [before it happened] that regulatory action will be taken against PCB's" [*Chemical Week* (37)]. A related substitution effect is "defensive" research to make existing products or processes acceptable as the probability of restrictions grows. Pesticide producers are exploring a variety of "slow release" techniques which reduce the quantities that must be used to achieve a given result and also take better advantage of biodegradability [Davis (52)]. The net impacts of these adjustments *might* be fairly sensible—*if* the regulatory authorities allocated their resources according to the *true* marginal productivity of alternative regulatory and enforcement efforts. Given the nonprofit incentives that shape regulatory laws and rules of thumb, however, a desirable net impact on R&D is not very likely. Adverse effects on R&D will not count heavily in this nonprofit milieu—unless bargaining pressures make them impinge on the regulatory officials.

2. *Knowledge of risks.* Knowledge of the toxicity of substances and of other risks is a second category of information that is affected, in part intentionally, by the regulatory apparatus. Such knowledge has positive value if we are to reduce health hazards, though, as with most information production, we cannot identify the optimal output. Existing regulations elicit considerable information (animal tests, reports on safety), yet fail to fill important gaps in our knowledge about the effects of chemicals on *human* health. Moreover, the regulatory climate sometimes inhibits the reporting of disease or adverse reactions to substances.

As in many other instances, the constraints pull government personnel toward the use of relatively measurable and monitorable proxies, even if their relationship to the "correct" objective is tenuous or unknown. Thus, the tests required for certification or approval of substances are largely animal tests. Unfortunately, animal tests may reveal relatively little regarding the effects of chemicals on *human* health. If a substance is said to be a carcinogen, this usually means that, when exposed to *some* dosage of the substance over *some* time periods, *some* test group of rats, mice, dogs, or monkeys developed a higher rate of malignancies than the control group did. Among the difficulties are the sensitivity to cancer of many test animals, especially mice. The mouse liver is so labile that changes in seemingly minor background conditions, such as the amount of oxygen in the air, can increase the incidence of tumors [Carter (33)]. Even when great care is exercised, duplicate tests do not always yield the same results; and the experiments are *not* always done with great care. Again, monitoring incentives and costs are pertinent; it is much easier to check on whether specified tests have been made than on whether they have been done in an appropriately careful fashion.

The major problem, however, is the metabolic and biological differences between those animal species and man. Substances may cause cancer in certain animals but not in others and not in human beings. Other chemicals may damage human beings, yet produce no ill effects on animals. Thus the notorious MER-29 passed its animal tests and was approved, yet turned out to be a potent cause of eye cataracts in people. At present we know little about the correlation between the results of animal tests and the probabilities of ill effects on people.[19] Another worrisome aspect of such tests is that the test animals are not simultaneously exposed to the multiplicity of chemicals and bodily conditions that people are exposed to and for which synergistic effects may exist. (The drug Marsalid turned out to be injurious if the user simultaneously ate Cheddar cheese, which might logically be in the mouse diet but usually is not.)

Few would really be willing to ignore the effects of chemicals on test animals; after all, these effects give good tips sometimes about the development of new drugs,[20] so maybe they yield good tips pertinent to the banning of substances. Almost everyone agrees, though, that our ability to interpret animal tests is appallingly poor and that more and better epidemiological studies (correlations between exposures and illness rates among *people*) are urgently needed.[21]

Given the present state of knowledge, it seems likely that the marginal worth of epidemiological studies and human experiments is higher than the marginal value of more animal studies. But it should not be surprising if nonprofit regulatory organizations purchase, or induce the production of, an uneconomical package of information. After all, personnel cannot usually capture rewards from pursuing economic efficiency. Regulations are geared to specific chores rather than overall net-benefit-maximization. Note too a possible penalty to regulators for epidemiological studies—political hostility toward correlations implying that certain localities are dangerous to health. "Cancer-mappers" may be regarded as "enemies of the people"; animal tests may be looked upon as less threatening actions, yet comforting proofs that something is being done.

In addition to requiring reports on animal reactions, the regulations require a few reports on people reactions to chemicals. Required clinical investigations and follow-up studies by drug manufacturers yield relevant data. Employers are required to report all instances of occupational disease, and pharmaceutical manufacturers are supposed to reveal any later adverse reactions to their products that they learn about. As far as physicians and their patients are concerned, reports of adverse reactions to drugs are voluntary (forms are provided). Physicians write in medical journals on ailments that may be related to chemical exposures, but otherwise such data are not collected in any systematic fashion.

A number of forces make the information output of this "system" relatively poor. The free-rider difficulty undermines the voluntary reporting. Next, where reports are required, program emphasis and monitoring costs frustrate the collection of epidemiological data. For instance, the emphasis of OSHA is on protecting workmen from occupational injury [Ashford (16), pp. 20–24, and R. S. Smith (157)], and employers are not under as much pressure to report occupational *illness* fully or systematically. One reason for this emphasis may be that it is easier to monitor the reporting of injuries (which are *relatively* certain as far as diagnosis and cause are concerned) than it is to monitor the reporting of diseases. Monitoring the latter is especially difficult if there are lags between exposure and illness and if the disease, while perhaps work related, often occurs anyway (such as cancer or heart disease). At the same time, fear of getting into the general duty clause may make employers reluctant to report diseases that may or may not be work related. Even with respect to safety, there has been little incentive to comply with the rules, at least in the early years of OSHA's existence, to wit: with an average fine per violation of $25 and an average expectation of seeing an OSHA inspector "once every seventy-seven years, about as often as we see Halley's comet" (*ibid.*), pp. 62–63.

3. *Dissemination to users.* Another "type" of information that is influenced by regulation is the dissemination of existing knowledge to the individuals exposed to products and chemicals. The acquisition of such information by individuals is important, because part of the task of protecting health has to be done by consumers in bidding for products and by job-seekers in bidding for jobs. Consider labels and the role of consumers. In a free market, one would expect competing producers to probe to see what kind and amount of information customers were willing to pay the cost of. After a while, one might hope, especially for

recurring purchases, to find the appropriate amount of information provided (on labels, warnings, brochures, and instruction sheets). What
customers would buy, of course, would be mainly information about
various dimensions of *performance* (including hazards), not about the
detailed chemical ingredients of foods or the inner workings of television sets. If transaction costs were low, it would be as difficult for firms
to sell "inadequate" information as it would be for them to sell rubber
crowbars. Transaction costs may, however, attenuate the abilities of the
traders to capture gains from such deals. Emergence of credible and
"correct" information may require numerous transactions, especially
since instructions and labels constitute only one of many jointly offered
features of a product. The case for intervening—for example, by requiring prescriptions or by requiring special information on labels, advertisements, or enclosures—should be stronger the less often the product
is purchased, the more costly it is to individuals to get accurate information, and the greater the damage from mistakes.

In most instances, however, it is by no means obvious that requiring
more detailed labeling and so forth will in fact bring improvement.
Perhaps the main difficulty is that when officials in nonprofit organizations begin to decide what information is worth having, they drift away
from what individual customers really value or can utilize. Moreover,
even putting "good" information on labels may result in low productivity: a government survey indicates that only 13 percent of consumers of nonprescription drugs study the labels. Furthermore, regulators,
divorced from worry about pleasing consumers, sometimes suppress
information that *they* believe is bad for consumers. The FDA called
advertising low-fat content "misbranding" and discouraged the development of low-fat candies and other products [Turner (173), pp. 59–
60].

Finally, something valuable may be lost if people are lulled into believing that the government is taking care of the store as far as their
protection is concerned. We should assume that producers will try to
fool consumers *wherever it is genuinely profitable to do so,* but vigilance by
numerous consumers in deciding what products to buy can usually
render misinformation or missing information unprofitable. The same
vigilance by voters in monitoring regulatory agencies might keep them
from neglecting consumers' interests, but note that in their capacities as
voters and government monitors, citizens are free riders. Real-life government will not succeed in protecting complacent or gullible or ill-
informed individuals. Yet if government appears to be taking responsi-
bility for safety and health, the marginal payoff to the consumer from
seeking or absorbing information will decline.

4. *An alternative.* In comparison with regulations designed by non-

profit government agencies, heavier and more certain penalties for damages attributable to products, working conditions, or procedures should be considered. By putting the profit system to work on the problem, such penalties would often elicit more valuable information than do detailed constraints that preclude sensible trade-offs. In some situations, at least, heavier liability could be substituted for detailed standards. Rewards (avoidance of liability) would then be for reductions of *actual serious* hazards rather than for compliance with specific inflexible rules that make dubious contributions to health or that deal with trivial hazards. Producers and others would have stronger reason to keep their eyes on the net benefits of damage reduction. They would redirect R&D, advertisements, consumer warnings and information, and warnings to employees in a more nearly appropriate manner than they would if guided by less relevant regulatory proxies. [22]

IV. GENERAL CONCLUSIONS

The main conclusion that I reach is that, in the nonprofit sector, the decisions to produce or influence information have a tenuous linkage with judgments about the prospective social value of that action.

A. Too Little or Too Much Nonprofit Research?

There is no way to demonstrate rigorously whether searches for unknown outputs should be increased or decreased. Any conclusion on this point has to be a judgment. My own judgment is that the incentive structure probably results in overspending on several types of research and especially overproduction of low-quality information. [23]

With my risk preferences and judgments about the payoffs from research in the social sciences, for example, my guess is that the marginal cost has in recent years exceeded the marginal gain. A decisive factor is of course the probability of success in any research. Needless to say, the gains from discovering information that would help us reduce war, unemployment, crime, injustice, and other social problems would be enormous, but, if the probabilities of success are low enough, our nonprofit institutions may be allocating too much effort to certain lines of inquiry. If this is so, let me emphasize that the culprit is not the personnel or their quality but rather the inherent difficulty of the problems and *thence the difficulties of peer (or any other) monitoring.* In these circumstances, nonprofit incentives are especially likely to lead to misallocations. From the standpoint of my argument, thus, the key difference between the physical sciences and the social sciences is the degree to which the research is appraisable and monitorable.

Even the most sophisticated econometric study could probably not produce useful estimates of the past returns from research or from "soft-science" research. It would be too difficult to measure the benefits (including information as a consumption good), to allow for the influence of other variables, and to allow for lags. It is hard for me to believe, however, that social science research is now generating *dramatic* returns. Consider research and information as inputs in the production of goods and services. In the past few decades, the information explosion has surely proceeded more rapidly than economic growth. Maybe the returns from this explosion, at least the social science portion, are diminishing, although returns on capital in general have not fallen. If one considers numerous nations, a *marked* connection between their growth rates and absorption of soft-science research seems quite far-fetched.

Since information and research are put to work mainly through being embodied in human capital, returns on the information explosion may be related to the returns on human investment. To the extent that these returns are correlated, the empirical work on human capital theory[24] casts doubt on the high productivity of information. (One contributor to that productivity, incidentally, is the extra demand for Ph.D.s that nonprofit institutions themselves generate.) For instance, rates of return on education have not been increasing as larger amounts of information became embodied in graduates. In fact, one recent study estimates that the return on a college degree fell from 11 or 12 percent in 1969 to 7 or 8 percent in 1974.[25] More significantly, the rate of return on graduate education in the United States appears to be low or even a negative 2 or 3 percent [Blaug (28), pp. 840, 842]. Furthermore, there has been increasing interest during the past few years in the "screening hypothesis," with a growing number of persons believing that education appeals to employers mainly because it screens out individuals who have desired attributes (such as above-average intelligence, motivation and drive, self-reliance, ability to get along with people); (*ibid.*), pp. 845–849. To the extent that this is so, the expanding body of journal articles and books contributes little to the returns on human investment.[26]

Such returns are, of course, a poor proxy for the full social returns on information. Widespread dissemination and the steady expansion in the number of graduates may have "competed away" most of the rents to possessors of the improved knowledge. More importantly, neither private nor estimated social returns would really capture the more subtle social benefits—the lagged serendipitous contributions of basic research to well-being, or the alleged improvements in citizenship and public decision-making. In the physical sciences the indirect productivity of university and government research may have made it highly worthwhile.[27] In the social sciences, I really wonder, though, about the magnitude of such subtle spillovers. Are political processes, social stability, individual choices, character development, concern for others, or collective choices being improved? Or, assuming that the difficulties are simultaneously growing, are the informational advances making things better than they would otherwise be? Is our expanding knowledge enabling us to stabilize economies, increase inner serenity, reduce social conflict, enjoy better government, or prevent wars? What *are* the fruits of the past fifty years' research in the "soft" sciences?[28]

As mentioned before, solutions to these social problems would be enormously valuable. Even Willmoore Kendall, who thought intelligence capabilities were poor and who never hesitated to take unpopular positions, fell back on a "Manhattan project in the social sciences" as one possible solution [Kendall (87), p. 552]. (Also it's hard to shake the view that, since we spend X billion dollars on liquor and Christmas tree lights, surely we can afford Y billion on Z.) But a possibility that we should at least *face* is that our limitations in some areas are so great and the object of our search is so elusive, that less, not more, research may be appropriate.

What policy changes would all this suggest? If this judgment has any merit, it suggests a reallocation of support away from selected "soft sciences," "trivial" topics, or "worthless" research. We might imagine government or some nonprofit association offering prizes for exposing worthless research, or government might levy a fine on publications judged to be worthless. One can easily visualize, however, the difficulties of designing a mechanism for judging the worth of research, the potential abuses, the threat to free inquiry. It's very hard to eliminate the hot air from any detonation, including the information explosion. Perhaps one could at least move toward stricter liability for damaging misinformation.

Maybe the best approach—if people judged that the marginal costs of across-the-board increments in research do exceed the marginal gains—is simply to reduce the size of the explosion. Government could reduce its grants and in-house expenditures for research, with or without reallocation. Government could also have a powerful impact on the scale of university and foundation activities, if voters wished to do so, by making, say, only 50 percent of contributions tax deductible. Universities might then increase teaching loads and give less weight to publications in connection with promotions and salary increases, thus reducing the net rewards from publishing. Or, a tax per page of publication might have a similar effect. (All this is of course somewhat fanciful. Unless the prevailing mood among citizens changed, such steps would presumably not occur; for otherwise the forces that lead to the current policies would continue to do so.)

If the volume of information production—even across the board, including nonprofit research in the physical sciences—were reduced, would it have serious adverse repercussions? Would damping of the publish-or-perish motivation or reduction of government research-support turn off the Adam Smiths, the Keyneses, the Pasteurs, the Einsteins? Did the weaker research support that formerly existed prevent *additional* such scholars from emerging? Even if we lost 50 percent of the truly worthwhile contributions, would the slower rate of advance have a 10 percent chance of disastrous consequences? Would it cost more than would be saved? Or, for those who have more confidence than I do in the nonprofit system, should we be spending more to stimulate research? We should at least be asking such questions. Given the nonprofit incentives that we cannot avoid employing, there is little reason to regard the present volume and type of research as being optimal.

B. "Market Failures" in Other Nonprofit Impacts on Information

In other respects, too, I am impressed with the reasons to expect nonoptimality from the nonprofit system. Utility maximization in the nonprofit world seems like a Rube Goldberg mechanism, when one considers the effective constraints (which depend heavily on the incentives to monitor subordinate agencies and the monitorability of their activities). Consider regulation. It is no doubt economical to make profit-seeking R&D more averse to "Kepone episodes," yet having nonprofit regulatory agencies guide the invisible hand is often like having a blind man direct traffic. Policy evaluations, government investigations, hearings, providing information to consumers—all these activities suggest again that getting away from the profit motive does not fill the gaps left by "market failures" in the private sector. Not surprisingly, markets fail to exist even more often in the nonmarket sector than in the market sector.

FOOTNOTES

The author is professor of economics, Department of Economics.

In one section I have drawn on my paper [McKean (115)]. I am also indebted to the National Science Foundation, Grant No. SOC-76-11263, for enabling me to pursue related research on which I have also drawn.

1. See Clarkson (42), Davies (50), De Alessi (54), whose pages 645–648 present a succinct, helpful summary of utility-maximization models, and Alchian (4).

2. Clarkson, *op. cit.* To derive even this implication requires a number of auxiliary assumptions, including the assumption that the technology is not rapidly changing, which might cause private firms to have widely varying inputs until old capital wore out. Yet this might leave public enterprises unchanged for a long time.

3. Some models, instead of regarding the pressures as constraining utility maximizers, assume that officials seek to maximize an intermediate good—namely, votes or support. In such models, public entrepreneurs will in effect equalize the marginal productivity of their actions in terms of net support. Leverage and monitoring costs again help determine the constraints or opportunity sets. Along these lines, see Peltzman (132).

4. Assistant professors must publish frantically to get tenure; older professors work frenziedly for salary increases (as they see inflation eroding their retirement income) and also to advertise that they are not dead. Associate professors allegedly take time for a little rest and rehabilitation [Katz (86)].

5. For an excellent, wider-ranging analysis of incentives in universities, see Manne (107).

6. Another related result of these institutions is that there is relatively little penalty for muddy, obscure exposition; see Degnan (57).

7. As in the private sector, information production in the nonprofit sector is sometimes completely fraudulent. Among the highly publicized instances are Piltdown man, and allegedly, the research on the IQs of identical twins by Sir Cyril Burt.

8. See Walker (176). His main point is that in political science, new techniques or not, the percentage of articles pertaining to general topics remained about the same during the 1960s.

9. Those that start out with a large endowment may have fewer or at least different constraints. Dwight MacDonald (104) once wrote that "The Ford Foundation, which in 1953 moved . . . from an estate in Pasadena that was known to the staff as Itching Palms, is a large body of money completely surrounded by people who want some."

10. I hasten to concede that many of the above points apply to the present paper. It is imprecise, with no implications derived in refutable form. The information presented will not alter any incentives or affect the course of events. And so on.

11. Hitch and McKean (77). Nonmilitary officials also tend to emphasize capturable short-run payoffs; see *Chemicals and Health* (38), pp. 87–101.

12. The results of rewarding people on the basis of such proxies have been described by Adam Smith and many others. For example: "According to a new rule made by the King, whenever they (the engineers) changed the position of their guns, they were entitled to a pecuniary recompense. Accordingly, they passed all their time in uselessly changing about from place to place . . ." [Duke of Saint Simon (142), p. 360].

13. See Schneider (146), pp. 102–113 and 145–147. There are exceptions to all of these propositions. In this connection, for example, NSF has sought outside evaluation of some of its programs, as noted below.

14. *Garrison Diversion Unit Irrigation Project: Prospects and Problems*, Hearings before a Subcommittee of the Committee on Government Operations, House of Representatives, 94th Congress, 1st Session, Part 1, Sept. 15, 1975, and Part 2, Nov. 19, 1975, Washington, D.C., 1975. See especially the objections of the Canadian government, the U.S. Environmental Protection Agency, and economist Thomas M. Power (various pages).

For an enlightening discussion of some reasons why we should not expect objective analyses (and appraisal of the government analysis of the Trinity River Project in Northern California), see Shapiro (151).

15. On incentives to distort information within a bureaucracy, with the reporting of bombing scores and military capabilities as an example, see Downs (60). On selective dissemination of information within bureaucratic hierarchies, see Tullock (170), pp. 137–141.

16. Much of Wilensky's book pertains to information-acquisition in general within government. His criticisms of government are not harsh, yet he does describe many of the limitations on public intelligence activities.

17. One does not necessarily expect nonprofits to have greater variety of *output* designs than profit-seeking enterprises, for the latter will cater more frequently to individual-consumer tastes, while nonprofit managers can usually gain from producing a few standardized products, such as public housing.

18. See *Chemical Week* (36), pp. 37–38. This search, incidentally, brings out again the interdependency between innovation and the level of venturesome research on other problems: the second substitute above was "discovered accidentally by a group of Lilly chemists researching an anti-fungal antibiotic."

19. We now at least have better fragmentary notions about possible correlations than at the time the Delaney clause was enacted. We have now observed several substances (tobacco, estrogen, VCM's, asbestos fiber) that are carcinogens in animal tests and that also appear at "human dosage" to cause malignancies in people.

20. For example, an important step toward the realization that lithium could help manic-depressives was the injection of uric acid from patients into guinea pigs, which produced agitation in the animals, and then the injection of a lithium compound, which quieted the animals; Kline (91), pp. 135–136.

21. For instance, see *Chemicals and Health* (38), various pages (e.g., pp. 5–25, 87–101). See also Ember (63), particularly p. 1117, concerning the additional emphasis gradually being placed on epidemiological studies by the National Cancer Institute.

22. Several assumptions about the functioning of the two arrangements obviously underlie such statements. Moreover, I am neglecting many of the costs and benefits of regulation and am focusing attention on only one set of consequences.

23. I do not mean that government or other nonprofits produce worrisome amounts of highly useful information. Often in fact there are pressures for government agencies to act without getting sufficient information in the sense of "pertinent" or "high quality" knowledge. See Cornell, Noll, and Weingast (48).

24. Blaug (28). Blaug's conclusion—that the work suggests the deterioration of the human-capital research program—may be more nearly correct. Perhaps then it casts doubt on the social value, at least thus far, of human-capital research, one illustrative component of social science research.

25. A study by Harvard economist Richard B. Freeman, cited in the *Wall Street Journal*, Nov. 18, 1976, p. 1.

26. Perhaps it should be mentioned that many nonprofit expenditures on this general information-producing process don't even affect the volume of information, whatever its quality or worth. For example, the National Science Foundation (whose programs have been, in my judgment, relatively useful and have certainly helped me personally) has had a large Science Development Program (over $200 million in total). Evaluation of the program (requested by NSF itself) suggests that the program did enable the grantees to expand the size of their faculties but did not significantly increase the publication rates of individual faculty members, the graduate student enrollments, Ph.D. outputs, or the attractiveness of Ph.D.'s to employers. See Drew (61).

27. Some would surely deny this if welfare a few hundred years hence rather than the well-being of existing populations were one's criterion. Some argue rather persuasively that we should hope the Green Revolution fails so as to induce population adjustments soon rather than late (to economize on other exhaustible resources) and that, to postpone ultimately disastrous thermal pollution, one must hope that we do not discover fusion power. For interesting discussions, see Heilbroner (74), pp. 31–58.

There is also a not-so-long-run question about the worth of progress because of the "treadmill effect." We apparently get used to a higher level of living quickly, adjust our expectations, and subsequently experience as much disappointment as before. Our unending lament is, "What has GNP done for me *lately*?" (Along such lines, see Scitovsky (149), pp. 133–145.)

28. It is not easy for me to ask such questions, for I am biting the hand that feeds me. Nor can I bring myself to give harsh answers; about as far as I can go is to say (switching figures of speech) that perhaps the Emperor has no pants.

DELIVERED COMMENTS

Andrew Whinston (Purdue University).   Most of my comments will be directed to Matt Lindsay's paper. Lindsay is investigating the problem of determining how government decides which services to provide relative to the private sector.

I think a more interesting endeavor would be to investigate this problem in the context of a mixed system with government intervention and other types of property rights arrangements for regulating private behavior.

Lindsay suggests we have to use a fixed allocation of costs if we are to avoid the misrepresentation of preferences inherent in public goods demand. We must have a mechanism for deciding on the level of the public good, such as the size of a bridge, if the project is to be completed in a private setting. In other words, we must have some kind of rule which takes preferences of the different individuals in the group and comes out with a resulting agreed-upon solution. In that context we get into a problem if we pick a social welfare function that violates one of Arrow's axioms, and is nondictatorial.

So if we pursue this question from a purely social choice point of view, we would face some problems. In the social welfare function, what Arrow axiom will be violated? What function will be selected? How susceptible is the function to misrepresentation? What is the information structure? Are logrolling and coalition formation present?

Alternatively, one can look at public goods determination by the use of taxes, where there is not initial fixed cost allocation. Here we find that revealed preferences of the individuals involved for the good which they are going to jointly agree upon leads us to the "Clark tax," to which Lindsay refers. The Clark tax is a tax which is placed on an individual but is a function of the effect of the individual on the rest of the group. Lindsay feels that it is unrealistic to count on a procedure that will yield this information and mentions that we don't see the tax being used.

There are some problems with the Clark tax. Suppose a corporation is counting on different division heads to give sincere information on the use of corporate resources; in such a situation the Clark tax reduces incentives, which may lead corporate managers to give completely random information because their payment is really a function of what other people are going to do. In this case individuals will reveal information which is strategically in their interest but not necessarily true information.

I also want to comment briefly on the bargaining question that Lindsay raised. I would place bargaining in the framework of game theory alluding to Jim Buchanan's club theory. If we are interested, for example, in the provision of collective goods and the allocation of benefits which are in the *core*, we might worry about subgroups of the participants pulling out and forming their own swimming club or building their own bridge. Thus, we want to look at the stability of the payment structure in the context of bargaining. We may also want to look at the optimal size of the collective group, since we may have a size of a group which is too large or too small in terms of the type of service. The cost involved in this determination in itself might be inherently unstable, so that we lose a core solution.

My final comment concerns the role of government. It seemed to me that one should use a game theoretic framework, with a particular producer and potential consumers of a good. The government in this model sets up some ground rule, some set of property rights, and we then observe the kind of solution that emerges, focusing on the particular gain and the stability properties of that gain. When we vary the property rights, we are going to get different types of allocation problems and different stability characteristics. It may be interesting to look at this type of parametric analysis to see if these lead to some interesting types of government control or intervention.

James M. Buchanan (Virginia Polytechnic Institute and State University). We can acknowledge, with Matt Lindsay, that early formulations of public goods theory, emerging directly from the "market failure" emphasis of theoretical welfare economics, embodied surprising naivete about the way governments function. We can go further and acknowledge, again with Lindsay, that early variants of public choice theory, directly inspired by Wicksell, unduly concentrated on demand-driven models of governmental processes to the neglect of supply-side influences. In recent years, however, an increasing number of public choice theorists have introduced supply-side influences into their models, including some in which these elements dominate the results. As things now stand, we do need more positive analysis of the way governments actually function. Lindsay is surely right when he argues that no case has been made for any direct connection between public goods, technologically defined, and government organization.

I want, however, to shift away from public goods theory to some basic issues in political philosophy that are suggested by Lindsay's paper. He defines governments as those entities that "have the undisputed power to redistribute rights (hence, wealth in the broadest sense) among their citizens." I should challenge this definitional statement. Governments, in fact, do not have "undisputed" powers. Here I would like to replace the word "undisputed" with "unlimited" or "unconstrained," words more in keeping with what I take to be Lindsay's basic intent. Governments possess *some* (perhaps considerable) powers to redistribute rights among citizens, but these powers, even in the years that are drawing increasingly close to 1984, are limited. The United States government today cannot take you bodily out of this conference room and put you in chains, merely on the whim of some bureaucrat. More importantly for my argument, it is questionable, in a normative sense, whether we as analysts should proceed on the "as if" presumption that such powers do exist. For all its battering, for all the subversion successfully carried out by the legal positivists, the United States Constitution still has meaningful power inherent in it as an institution.

Why do we need a positive analysis of government enterprise? Surely, we must answer this question as follows: We need to understand how governments operate, or may be predicted to operate, under differing institutional conditions, in order to construct and then to choose a set of institutions that will *constrain* governmental powers.

My essential problem with Lindsay's paper (and, indeed, with most monopoly-state models) is that I do not see how we can move readily from his definitional base to any analysis and discussion of this fundamental constitutional issue. And who here can deny that this is *the* issue of our time?

Let me now move to Rol McKean's paper. As usual when I see a paper by McKean, I was informed, impressed, and amused. Rol's wit shines through these papers, and his mildly cynical skepticism is appealing. But I am assigned a role as critic, and I do have a fundamental criticism of the paper in the large.

My concern may be summarized by saying that Rol McKean has forgotten what Frank Knight tried to teach him. By saying that Rol has forgotten what Knight taught him, I mean that his paper seems to be based on the adoption of what Knight, and Hayek, have called the "scientistic" interpretation of social science, including economics. This is the interpretation or attitude which suggests, at least by implication, that "scientific solutions" to "problems" offer potential salvation. I recall that one of Knight's critical review articles was entitled, "Salvation by Science." But, as he so well emphasized, the problems of political economy are only to a very limited extent "scientific" in the standard sense of the term. Is there really any "scientific" content to the problem of minimum-wage legislation, and by inference to teen-aged minority unemployment? Of course not. There is, however, a *problem* of "Intelligence and Democratic Action," again to use the title of Knight's last book.

McKean is at least somewhat ambivalent toward the "scientistic" position; he should be given credit where credit is due. And I should make clear that Rol McKean probably would fall toward the Knight-Hayek end of the "scientistic" spectrum if we tried to array economists methodologically. But the observed fact that Rol slips so easily into the "scientistic" camp serves both to illustrate and to emphasize my basic critique. Let me cite but one passage from McKean's paper:

> Needless to say, the gains from discovering information that would help us reduce war, unemployment, crime, injustice, and other social problems would be enormous, but, if the probabilities of success are low enough, our nonprofit institutions may be allocating too much effort to certain lines of inquiry. If this is so, let me emphasize that the culprit is not the personnel or their quality but rather the inherent difficulty of the problems and *thence the difficulties of peer (or any other) monitoring.* In these circumstances, nonprofit incentives are especially likely to lead to misallocations. From the standpoint of my argument, thus, the key difference between the physical sciences and the social sciences is the degree to which research is appraisable and monitorable.

I do not for a moment think that McKean means to say what he appears to me to be saying in this passage. Surely he must agree with me that monitoring (or its absence) has very little to do with the alleged "failures" of social science to resolve socioeconomic-political difficulties. Surely he must agree that, if some perfect monitor were to be invented tomorrow, there would be very little change in our progress toward the "solution" of problems of social order. We might, as a result, be able to eliminate more easily a lot of wasted research effort, but we should not move one whit closer to the ultimate objective of living together in a more prosperous, more peaceful, more orderly, and more just world.

It should be evident that I share McKean's conclusions about the wastage of research effort in the soft sciences. And I tend to support his proposal for across-the-board cuts in support of such research. But before we go too far in this direction, let us look at some of the spillover effects. It would do little good to reduce research support and to increase teaching loads if the subject matter taught remains that which the wasted research has been falsely aimed at resolving. If the basic problems are not "scientific," education based on the premise that they are will surely do more harm than good.

I am not suggesting that education, in what we call the social or soft sciences, be abandoned as socially unproductive. Far from it. I am suggesting that education "as positive science" be redirected. There are *principles* of economics to be taught, the most important of which is the principle of the spontaneous coordination of the market. The economist who succeeds in conveying some understanding of this principle to his students (or his readers) has earned his bread. But this principle has little or nothing to do with the testing of hypotheses, and it can be transmitted without so much as a mention of a regression routine. A general understanding of this principle may, nonetheless, lead to consensus and agreement on social (governmental) action that can do something toward "solving" the problems of social order just noted. *There is no other way.* Which returns me to Matt Lindsay's definition of government. How can education research and analysis help us do anything but "know" if the government's powers are, in fact, unlimited? And beyond control?

GOVERNMENTAL ORGANIZATIONS: DISCUSSION

Lindsay. In response to Andy Whinston's comments, there were a considerable number of topics that I couldn't cover in the circulated paper. One of these topics is how government or private organizations decide how much to provide. Since most of my discussion was framed in the context of perfect information where everyone knew individual demand functions for public goods, the important question that emerges is: how is the surplus that is produced by providing public goods distributed among the various users? A lot of time has been devoted to discussing whether people are going to reveal their preferences or reveal their demand for public goods and how this information problem rules the outcomes that emerge from these particular transactions, regardless of whether they are governmentally or privately organized. It seems to me that this conflict is a bit misplaced. In the provision of most public goods, we see that the valuations of the people involved, such as a water-flood control project, are obvious. In this case you simply esti-

Economics of Nonproprietary Organizations
Research in Law and Economics, Supplement 1, pages 239-242
Copyright © 1980 by JAI Press Inc.
All rights of reproduction in any form reserved.
ISBN: 0-89232-132-6

mate the damage on people's property from a particular flood. This estimate is probably a good measure of the value individuals place on a water control project. This is why I didn't spend much time talking about this type of problem in the paper.

For different reasons, I agree that the demand revelation literature is currently in the area of negative marginal productivity. Before more resources are devoted to the exploration of these schemes, I would like to see some groups actually attempt to employ Clark-type taxes to make decisions.

With respect to Buchanan's comments, I don't really disagree with his charge that I've oversimplified the definition of the government. Obviously no government has undisputed or unlimited power over its citizens. It is an oversimplification, though, to say that the proof of that assertion is that any bureaucrat does not have the right to whisk us out of this room and throw us into prison. My argument is that an agency is a government if someone in it may throw me into jail, and this is true regardless of the decision process of that agency.

McKean.   It is difficult to respond to Buchanan's criticism. There is, however, an issue of what kind of information that is likely to be produced in the various disciplines or research programs. Each of us then has to make up his mind on the basis of those expected values. This topic was prompted by individuals who have said that our physical science capabilities have outstripped our knowledge of how to live together. My judgment is that this observation is correct and our inability to solve some of the problems of living together in large groups is likely to have a tragic outcome. Unfortunately, many people have jumped to the conclusion that a Manhattan project in the social sciences, to improve our knowledge, is in order. I would like to have better information to feed into the decision-making apparatus, but have lost hope that any will shed light on some of the basic problems about how to live together in large groups.

Kenneth Clarkson (University of Miami).   One of McKean's major conclusions is that we cannot test most of the propositions about government enterprises. I would like to suggest that some testing is possible. Government can be viewed as a collection of different ownership arrangements with different objectives and different constraints. Within this context is a complete spectrum of constantly changing rules. In many cases we can derive how those rules are going to change the opportunity sets of decision-makers as they become more or less binding for certain activities. In addition many of these rules do not apply to all governmental units. We may be able to test for differences in the types of information that are produced, inputs that are used, and other dimensions of economic activity. One only has to look at the Federal Register for one week to find that governmental rules are changed very frequently and in many cases in significant ways. Consequently I am more optimistic since I believe there are a large number of possible good research topics.

Burton Weisbrod (University of Wisconsin). Jim Buchanan pointed out in his comment that the power of government is not unlimited. In Lindsay's paper, there's a discussion of the fundamental difference between private and governmental organizations. Governments do have at least one attribute which differentiates them from that set of institutions regarded as private. They have the power to redistribute rights among their citizens. The use of this power is unavailable to private institutions in their normal dealings, hence transactions with and among them may not result in decreased wealth for anyone. I think we may exaggerate the difference between governments and private markets. Consider the institutional form of private governments, such as professional baseball leagues. Since there is no compulsion in these organizations, no one voluntarily becomes a party to these private governments unless he anticipates being better off. However, we should distinguish between the anticipation of being made better off and actuality of being made better off. I suspect that Charlie Finley, the owner of the Oakland A's, was very upset when the private government to which he belongs said that he could not sell certain baseball players. The point is that he made a decision to buy a baseball franchise and that decision caused him to be a part of a private institution which acts very much like governments. It imposes fines, it establishes rules, and it has power. The existence of private governments illustrates the proposition that the distinction between a governmental mechanism and the private one is not quite as sharp as we have generally suggested.

Steven Cheung (University of Washington). Just about every country in the noncommunist world has high-rise buildings which are owned by separate individuals. In the United States they are called condominiums. But, as a rule, there is usually some kind of organization with every owner getting one vote. The organization establishes which activities are permitted or prohibited in their set of bylaws, which are determined by the majority rule. People entering into this kind of contract know the set of rights when they buy the building. Is this a government? If you tell me that it is not, then I can show you conclusively that there is no such thing as a government. If you tell me that the condominium is a government, then government is simply a formal contract which you sometimes sign yourself and other times you don't. I've gone through half a dozen high-rise contracts in various Asian countries and have found that one vote per household apparently is common. Sometimes the vote is proportionate to the value of the asset involved. What I'm suggesting here is that it is difficult to get a definition of government. Furthermore, it is no good defining government by coercion, because there is no higher coercive power than that which we have over our kids, but we don't call this relationship government.

GENERAL DISCUSSION

Henry Manne (University of Miami). I have placed a couple of shills in the audience to review, in provocative fashion, our progress to date and, perhaps, state where they think we would like to go. I have reference to Ken Clarkson and Donald Martin.

Clarkson. The development of theorems about nonproprietary status is fairly new to the profession. Most of our research and knowledge about nonproprietary organizations can be divided into two main categories. The first examines the effects of alternative constraints on incentives by deriving implications from utility maximization. The second attempts to explain how various institutions have evolved, including the economic rationale for the formulation of various organizational rules. It is clear, from the literature, that we have begun to identify some of the more crucial elements for analysis. It turns out that certain characteristics of organizations, such as the profit status, affect decision-makers' incentive structures and influence behavior. Yet we have a long way to go for a complete understanding of nonproprietary organizations. There are a large variety of constraints, both natural and institutional, that have not been analyzed and can affect implications. Steve Cheung's paper, for example, shows us that other factors, such as transactions costs, must be incorporated when we examine pricing in nonproprietary organizations.

I'd like to try to identify some questions that are important for understanding institutional rules and their development. Weisbrod's paper

Economics of Nonproprietary Organizations
Research in Law and Economics, Supplement 1, pages 243-256
Copyright © 1980 by JAI Press, Inc.
All rights of reproduction in any form reserved.
ISBN: 0-89232-132-6

suggests that organizations' characteristics are useful for explaining behavior and that collectiveness is the key variable. But that variable is difficult to link with actual behavior. I'd like to suggest that there are other factors that yield a much richer set of implications. First, the form of the organization, such as governmental or mutual, will be important in the model. Second, the structure of financing such as lump sum or per unit, as well as the source of financing, such as endowment or government grant, will be included in the model. Third, the method for "selling" the output will be part of the model. For example, do the individuals who finance the output actually purchase it? Finally, the tax status of the organization will also be important. In each case these attributes can be linked to the incentive structures of nonproprietary organizations.

Martin.   One thing that struck me about the conference, and I must confess, about my own work as well, was our inability to come up with a good understanding of why some organizational forms are chosen over others. Some of us have suggested that nonprofits and nonproprietaries arise because of tax reasons. This seems very obvious at first blush. But taxing ownership characteristics, or ownership forms, is a relatively new phenomenon and nonproprietaries and nonprofits have existed for quite a long time before such taxes were introduced. This is the case not only in our own society, but in other societies as well. Other conferees have suggested that nonprofits and nonproprietaries exist for reasons of collectiveness of output. This, of course, was explicit in Burt Weisbrod's paper. Still others have suggested that there are differences in the cost of monitoring output, relative to the cost of monitoring contracts. Here I am referring to Thompson's work. Maybe that is a fruitful area to probe. A few have suggested that it's really government pressure that prevents some organizations from being proprietary. The relevant and important point is that the ownership form is not an exogenous factor. If we're going to predict behavior of organizations based on their differences in ownership form, or differences in constraints, one must ultimately answer the question why those constraints were chosen in the first place.

Whinston.   I think most of us in economics realize that nowadays economics, at least as it is reported in the journals, has become extremely formal. Even at the level of graduate training we usually look at economic questions in terms of the Arrow-DeBreu model. You have the feeling that students will spit on you if you are not in Hilbert space. I certainly don't want to argue that this is what this group should be doing. But it seems to me that we have people at this conference with very strong *intuitive* feelings about different aspects of resource allocation economics. Perhaps there should be some attempt in the future to use a more formal means of presenting these feelings than, I felt, was available in the papers. I would also like to suggest that the authors consider using game theory as a tool in analyzing these problems. I have no specific suggestions—it's just that many of you have not thought about it. It may be worthwhile to give it a little thought.

On the distinction between proprietary and nonproprietary organizational forms, several people have raised the issue that the distinction really isn't that clearly defined and I find myself uncomfortable with it. I think that every once in a while we lapse into the notion of profit and nonprofit, and I don't think that is really what we have in mind. In fact, in abstract theory, the competitive firm should earn zero abnormal profits in the long run. The distinction seems to relate more to the nature of the firm's financing. This may be a fruitful avenue for nonproprietary studies. I think some of the ideas from the finance literature will be useful to you. I don't say that these ideas will carry over, but I think they should be understood by people at this conference and the kinds of problems that are facing finance theories should have equivalents in the nonproprietary area.

John Osborn (University of Miami). I've been trying to think about this a little bit from the legal side, which has been hard because I haven't understood a lot of the economics that has been presented. The paper that really impressed me was the one by Burton Weisbrod. He has developed a definition of the charitable firm. That is one of the critical problems now facing lawyers. From a legal standpoint, the way you determine whether an organization is charitable is by going to the IRS and asking them to issue a ruling, that you are a charitable organization under Section 501(c)(3). In important cases, the IRS issues a revenue ruling which is like a little case that a judge would write out. The IRS has finally issued so many of those rulings that there is now, collected into a kind of critical mass, a sufficient body of law that you can draw out general principles, and for the first time get real understanding of what is the fundamental nature of the charitable organization. Developing an overall index has become a very important thing to do, in the legal field, and I think this is the thrust of Burton's paper.

Manne. Although it's true, as Don Martin suggests, that the influence of the present tax laws alters property rights structures, and we know that this may in turn affect behavior, nevertheless this cannot get us any closer to a general theory of ownership or to the discovery of some overriding characteristics that are worthy of deeper exploration.

On the other hand, it seems to me that Martin and Clarkson have missed an important question that Bill Meckling had answered for us the other day. Perhaps an illustration will set us all in the right direction. Roughly 80 percent or more of all the private colleges and universities that exist in this country today were founded in the early to middle years of the nineteenth century. Subsequent study done at the Columbia School of Education indicated that (there may be some overlap here) of all private universities, about 98 or 99 percent of them had religious origins in one sense or another. Either they were theological schools, training ministers, or they were designed to inculcate children with a certain faith or simply to guarantee that people of a particular belief exposed their children only to children of similar backgrounds. What can we learn from that experience? It seems to me that the founders of such organizations were trying to escape the consumer sovereignty discipline or influence of the market. What they attempted to do was set up a trust device, a charitable trust device, that could exist in perpetuity. The Baptist church established the colleges that it wanted, the Catholic church established the colleges it wanted and Pierre Goodrich established the Liberty Fund, all under this doctrine, and all protected from the influence of market forces. The significant thing to realize, and as far as I can see, the universal characteristic of everything we have talked about, is that the charitable trust does this by preventing anyone's being able to capture a present capitalized value by transferring nonproprietary assets. That is what the founders of these organizations wanted. The managers of foundations and charitable organizations also do not want to compete; they want to make decisions free of market forces.

Martin.   That is an attractive hypothesis, but I have problems understanding why is it always the case that they want to avoid those market consequences to which you refer.

Alchian.   For the same reason I don't give my children all my wealth until I die, I will try to impose my preference pattern on succeeding generations. One way to do that is to not let them have private property rights. And when I do die, if I want to make sure that wealth is used the way I want it to be used in the succeeding generations, one way to be able to do that is to *not* assign private property rights to the assets I leave behind. If I can put it in one of these trusts that Manne mentions, I've got that future generation tied up. I don't know of any other explanation.

Meckling.   Governments that promote labor-managed firms never want to give the laborers ownership of the assets. They want to give them rights in the stream, which depends on their employment, but they never really want to give them title to the firm in the sense of capitalized value. This is Alchian's point. Once government gives labor those titles it loses control over the firm.

Martin.   I'm very sympathetic to that view, but the thing that makes me uneasy is that it sounds adversarial. Take the example of a club. I have a group of members of that club that is making decisions. I have a collectivity of individuals who are voluntarily constraining their rights to transfer ownership, or transfer use of rights, in that organization. They themselves choose to do that. Now, are they doing so because they are afraid their partners will transfer rights in a way that they do not appreciate or are they doing it for some other reason? It is not just a single individual who wants to make sure that his children or his dependents behave in a way consistent with his performance. I would like to be able to sell my union card, for example, to someone else. I just do not want anybody else to do it.

Alchian. That's a different proposition than the one Meckling was talking about, but it's not inconsistent. There are other reasons also for using nonproprietary organizations.

McKean. There has been some discussion of nonprofit versus non-proprietary or noncapitalist. I am certain we do not have in mind the railroads or something like that when we speak of a nonprofit organization. But what is difficult, and is the problem on which Weisbrod and others have focused, is trying to decide what organizations, in effect, are profit-seekers in disguise. Which organizations have the ability to appropriate residuals and which do not? Even among the churches, which we think of as nonproprietary, there are some borderline cases—the Moonies, Reverend Ike, Oral Roberts, perhaps. Some of the organizations seem to be awfully close to profit-seekers in disguise and yet others certainly are not. Now maybe I'm wrong about that, but I think there are some ambiguities.

Whinston. On the question of market forces, again I'm not sure I completely understood what Professors Manne and Alchian had in mind. If we take charities as an example of nonproprietaries, they seem to be extremely competitive. One case I'm familiar with is the National Foundation of Muscular Dystrophy and the Muscular Dystrophy Association. They are constantly suing each other in court for infringement on markets. One has a Jerry Lewis telethon and the other will run some other telethon during the same time and each is suing the other for a variety of reasons.

Alchian. I want to make two comments to Whinston. First, in a trivial, but fundamental sense, everybody is competitive whether they are proprietor, bureaucrat, laborer, or homemaker. We should not be surprised to observe competition when resources are scarce. Second, I want to address attention to the comments you made yesterday and with which I have sympathy. I refer to your plea for a little more formalism. I am discouraged because we have made so little progress in using the techniques of mathematics or any kind of formal logical analysis. Let me indicate the nature of the problem that has been so difficult to solve. We go to the blackboard and write on the blackboard a utility function for somebody, subject to a wealth constraint. Every student can go through that and derive implications symbolically. But when I ask them what that X, the good, means, I get statements like, "that's the number of potatoes, or the number of cars you have." I ask them, then, "What do you mean by have?" They say nothing. I have observed no success, so far, in defining what "have" means, or what that X means in the utility function. For example, I have a typewriter in my office but it isn't my typewriter. I have one at home; that is my typewriter. Nothing in economic theory distinguishes those two goods.

All our current economic theory is based on the private property constraint. The utility function and the constraint are based on the private property model. What we are trying to do here is to get away from that model and see if we can formalize the concept of "have" in some other sense than the private property sense which is itself never defined, except in terms of PX_1 plus PX_2 plus $PX_3 = W$. When you dig beneath that, you get all these ambiguities. If anybody can suggest a way to make those concepts analytically tractable, I'd like to see them. The same is true for all our mathematical methods because we just have not got a clear understanding of what the word "have" means. The lawyers talk about it, but they have no analytical techniques.

Whinston identifies what I think is the main obstacle: the ability to formalize through analytical techniques which we can then run through and get implications. It is a tough problem, but I don't want to let that difficulty go unemphasized here.

Clarkson. That's just half the problem, because we find when we move to the nonproprietary status, we move from the wealth-maximization all-encompassing rule, which is relatively easy to specify mathematically, to one in which we have a large number of rules that have been placed by administering authorities to prevent certain types of deviations. When you look at government bureaus, for example, instead of observing just cost minimization, you find out that you are faced with the Code of Federal Regulations that slap thousands of additional constraints on the production function, and you have Office of Management and Budget circulars and budget procedures. These rules and procedures complicate things considerably more than a simple constraint. We have literally, a very complex set of constraints sitting on top of this other problem.

Meckling. I simply want to make a point about what McKean said earlier in terms of how you look at this whole business. He suggested thinking about motives of organizations. He was talking about the motives of churches; which were the profit-seekers and which were not. Viewing organizations as if they were human beings with motives has very serious limitations. As I said earlier, you really ought to be looking at those organizations as a *process* within which there exists individuals who are trying to maximize utility. I'm not saying that it's useless to use anthropomorphic assumptions, but I think for many kinds of problems, especially the one we are talking about, you are going to be strictly limited in what you can say. If you go around treating the organization as if it were a human being having motives of its own, you will in some ways confuse positive and normative concepts in examining different kinds of organizations. As long as there is uncertainty in economic activity, the residuals (difference between revenue and costs) are going to be there and somebody is going to bear the costs or get the benefits. It doesn't really make any difference. All that really matters is what kind of rules there are about how residuals are to be allocated.

Buchanan.   I'd like to make a point that I think represents a disagreement with the philosophy behind several comments made today. I think the lawyer and the economist have different purposes here. On the one hand, I can understand the legal interest in trying to develop a taxonomy of profit and nonprofit characteristics for tax purposes. To the economist, on the other hand, this is just wasted energy. It seems to me that to try to distinguish and sharply categorize ownership forms is pretty much wasted effort. There are no pure profit institutions, there are no pure nonprofit institutions; they all fall in along an array. We recognize that constraints matter, that constraints differ as between institutions, and that this has effects on behavior. But I don't think we are going in the right direction if we try to create sharp distinctions.

On another note, the one thing that I have found lacking at this conference, except for Earl Thompson's paper and some of Alchian's remarks, is reference to "rent-seeking." That is the area where, it seems to me, there is some theoretical progress of late. There is more development still to come, of course, in these formal models. Rent-seeking objectives are surely applicable where you have constraints diverge from those consistent with pure profit motivation, and yet there has been very little of it discussed here. I'm thinking of the work of Gordon Tullock, Dick Posner, and Ann Krueger, in particular. There have been four of five basic articles where the investigators have looked at the particular opportunity sets that are imposed on decision-makers and derived implications that suggest that people are going to try to compete away existing rents whether or not entry is permitted. In other words, you are going to get dissipation of those rents as a result of competition. In some cases, this process is going to lead to a worse situation than otherwise. It is very important to model these rent-seeking institutions and to generate implications about where you can expect rent-seeking to emerge. I think this is an area, to echo earlier comments by Andy Whinston, where the comparative statics simply have not been worked out. Nobody has really worked out the formal model.

Martin.   I don't think that I have worked out a formal model to my satisfaction, or for that matter to Professor Oi's satisfaction, but I thought that it was clear from my paper that that was my intention. I specifically discussed the comparative advantage that unions had in producing rents for their members and how they would be concerned about those rents being dissipated by competition among members. I further conjectured that one of the reasons that unions prohibit the transfer of property rights—pardon me—the transfer of membership cards to would-be members was to economize on the cost of monitoring or policing rent dissipation.

Alchian.   Is your proposition that the unions do not allow cards to be sold because that will destroy their rents?

Martin.   I said that if the collective action of members, that is, strike threats, can result in the creation of rents, there is going to be competition among individual members and would-be members to capture those rents by methods that will threaten the union as a cartel.

Alchian.   The reason, I conjecture, why they don't let them have private property in membership is that they will buy and sell that rent and reveal to society the monopoly value of labor legislation. Once this has occurred, unions will be subject to a tightening of regulation.

Martin.   I don't believe that.

Alchian.   I make the proposition that as soon as unions permit private property in cards, they become an *explicit* cartel, obtaining rents in that fashion and we, society, may not tolerate that. Now you have an alternative theory: how do we go about verifying one or the other? All members should want those rights, *so long as society lets us keep those rights.* I thought you were denying that proposition, were you?

Martin.   Yes! But not all legitimate cartels recognized by society enjoy proprietary rights in the rents they generate. For example, airlines do not have private property in their monopoly routes and TV stations do not have private property in their licenses. Isn't your proposition rejected by the evidence?

As a union member, I'm worrying about my neighbor. I am worried that his activity or his action is going to dissipate some of my rent through competition. He may sell his card to an undesirable person, one that cheats on the "standard rate," or curries favor with the boss, or supplies some other threat to the solidarity of the union.

Alchian.   How is he going to cheat if you have controls on him?

Martin.   Prohibition of union card sales is part of the control mechanism, a manifestation of economizing on the costs of rent dissipation. Other controls, such as union discipline, premembership screening, violence, may be relatively costly at the margin for unions whose membership numbers in the tens of thousands.

De Alessi.   Current dissatisfaction with the apparent failure of received economic theory to explain certain classes of phenomena has led to a reappraisal of various conditions underlying the formal structure of the theory. Until recently, pure theorists typically hypothesized, explicitly or implicitly, that all property rights were private and fully allocated, and that search, transaction, and enforcement costs were equal to zero. Relaxing these conditions has permitted some dramatic extensions of economic theory and opened the way for further advances.

This conference is focusing on the economic behavior of proprietary and nonproprietary organizations. What is really at issue, however, is the economic effect of differences in institutional constraints which alter the incentive structures and, therefore, the choices of individuals within organizations characterized by different structures of property rights. Another important issue is the choice and survival of alternative institutional arrangements.

Weisbrod. I wanted to comment on a point that Don Martin raised in his opening remarks, and I think it was really a very important question. Namely, why a particular organizational structure is chosen. He pointed out, I think absolutely correctly, that the form of an institution is not appropriately treated as an exogenous variable, but rather as something which is itself a response to both the opportunities that are technologically available on the one hand, and demands on the other. I'd like to suggest one possible explanation, among many, for why a nonprofit form—and here I'm talking about private rather than governmental units—may be preferred. My hypothesis is focused on the points that Don Martin and Louis De Alessi raised a few moments ago: monitoring costs, information costs and, to use a word that I used in a comment yesterday, *trust.* I speak of the need for trusting in a relationship in which one party to a transaction has considerably more information than the other, regarding characteristics of the commodity being traded.

I suggest a hypothetical experiment we might all perform in our minds—to consider how, as individuals, we would react if a for-profit firm went into the charity business. The kind of example I have in mind, is to imagine a firm, Charity Incorporated, that opens up a shop somewhere in our neighborhood and sells units of charity for, taking an arbitrary price, $10.00 per unit. What I mean by selling charity is the following. You go into that store, it looks just like any other store, there is a clerk behind the counter, and you say I'd like to buy X units of charity. That is, you are proposing to give, say three units or $30.00 to some deserving person. The clerk writes out a receipt, three units at $10.00 per unit and he says $30.00 please, and he gives you a receipt. You have purchased three units of charity. My question is, do you think that such an institution would do well? Indeed, would it even survive? Let me add the assumption that there are no special tax laws. I think the reason that Charity Incorporated would not long endure, relative to United Fund, a competitor, is that we wouldn't trust it. That is to say, the costs of monitoring its output, the costs of determining whether in fact it is giving the money in ways that we would like, are so high that we would not want to deal with that organization. By contrast, if we could find an organization in which we have reason to believe that the managers are not trying to maximize their money income, there may be some reason for believing that what they would do would be closer to what we would like to see them doing. Some anecdotal evidence consistent with this theme is the organizational structure of nursing homes today; it is heavily "nonprofit."

Meckling.   I don't believe that I can infer from what you said anything different about the behavior of the managers who run the Community Chest from those that would run a for-profit charity. It may be true that there is some difference, but I don't believe you can explain it in terms of information cost or anything that you presented in your own discussion.

Lindsay.   They don't really act like everybody else. I think if you look at charitable organizations, particularly churches, they are populated by a very special sort of person. This goes back to what Thompson was talking about earlier and Weisbrod had stated just a few moments ago. I mean, *trust* is important and proprietary organizations typically are not populated by people that are trustworthy. There are very special dedicated people in these organizations, they are very interested in the welfare of other people.

Alchian.   What do you mean by trustworthy?

Lindsay.   You can predict how these people are going to behave. They are not going to take the money and put it in their own pocket and spend it on Cadillacs.

Alchian.   There *are* Charities Incorporated! If you want to get money for a charity there are private firms that will do so for a profit and distribute that money for you. They exist. Look in the yellow pages. You can hire people to go out and collect funds for you. Then you hire someone else to distribute them. They are just like a standard business firm. We just do not recognize them as such.

Whinston.   When I went out in the world, the one thing my father told me was don't give to charity. This advice reflected the years he spent auditing one of those New York charities, and as far as he could tell they were operating, as many of us have said, as a secret profit-making organization, but they had this aura of a nonprofit firm.

McKean.   Unless you could have competition among numerous Charities Incorporated, it's a little hard to see how that residual profit would be determined other than as a contract between donors and this firm, saying in effect, we guarantee to deliver X dollars to charities. You would have to monitor that arrangement just as you monitor, or to the same extent, the nonproprietary charitable organizations.

Clarkson. Another kind of institutional arrangement is one where entrepreneurs go to the various organizations that are engaged in charitable activities, such as hospitals and the YMCA, and ask how much these organizations are currently collecting from their individual fundraising efforts. Entrepreneurs of this Charity Incorporated could then offer a higher guaranteed level of funds if they were given exclusive collection rights. Acceptance of the offer would permit Charity Incorporated to approach employers and employees with a cost-reducing method of donating to various charities. The method would permit the parties to allocate charity donations the way they want them, and would save significant transaction costs. Charity Incorporated would provide a minimum level of donations to each charity, but these entrepreneurial middlemen would take a residual payment which often turns out to be quite large. This residual, however, doesn't threaten their nonprofit status because they can pay themselves high wages and high nonpecuniary benefits. I assert that this describes the United Fund and, to me, they are about as distrustful as anything that I have run across. The question I raise is, why would a different form of Charity Incorporated be any more distrustful?

Weisbrod. It seems important to me to distinguish between those cases in which monitoring costs are small; that is to say, where it is very easy for the buyer to know when he is getting what he wishes to get, and those cases in which that assumption does not hold very closely. In the former case, ownership distinctions may not be important. In the latter case, the prospective buyer may have to choose between taking his chances because he doesn't really know what he is getting, or incurring some costs in another form, perhaps more explicit, to gain more certainty about what he is getting. With respect to this latter class of cases, it seems to me the issue arises as to whether one type of institutional arrangement might generate different kinds of behavior in a systematic way which would result in consumers having a basis for preferring one type or another.

To illustrate, assume that there are two kinds of people in the world. There are those people whose utility functions are of the type in which money income is extraordinarily important, essentially the only thing they care about in addition to leisure. There is another group of people who care about leisure, money income, and "altruism." These groups are going to behave differently because they have different preference functions. Furthermore, assume that all of one of these types of people happen to gravitate into the for-profit sector of some industry and all of the other type of people just happen to gravitate into organizations that are organized as nonprofits. Wouldn't you expect the organization to be different? I would expect different behavior because the people making the crucial decisions have different kinds of utility functions. I don't know whether all of these assumptions hold up, but I don't find them ridiculous a priori. I don't find it absurd to assume that there may be some systematic sorting out in which people with different kinds of preferences gravitate toward different kinds of organizations. If that were true, then there would be differences in behavior depending on the organizational institutional structure.

Alchian.   You do not have to have different organizational forms to get firms to behave differently if their purposes are not the same. The interesting problem should be formulated in terms of the same purposes, but asking why one particular institutional arrangement or organizational form gets different results.

Weisbrod.   If people have the same preferences, then in this model there would not be any difference in behavior.

Alchian.   I agree that if the costs of using markets are high, for certain resources, you may not rent them. You would rather buy them, because an owner will not rent them to you. The same logic can be used to explain why there are certain forms of business organizations. I don't have to rely on differences in preferences to explain that. That is why I hesitate to use the difference in preference assumption without denying that they exist. There is a methodological problem in your approach. As soon as you introduce differences in preferences *anything* can be explained and that bothers me. Until you tell me something more about how you identify, in advance, which people have these preferences and then say, "hence I can tell you all redheads have this preference, and that they are going to be part of this kind of organization," I can't test your proposition.

Thompson.   Weisbrod's theory is essentially the same as mine and I don't think that too many people here have really disagreed with him. I think there are a few that have questioned it and I think it reflects a lack of willingness to seriously consider the hypothesis. The point is simply that, in a nonprofit organization, it is illegal to take the money home and you have some legal basis for suing someone that does not perform by giving away your contribution. In a profit organization the manager agrees to distribute donations but you do not have any legal assurance that he will do it. On the other hand, a nonprofit organization does provide some legal basis for your expectation.

Meckling.   There is absolutely no reason why a private organization, a private proprietary organization, cannot write contracts which say that for every $10.00 you give me, I will guarantee you that I will give away $9.50; and that would be legally enforceable.

Thompson.   That is a nonprofit organization and that is what we are talking about.

Meckling. No, I am describing a proprietary organization.

Thompson. But, we are talking about the manager's salary being a fixed number, a competitive salary for his kind of services, and then he has to give away the rest. A customer has legal assurance in that case, that even if this manager is not too benevolent, more of his money is going to go to a charity than otherwise. I don't think it's a very tricky point.

Whinston. Suppose for the sake of doing positive economics, we looked at an industry where we had firms operating with different ownership structures simultaneously. For example, many of us are familiar with Rand Corporation, which is a nonproprietary organization. For some reason, the Air Force felt that it would be more effective to conduct research through Rand, so it took what funds it would use in a governmental agency and set up a nonproprietary organization. Rand had a spin-off called SDC (System Development Corporation), which started out as a nonproprietary firm and at some point in its life decided it would be better off as a proprietary organization. It is now trying to go public. There must have been some soul searching and thinking about the relative desirability of organizational structures. On the other hand, we have a company, in the same line of business, which was started by university people and they, for whatever reason, felt that they should choose a proprietary form of organization. All of these companies compete with each other. They all, as far as I can tell, are interested in developing new markets, they hustle contracts, they recruit staff, and pay probably comfortable salaries. I would ask what is going on here? Why do we have competitive organizations with different organizational structures? Can we really discern any differences in efficiency of operation, so-called monitoring advantages that have been derived? Maybe these were accidents, random events.

Thomas Borcherding (Simon Fraser University). We have been spending a lot of time comparing the private firm with the so-called nonproprietary firm in the private sector. With the exception of Thompson, I'm not convinced that we have given sufficient time to comparing the nonproprietary firm that is in the private sector with that same type of activity when it is done by government. I recently had occasion to examine some interesting data relevant to such a comparison. The figures were like this. For every dollar of charity that is delivered to worthy people by a church group, it takes about 13 cents worth of resources. Next, the same activity conducted by groups such as the Community Chest involved a figure quite a bit higher. Finally, there is the government figure. For something like the war on poverty, it may take as much as eighty cents to give a dollar to some poor person. If these comparisons are true, that represents a great difference in marginal costs. Why any charity is done through the public sector is a mystery, unless choice of that sector has nothing to do with the articulation of this demand.

Senator Moynihan said that the chief beneficiaries of the war on poverty were the poverty workers. During the period when inflation went up by something like 40 percent, their incomes went up by about 250 percent. I wonder if that is not a relevant point to consider. We have a number of people who are articulating their demands for charity in the nonprofit sector, not all of which are citizens wishing to do good, but people who in fact want to have good done for them.

Meckling. Can I just add that a lot of those people that Borcherding is talking about now are not necessarily government employees. That is, if you start looking at the private charitable organizations that we have been talking about, many of them are the agencies through whom federal money is distributed. They are the ones who manage the local housing projects, and they are the ones who manage the educational projects, the training projects and so on. A lot of what Borcherding is talking about is, in fact, done by what are supposedly charitable, voluntary organizations.

SELECTED REFERENCES

1. Ackerman, Bruce A., Ackerman, Susan R., Sawyer, James W., Jr., and Henderson, Dale W. (1974) *The Uncertain Search for Environmental Quality*, New York, Free Press.
2. Alchian, Armen A. (1961) "Some Economics of Property," Rand Corporation Working Paper P-2316, Santa Monica, Calif.
3. ———. (Nov. 1965) "The Basis for Some Recent Advances in the Theory of Management of the Firm," *Journal of Industrial Economics*, Vol. 14:30–41.
4. ———. (Dec. 1965) "Some Economics of Property Rights," *Il Politico*, Vol. 30:816–829.
5. ———. (1967) "Cost Effectiveness of Cost Effectiveness," pp. 74–86 in *Defense Management*, Englewood Cliffs, N.J., Prentice-Hall.
6. ———. (June 1967) "How Should Prices Be Set," *Il Politico*, Vol. 32:369–382.
7. ———. (1969) "Corporate Management and Property Rights," in *Economic Policy and the Regulation of Corporate Securities*, Washington, D.C., American Enterprise Institute.
8. ———, and Allen, William R. (1969) *Exchange and Production: Theory in Use*, Belmont, Calif., Wadsworth.
9. ———, and Demsetz, Harold. (Dec. 1972) "Production, Information Costs, and Economic Organization," *American Economic Review*, Vol. 62:777–795.
10. ———, and Kessel, Reuben A. (1962) "Competition, Monopoly, and the Pursuit of Money," in *Aspects of Labor Economics*, National Bureau of Economic Research, Special Conference Series, Vol. 14, Princeton, N.J.
11. *Americans Volunteer*. (April 1969) Manpower Administration Research Monograph No. 10, Washington, D.C., Government Printing Office.
12. Arrow, Kenneth. (1969) "The Organization of Economic Activity," in *The Analysis and Evaluation of Public Expenditures*, Vol. I, Washington, D.C., Government Printing Office.
13. ———. (1971) "The Political and Economic Evaluation of Social Effects and Externalities," in *Frontiers of Quantitative Economics*, Amsterdam, North-Holland.
14. Ashenfelter, Orley. (1973) "Discrimination and Trade Unions," pp. 88–112 in *Discrimination in Labor Markets*, Princeton, N.J., Princeton University Press.
15. ———, and Johnson, George. (March 1969) "Bargaining Theory, Trade Unions, and Industrial Strike Activity," *American Economic Review*, Vol. 59:35–49.
16. Ashford, Nicholas A. (1976) *Crisis in the Workplace: Occupational Disease and Injury*, Cambridge, Mass., M.I.T. Outing Club, Inc.

257

17. Atherton, Wallace. (1973) *A Theory of Union Bargaining Goals*, Princeton, N.J., Princeton University Press.

18. Averch, Harvey, and Johnson, Leland L. (Dec. 1962) "Behavior of the Firm under Regulatory Constraint," *American Economic Review*, Vol. 52:1052–1069.

19. Bailey, E. (1973) *Economic Theory of Regulatory Constraint*, Lexington, Mass., Lexington Books.

20. Bays, C. (1976) "Cost and Efficiency of For-Profit and Nonprofit Hospitals," unpublished paper presented at the American Economic Association meetings.

21. Becker, Gary S. (1957) *The Economics of Discrimination*, Chicago, University of Chicago Press.

22. _____. (1959) "Union Restrictions on Entry," pp. 209–244 in *The Public Stake in Union Power*, Charlottesville, Va., University Press of Virginia.

23. _____. (Feb. 1962) "Irrational Behavior and Economic Theory," *Journal of Political Economy*, Vol. 70:1–13.

24. _____. (Sept. 1965) "A Theory of the Allocation of Time," *Economic Journal*, Vol. 75:493–517.

25. Berkowitz, Monroe. (July 1954) "The Economics of Trade Union Organization and Administration," *Industrial Labor Relations Review*, Vol. 7:575–592.

26. Blair, R. D., Ginsburg, P. B., and Vogel, R. J. (June 1975) "Blue Cross—Blue Shield Administrative Costs: A Study of Nonprofit Health Insurers," *Economic Inquiry*, Vol. 13:237–251.

27. _____, Jackson, Jerry R., and Vogel, Ronald J. (May 1975) "Economies of Scale in the Administration of Health Insurance," *Review of Economics and Statistics*, Vol. 57:185–189.

28. Blaug, Mark. (Sept. 1976) "The Empirical Status of Human Capital Theory: A Slightly Jaundiced Survey," *Journal of Economic Literature*, Vol. 14:827–855.

29. Buchanan, James M. (1968) *The Demand and Supply of Public Goods*, Chicago, University of Chicago Press.

30. _____. (1975) "The Samaritan's Dilemma," in *Altruism, Morality, and Economic Theory*, New York, Russell Sage Foundation.

31. _____, and Tullock, Gordon. (1962) *The Calculus of Consent*, Ann Arbor, University of Michigan Press.

32. Carlsson, R., Robinson, J., and Ryan, J. (March 1971) "An Optimization Model for a 'Nonprofit' Agency," *Western Economic Journal*, Vol. 9:78–86.

33. Carter, Luther J. (Oct. 1974) "Cancer and the Environment (I): A Creaky System Grinds On," *Science*, Vol. 186:239–242.

34. Cartter, Alan. (1959) *Theory of Wages and Employment*, Homewood, Ill., Greenwood Press.

35. Charnovitz, D. (1972) "The Economics of Etiquette and Customs: The Theory of Property Rights as Applied to Rules of Behavior," M.A. thesis, University of Virginia, Charlottesville.

36. *Chemical Week*. (Nov. 6, 1974) "Uncertain Future for Saccharin Spurs Synthetic Sweetener Research," Vol. 115, No. 19.

37. _____. (Dec. 10, 1975), Vol. 117.

38. *Chemicals and Health*. (1973) Report to the Panel on Chemicals and Health of the President's Science Advisory Committee, Washington, D.C.

39. Clarke, E. H. (Fall 1971) "Multipart Pricing of Public Goods," *Public Choice*, Vol. 11:17–33.

40. _____. (1972) "Multipart Pricing of Public Goods: An Example," in S. Mushkin, ed., *Public Prices for Public Products*, Washington, D.C., Urban Institute.

41. Clarkson, Kenneth W. (1971) *Property Rights, Institutional Constraints, and Individual Behavior: An Application to Short Term General Hospitals.* Ph.D. dissertation, UCLA.
42. _____. (Oct. 1972) "Some Implications of Property Rights in Hospital Management," *Journal of Law and Economics,* Vol. 15:363–384.
43. _____. (Fall 1974) "The Right Way, the Wrong Way and the Government Way," *Res Publica,* Vol. 2:14–19.
44. _____. (1976) "Economics of Art Museums," unpublished paper presented at the Western Economic Association meetings.
45. _____. (April/May 1977) "Organizational Constraints and Models of Managerial Behavior," paper presented at the Liberty Fund Seminar on The Economics of Nonproprietary Organizations, Miami, Fla.
46. Coase, Ronald H. (Nov. 1937) "The Nature of the Firm," *Economica,* Vol. 4:386–405.
47. _____. (Oct. 1960) "The Problem of Social Cost," *Journal of Law and Economics,* Vol. 3:1–44.
48. Cornell, Nina W., Noll, Roger G., and Weingast, Barry. (1976) "Safety Regulation," pp. 479–483 in *Setting National Priorities: The Next Ten Years,* Washington, D.C., Brookings Institution.
49. Daly, G., and Giertz, J. F. (Fall 1972) "Benevolence, Malevolence, and Economic Theory," *Public Choice,* Vol. 13:1–20.
50. Davies, David G. (April 1971) "The Efficiency of Public versus Private Firms: The Case of Australia's Two Airlines," *Journal of Law and Economics,* Vol. 14:149–165.
51. _____. (April 1977) "Property Rights and Economic Efficiency: The Australian Airlines Revisited," *Journal of Law and Economics,* Vol. 20:223–226.
52. Davis, John C. (Jan. 1976) "Pesticides: The Accent Is on Delivery," *Chemical Engineering,* Vol. 83:57–59.
53. De Alessi, Louis. (March 1969) "Some Implications of Property Rights for Government Investment Choices," *American Economic Review,* Vol. 59: 16–23.
54. _____. (May/June 1974) "Managerial Tenure under Private and Government Ownership in the Electric Power Industry," *Journal of Political Economy,* Vol. 82:645–653.
55. _____. (Fall 1974) "An Economic Analysis of Government Ownership and Regulation: Theory and Evidence from the Electric Power Industry," *Public Choice,* Vol. 19:1–42.
56. De Graaff, J. (1967) *Theoretical Welfare Economics,* Cambridge, Cambridge University Press.
57. Degnan, James P. (Sept. 1976) "Masters of Babble," *Harper's,* Vol. 253:37–39.
57a. Demsetz, H. (1977) "The Growth of Bureaucracy," unpublished manuscript, UCLA.
58. De Vany, Arthur S. (1970) *Time in the Budget of the Consumer: The Theory of Consumer Demand and Labor Supply under a Time Constraint,* Ph.D. dissertation, UCLA.
59. Downs, Anthony. (1957) *An Economic Theory of Democracy,* New York, Harper and Row.
60. _____. (1967) "Communications in Bureaus," pp. 112–131 in *Inside Bureaucracy,* Boston, Little, Brown.
61. Drew, David E. (1975) *Science Development: An Evaluation Study,* A Technical Report to the National Board on Graduate Education, Washington, D.C.
62. Dunlop, John. (1950) *Wage Determination under Trade Unionism,* New York, Agustus M. Kelley.
63. Ember, Lois. (Dec. 1975) "The Specter of Cancer," *Environmental Science and Technology,* Vol. 9:1116–1121.
64. Feinberg, Robert. (July 1975) "Profit Maximization vs. Utility Maximization," *Southern Economic Journal,* Vol. 42:130–132.

65. Fellner, William. (1949) *Competition among the Few*, New York, Agustus M. Kelley.

66. Frech, Harry E., III. (1974) *The Regulation of Health Insurance*, Ph.D. dissertation, UCLA.

67. _____. (Feb. 1976) "The Property Rights Theory of the Firm: Empirical Results from a Natural Experiment," *Journal of Political Economy*, Vol. 84:143–152.

68. _____. (1977) "The Property Rights Theory of the Firm and Competitive Markets for Top Decision-makers," unpublished manuscript, Harvard University.

69. _____, and Ginsburg, Paul B. (March 1978) "Competition among Health Insurers," pp. 210–237 in *Competition in the Health Care Sector: Past, Present and Future*, Warren Greenberg, ed., Washington, D.C., Federal Trade Commission.

70. Furubotn, Eirik, and Pejovich, Svetozar. (Dec. 1972) "Property Rights and Economic Theory: A Survey of Recent Literature," *Journal of Economic Literature*, Vol. 10:1137–1162.

71. *Gale's Encyclopedia of Associations*. (1975) 9th ed. Detroit, Mich., Gale Research Company.

72. Hanke, Steve H., and Walker, Richard A. (Oct. 1975) "Benefit-Cost Analysis Reconsidered: An Evaluation of the Mid-State Project," *Water Resources Research*, Vol. 10:898–908.

73. Hayek, F. A., ed. (1935) *Collectivist Economic Planning*, London: Routledge Kegan Paul.

74. Heilbroner, Robert L. (1975) *An Inquiry into the Human Prospect*, New York, Norton.

75. Hetherington, J. A. C. (1969) "Fact v. Fiction: Who Owns Mutual Insurance Companies," *Wisconsin Law Review*, Vol. 196:1068–1103.

76. Hill, Herbert. (1973) "Discrimination and Trade Unions: Comment," pp. 113–123 in *Discrimination in Labor Markets*, Princeton, N.J., Princeton University Press.

77. Hitch, Charles J., and McKean, Roland N. (1960) *Economics of Defense in the Nuclear Age*, Cambridge, Mass., Atheneum.

78. Hochman, Harold, and Rodgers, James D. (Sept. 1969) "Pareto Optimal Redistribution," *American Economic Review*, Vol. 59:542–557.

79. Houston, David B., and Simon, Richard M. (Nov. 1970) "Economies of Scale in Financial Institutions: A Study in Life Insurance," *Econometrica*, Vol. 38:856–864.

80. Ireland, T. R., and Johnson, D. B. (1970) *The Economics of Charity*, Center for the Study of Public Choice, Levittown, N.Y., Transatlantic Charity Corp.

81. James, Estelle. (1976) "A Contribution to the Theory of the Nonprofit Organization," SUNY at Stony Brook.

82. _____. (1976) "The University Department as a Nonprofit Collective," SUNY at Stony Brook.

83. Jensen, Michael C., and Meckling, William H. (Oct. 1976) "Theory of the Firm: Managerial Behavior, Agency Costs and Ownership Structure," *Journal of Financial Economics*, Vol. 3:306–360.

84. Joskow, Paul L. (Autumn 1973) "Cartels, Competition and Regulation in the Property-Liability Insurance Industry," *Bell Journal of Economics and Management Science*, Vol. 4:375–428.

85. Kaplan, A. D. H., Dirlan, J. B., and Lanzilotti, R. F. (1958) *Pricing in Big Business: A Case Approach*, Washington, D.C., Brookings Institution.

86. Katz, David A. (June 1973) "Faculty Salaries, Promotions, and Productivity at a Large University," *American Economic Review*, Vol. 63:469–477.

87. Kendall, Willmoore. (July 1949) "The Function of Intelligence," *World Politics*, Vol. 1:542–552.

88. Kershaw, J., and McKean, R. (1962) *Teacher Shortages and Salary Schedules*, New York: McGraw-Hill Book Co.

89. Kilby, P. (May 1962) "Organization and Productivity in Backward Economies," *Quarterly Journal of Economics*, Vol. 76:303–310.

90. Kimball, S. L. (1960) *Insurance and Public Policy: A Study in the Legal Implication of Social and Economic Public Policy, Based on Wisconsin Records 1835–1959*, Madison, Wis.

91. Kline, Nathan S. (1974) *From Sad to Glad*. New York, G. P. Putnam.

92. Kwitny, Jonathan. (Nov. 1976) "Ford Foundation Mulls Crime Fight . . . ," *Wall Street Journal*.

93. Lahne, Herbert. (Sept. 1951) "The Union Work Permit," *Political Science Quarterly*, pp. 350–380.

94. Larrowe, C. P. (1955) *Shape-Up and Hiring Hall*, Berkeley: Univ. of California Press.

95. Lee, M. L. (July 1971) "A Conspicuous Production Theory of Hospital Behavior," *Southern Economic Journal*, Vol. 38:48–59.

96. Leibenstein, H. (June 1966) "Allocative Efficiency v. X-Efficiency," *American Economic Review*, Vol. 56:392–415.

97. ———. (Autumn 1975) "Aspects of the X-Efficiency Theory of the Firm," *Bell Journal of Economics*, Vol. 6:580–606.

98. Lester, Richard A. (April 1967) "Benefits as a Preferred Form of Compensation," *Southern Economic Journal*, Vol. 33:488–495.

99. Levy, Ferdinand K. (Spring 1968) "Economic Analysis of the Nonprofit Institution: The Case of the Private University," *Public Choice*, Vol. 4:3–17.

100. Lewis, H. G. (1963) *Unionism and Relative Wages in the United States: An Empirical Inquiry*, Chicago, University of Chicago Press.

101. Lindsay, Cotton M. (1972) "Impurities in the Theory of Public Expenditure," Discussion Paper No. 20, rev., UCLA.

102. ———. (Oct. 1976) "A Theory of Government Enterprise," *Journal of Political Economy*, Vol. 84:1061–1078.

103. Macaulay, S. (Feb. 1963) "Noncontractual Relations in Business: A Preliminary Study," *American Sociological Review*, Vol. 28:55–67.

104. MacDonald, Dwight. (1956) *The Ford Foundation*, New York, Macmillan.

105. Machlup, F. (March 1967) "Theories of the Firm: Marginalist, Behavioral, Managerial," *American Economic Review*, Vol. 57:1–33.

106. Manne, Henry G. (April 1965) "Mergers and the Market for Corporate Control," *Journal of Political Economy*, Vol. 73:110–120.

107. ———. (1975) "The Political Economy of Modern Universities," pp. 614–630 in *The Economics of Legal Relationships*, St. Paul, Minn., West Pub.

108. Martin, Donald L. (Oct. 1972) "Job Property Rights and Job Defections," *Journal of Law and Economics*, Vol. 15:385–410.

109. ———. (Winter 1973) "Some Economics of Job Rights in the Longshore Industry," *Journal of Economics and Business*, Vol. 25:83–100.

110. ———. (1976) "An Economic Theory of the Trade Union: A New Approach," unpublished manuscript.

111. ———. (April 1977) "The Economics of Employment Termination Rights," *Journal of Law and Economics*, Vol. 20:187–204.

112. McEachern, William A. (1975) *Managerial Control and Performance*, Lexington, Mass., Lexington Books.

113. McKean, Roland. (May 1964) "Divergences between Individual and Total Costs within Government," *American Economic Review*, Vol. 54:243–249.

114. ———. (Oct. 1972) "Property Rights in Government, and Devices to Increase Governmental Efficiency," *Southern Economic Journal*, Vol. 39:177–186.

115. ———. (June 1976) "The Regulation of Chemicals and the Production of Informa-

tion," Center for the Study of American Business, Working Paper No. 13, Washington University, St. Louis, Mo.

116. _____, and Minasian, J. (Dec. 1966) "On Achieving Pareto Optimality—Regardless of Cost!" *Western Economic Journal*, Vol. 5:14–23.

117. Minasian, J. (1967) "Land Utilization for Defense," pp. 232–245 in *Defense Management*, Englewood Cliffs, N.J., Prentice-Hall.

118. Mises, Ludwig von. (1944) *Bureaucracy*, New Haven, Conn., Yale University Press.

119. Mofsky, J. (1977) *Market Constraints on Corporate Behavior*, Law and Economics Center, University of Miami School of Law, Coral Gables, Fla.

120. Moore, J. (1974) "Aspects of Managerial Behavior in the Yugoslav Enterprise," unpublished paper, University of Virginia, Charlottesville.

121. Morgan, James N., Dye, Richard F., and Hybels, Judith. (1977) "Results from Two National Surveys of Philanthropic Activity," *Research Papers Sponsored by the Commission on Private Philanthropy and Public Needs*, Department of the Treasury, Washington, D.C., Vol. 1:157–323.

122. Musgrave, Richard A., and Musgrave, Peggy B. (1976) *Public Finance in Theory and Practice*, 2nd ed., New York, McGraw-Hill.

123. Needham, Douglas. (1968) *Economic Analysis and Industrial Structure*, New York, Holt, Rinehart & Winston.

124. Newhouse, Joseph. (March 1970) "Toward a Theory of Nonprofit Institutions: An Economic Model of a Hospital," *American Economic Review*, Vol. 60:64–73.

125. Nicols, Alfred. (May 1967) "Stock versus Mutual Savings and Loan Associations: Some Evidence of Differences in Behavior," *American Economic Review*, Vol. 57:337–347.

126. _____. (1972) *Management and Control in the Mutual Savings and Loan Association*, Lexington, Mass., Lexington Books.

127. Niskanen, William A. (1971) *Bureaucracy and Representative Government*, Chicago, Aldine.

128. O'Leary, Brian. (Oct. 1975) "R & D: The Thin Edge of the Wedge," *Bulletin of the Atomic Scientists*, Vol. 31:8–14.

129. Olson, Mancur. (1965) *The Logic of Collective Action*, Cambridge, Mass., Harvard University Press.

130. Pauly, Mark, and Redisch, Michael. (March 1973) "The Not-for-Profit Hospital as a Physicians' Cooperative," *American Economic Review*, Vol. 63:87–99.

131. Peltzman, Sam. (1974) *Regulation of Pharmaceutical Innovation: The 1962 Amendments*, monograph, American Enterprise Institute, Washington, D.C.

132. _____. (Aug. 1976) "Toward a More General Theory of Regulation," *Journal of Law and Economics*, Vol. 19:211–240.

133. Pencavel, John. (Jan. 1971) "The Demand for Union Services: An Exercise," *Industrial Labor Relations Review*, Vol. 24:180–190.

134. Pfeffer, Irving, and Klock, David R. (1974) *Perspectives on Insurance*, Englewood Cliffs, N.J., Prentice-Hall.

135. Piron, R. (May/June 1974) "Utility Maximization Sufficient for Competitive Survival: Comment," *Journal of Political Economy*, Vol. 82:654–656.

136. Powel, John. (1973) *A Theory of Union Behavior Applied to the Medical Profession*, Ph.D. dissertation, University of Washington.

137. Pryor, F. (1968) *Public Expenditures in Communist and Capitalist Nations*, New Haven, Conn., Yale University Press.

138. Reder, Melvin. (April 1960) "Job Scarcity and the Nature of Union Power," *Industrial Labor Relations Review*, Vol. 13:348–362.

139. Rice, Robert. (May 1966) "Skill, Earnings and the Growth of Wage Supplements, American Economic Review, Vol. 56:583–593.

140. Rosenberg, N. (Dec. 1960) "Some Institutional Aspects of the Wealth of Nations," *Journal of Political Economy*, Vol. 68:557–570.
141. Ross, Arthur. (1948) *Trade Union Wage Policy*, Berkeley, University of California Press.
142. Saint-Simon, duc de. (1901) *Memoirs of Louis XIV and the Regency*, Vol. 1, trans. Bayle St. John, Akron, Ohio, St. Dunstan Society.
143. Samprone, Joseph C., Jr. (1975) *State Rate Regulation of the Property-Liability Insurance Industry*, Ph.D. dissertation, University of California, Santa Barbara.
144. Samuelson, P. A. (1954) "The Pure Theory of Public Expenditure," *Review of Economics and Statistics*, Vol. 36:387–389.
145. Schelling, Thomas C. (1960) *The Strategy of Conflict*, Cambridge, Mass., Harvard University Press.
146. Schneider, Howard C. (1974) *An Economic Analysis of Selected Grant-in-Aid Programs*, Ph.D. dissertation, University of Virginia, Charlottesville.
147. Schwartz, R. A. (Nov.–Dec. 1970) "Personal Philanthropic Contributions," *Journal of Political Economy*, Vol. 78:1264–1291.
148. Scitovsky, Tibor. (1952) "A Note on Profit Maximization and Its Implications," in *Readings in Price Theory*, Cincinnati, South-western.
149. ———. (1976) *The Joyless Economy*, New York, Oxford University Press.
150. Shalit, S. (1971) *Barriers to Entry in the American Hospital Industry*, Ph.D. dissertation, University of Chicago.
151. Shapiro, David L. (March/April 1973) "Can Public Investment Have a Positive Rate of Return?" *Journal of Political Economy*, Vol. 81:401–413.
152. Shelton, John. (Dec. 1967) "Allocative Efficiency v. 'X-Efficiency': Comment," *American Economic Review*, Vol. 57:1252–1258.
153. Shibata, Hirofumi. (Jan.–Feb. 1971) "A Bargaining Model of the Pure Theory of Public Expenditure," *Journal of Political Economy*, Vol. 79:1–29.
154. Simon, H. (June 1964) "On the Concept of Organizational Goal," *Administrative Science Quarterly*, Vol. 9:1–22.
155. Simons, Henry. (1948) *Economic Policy for a Free Society*, Chicago, University of Chicago Press.
156. Smith, Adam. (1937) *An Inquiry into the Nature and Causes of the Wealth of Nations*, New York, Oxford University Press.
157. Smith, Robert S. (1976) *The Occupational Safety and Health Act*, Washington, D.C., American Enterprise Institute for Public Policy Research.
158. Solnick, L. M., and Staller, J. M. (June 1976) "The Effect of Unionism on Employer Fringe Benefit Expenditures," paper presented at the Labor Union Session of the Western Economic Association meetings, San Francisco.
159. Spiller, R. (March 1972) "Ownership and Performance: Stock and Mutual Life Insurance Companies," *Journal of Risk and Insurance*, Vol. 34:17–25.
160. Stigler, George J. (Oct. 1958) "The Economies of Scale," *Journal of Law and Economics*, Vol. 1:54–71.
161. ———. (1966) *The Theory of Price*, 3rd ed., New York, Macmillan.
162. Stockfisch, J. A. (Aug. 1976) "Incentives and Information Quality in Defense Management," Santa Monica, Rand Corp.
163. Strauch, Ralph E. (Aug. 1974) "A Critical Assessment of Quantitative Methodology as a Policy Analysis Tool," Working Paper P-5282, Rand Corporation.
164. Taft, Philip. (1954) *The Structure and Government of Labor Unions*, Cambridge, Mass., Harvard University Press.
165. Thompson, Earl A. (Spring 1968) "Do Freely Competitive Markets Misallocate Charity?" *Public Choice*, Vol. 4:67–74.
166. ———. (Feb. 1968) "The Perfectly Competitive Production of Collective Goods," *Review of Economics and Statistics*, Vol. 50:1–12.

167. _____. (July–Aug. 1974) "Taxation and National Defense," *Journal of Political Economy*, Vol. 82:755–782.
168. _____. (1977) "The Optimal Role of the Government in a Competitive Equilibrium with Transaction Costs," *American Revolution*, Tucson, Ariz.
169. Tideman, T. Nicolaus, and Tullock, Gordon. (Dec. 1976) "A New and Superior Process for Making Social Choices," *Journal of Political Economy*, Vol. 84:1145–1160.
170. Tullock, Gordon. (1965) *The Politics of Bureaucracy*. Washington, D.C., Public Affairs Press.
171. _____. (1966) "Information without Profit," in *Papers in Nonmarket Decision Making*, University of Virginia, Charlottesville.
172. _____. (1970) *Private Wants, Public Means*, New York, Basic Books.
173. Turner, James S. (1970) *The Chemical Feast*, New York, Viking.
174. U.S. Department of Health, Education and Welfare, Office of Research and Statistics. (1973) *Medicare: Health Insurance for the Aged, 1971, Section 2: Enrollment*, Washington, D.C., Government Printing Office.
175. Vogel, Ronald J., and Blair, Roger D. (1976) *Health Insurance Administrative Costs*, Washington, D.C.
176. Walker, Jack L. (Fall 1972) "Brother, Can You Paradigm?" *PS*, pp. 419–422.
177. Wardell, William M., and Lasagna, Louis. (1975) *Regulation and Drug Development*, Washington, D.C., American Enterprise Institute.
178. Weinberger, P. E. (1969) *Perspectives on Social Welfare*, New York, Macmillan.
179. Weinstein, Paul. (April 1966) "Racketeering and Labor: An Economic Analysis," *Industrial Labor Relations Review*, Vol. 19:402–413.
180. Weisbrod, Burton A. (1975) "Toward a Theory of Voluntary Nonprofit Sector in a Three Sector Economy," pp. 171–195 in *Altruism, Morality, and Economic Theory*, New York, Russell Sage Foundation.
181. _____. (1978) "Conceptual Perspective on the Public Interest: An Economic Analysis," in *Public Interest Law*, ed. Burton A. Weisbrod, Joel F. Handler, and Neil K. Komesar, Berkeley, University of California Press.
182. _____. (1978) "Problems of Enhancing the Public Interest: Toward a Model of Government Failures," in *Public Interest Law, op. cit.*
183. _____, Handler, J. F., and Komesar, Neil K. (1978) "The Public Interest Law Firm: A Behavioral Analysis," in *Public Interest Law, op. cit.*
184. _____, and Long, Stephen H. (1977) "The Size of the Voluntary Nonprofit Sector: Concepts and Measures," *Research Papers Sponsored by the Commission on Private Philanthropy and Public Needs*, Department of the Treasury, Washington, D.C., Vol. 1:339–364.
185. Whinston, A. (1964) "Price Guides in Decentralized Organizations," in *New Perspectives in Organization Research*, New York, John Wiley.
186. Wildavsky, Aaron. (Dec. 1966) "The Political Economy of Efficiency: Cost-Benefit Analysis, Systems Analysis, and Program Budgeting," *Public Administration Review*, Vol. 26:292–311.
187. Wilensky, Harold L. (1967) *Organizational Intelligence: Knowledge and Policy in Government and Industry*, New York, Basic Books.
188. Williamson, Oliver E. (1969) "Corporate Control and the Theory of the Firm," in *Economic Policy and the Regulation of Corporate Securities*, Washington, D.C., American Enterprise Institute.
189. _____. (1970) *Corporate Control and Business Behavior: An Inquiry into the Effects of Organizational Form on Enterprise Behavior*, Englewood Cliffs, N.J., Prentice-Hall.
190. Yamane, T. (1967) *Statistics: An Introductory Analysis*, New York, Harper and Row.

SUBJECT INDEX

265

Transaction costs (cont.)
  model of charity, 135–137, 174
  types, 196–197

Underpricing:
  as enforcement method, 31, 34–37, 42, 46
  optimality of, 46–47
  theories of, 28–30, 41, 45
  union membership, 93
Unions:
  bargaining rights, 77, 78, 92n.2, 111–112
  economic theory, 77ff, 113
  job rights, 79, 81–83
  nonproprietary defined, 81–85, 108, 112
  utility maximization, 79–81
  wage rates, 76, 77–79, 113–114
Universities:
  constraints in, 215
  decision making in, 56
  utility maximization in, 57
Utility maximization:
  achieving, 211–212
  charity, 136–137, 174–175, 184

differences, 9–10
information, 212–213
neoclassical theory, 7–9
predictive value, 180
pricing, 28, 83
producer behavior, 8, 24, 57
universities, 214–217
wealth maximization, 8, 58, 76
working environment, 79–83, 96–97,
  98nn 7–12, 109, 112
unions, 79–81

Wealth maximization:
  decision makers, 11–12, 45
  franchise, 12–20
  identifying, 46
  joint, 180
  vs. profit maximization, 114–117
  and underpricing, 31–32
  and uniform pricing, 32–34
  in proprietary firms, 6
  utility maximization, 7–8, 58, 76

Research in Law and Economics

A Research Annual

Series Editor: **Richard O. Zerbe, Jr., SMT Program, University of Washington.**

The contributions to be included in this series represent original research by scholars internationally known in their fields. A few articles generally based on outstanding dissertations by younger scholars will also be included. The contributions will include theoretical, empirical and legal studies considered to belong to the law-economics genre.

Volume 1. April 1979 Cloth Institutions: $ 27.50
ISBN 0-89232-028-1 285 pages Individuals: $ 14.00

CONTENTS: State Occupational Licensing Provisions and Quality of Service: The Real Estate Business, *Sidney L. Carroll and Robert J. Gaston, University of Tennessee, Knoxville.* Dynamic Elements of Regulation: The Case of Occupational Licensure, *William D. White, University of Illinois, Chicago Circle.* Airline Performance Under Regulation: Canada vs. the United States, *William A. Jordon, York University.* Airline Market Shares vs. Capacity Shares and the Possibility of Short-Run Loss Equilibria, *James C. Miller, III, American Enterprise Institute flr Public Policy Research.* The Political Rationality of Federal Transportation Policy, *Ann F. Friedlaender and Richard de Neufville, Massachusetts Institute of Technology.* A New Remedy for the Free Rider Problem? Flies in the Ointment, *Roger C. Kormendi, University of Chicago.* Toward a Theory of Government Advertising, *Kenneth W. Clarkson, University of Miami School of Law, and Robert Tollison, Virginia Polytechnic Institute and State University.* Protecting the Right to Be Served by Public Utilities, *Victor P. Goldberg, University of California, Davis.* The Role and Resolution of the Compensation Principle in Society: Part One - The Role, *Warren J. Samuels, Michigan State University, and Nicholas Mercuro, University of New Orleans.* The Dynamics of Traditional Rate Regulation, *Patrick C. Mann, Regional Research Institute, West Virginia University.* Price Discrimination and Peak-Load Pricing Subject to Rate of Return Constraint, *David L. McNichol, U.S. Treasury Department.* Index.

Volume 2. Spring 1980 Cloth Institutions: $ 27.50
ISBN 0-89232-131-8 Ca. 250 pages Individuals: $ 14.00

CONTENTS: Economic Analysis of Federal Election Campaign Regulation. *Burton A. Abrams and Russel F. Settle, University of Delaware.* The Quality of Legal Services: Peer Review, Insurance and Disciplinary Evidence, *Sidney L. Carrol and Robert J. Gaston, University of Tennessee.* Price Discrimination in the Municipal Electric Industry, *Daniel R. Hollas, University of Michigan and Thomas S. Friedland, University of Illinois.* The Resolution of the Compensation Problem in Society, *Warren J. Samuels and Nicholas Mercuro, Michigan State University.* Monopoly Profits and Social Losses, *Levis A. Kochin, University of Washington.* The Evaluation of Rules for Making Collective Decisions: A Reply to Kormendi, *T. Nicholas Tideman, Virginia Polytechnic Institute and State University.* Tort Liability for Negligent Inspection by Insurers, *Victor P. Goldberg, University of California - Davis.* The Economics of Property Rights: A Review of the Evidence, *Louis De Alessi, University of Miami.* The Problem of Social Cost in Retrospect, *Richard O. Zerbe, University of Washington.*

JAI PRESS INC., P.O. Box 1678, 165 West Putnam Avenue, Greenwich, Connecticut 06830

Telephone: 203-661-7602 Cable Address: JAIPUBL

OTHER SERIES OF INTEREST FROM JAI PRESS INC.

Consulting Editor for Economics: Paul Uselding, University of Illinois

ADVANCES IN ACCOUNTING
Series Editor: George H. Sorter, New York University

ADVANCES IN APPLIED MICRO-ECONOMICS
Series Editor: V. Kerry Smith, Resources for the Future, Washington, D.C.

**ADVANCES IN DOMESTIC AND INTERNATIONAL AGRIBUSINESS
MANAGEMENT**
Series Editor: Ray A. Goldberg, Graduate School of Business Administration,
   Harvard University

ADVANCES IN ECONOMETRICS
Series Editors: R.L. Basmann, Texas A & M University, and George F. Rhodes, Jr.,
   Colorado State University

ADVANCES IN THE ECONOMICS OF ENERGY AND RESOURCES
Series Editor: John R. Moroney, Tulane University

APPLICATIONS OF MANAGEMENT SCIENCE
Series Editor: Randall L. Schultz, Krannert Graduate School of Management,
   Purdue University

RESEARCH IN CORPORATE SOCIAL   RFORMANCE AND POLICY
Series Editor: Lee E. Preston, School of Management and Center for Policy
   Studies, State University of New York - Buffalo

RESEARCH IN ECONOMIC ANTHROPOLOGY
Series Editor: George Dalton, Northwestern University

RESEARCH IN ECONOMIC HISTORY
Series Editor: Paul Uselding, University of Illinois

RESEARCH IN EXPERIMENTAL ECONOMICS
Series Editor: Vernon L. Smith, College of Business and Public Administration,
   University of Arizona

RESEARCH IN FINANCE
Series Editor: Haim Levy, School of Business, The Hebrew University

RESEARCH IN HEALTH ECONOMICS
Series Editor: Richard M. Scheffler, George Washington University

RESEARCH IN HUMAN CAPITAL AND DEVELOPMENT
Series Editor: Ismail Sirageldin, The Johns Hopkins University

RESEARCH IN INTERNATIONAL BUSINESS AND FINANCE
Series Editor: Robert G. Hawkins, Graduate School of Business Administration,
   New York University

RESEARCH IN LABOR ECONOMICS
Series Editor: Ronald G. Ehrenberg, School of Industrial and Labor Relations,
   Cornell University

RESEARCH IN LAW AND ECONOMICS
Series Editor: Richard O. Zerbe, Jr., SMT Program, University of Washington

RESEARCH IN MARKETING
Series Editor: Jagdish N. Sheth, University of Illinois

RESEARCH IN ORGANIZATIONAL BEHAVIOR
Series Editors: Barry M. Staw, Graduate School of Management, Northwestern University, and L.L. Cummings, Graduate School of Business, University of Wisconsin

RESEARCH IN PHILOSOPHY AND TECHNOLOGY
Series Editor: Paul T. Durbin, Center for Science and Culture, University of Delaware

RESEARCH IN POLITICAL ECONOMY
Series Editor: Paul Zarembka, State University of New York - Buffalo

RESEARCH IN POPULATION ECONOMICS
Series Editors: Julian L. Simon, University of Illinois, and Julie DaVanzo, The Rand Corporation

RESEARCH IN PUBLIC POLICY AND MANAGEMENT
Series Editor: John P. Crecine, College of Humanities and Social Sciences, Carnegie-Mellon University

RESEARCH IN URBAN ECONOMICS
Series Editor: J. Vernon Henderson, Brown University

ALL VOLUMES IN THESE ANNUAL SERIES ARE AVAILABLE AT
INSTITUTIONAL AND INDIVIDUAL RATES.
PLEASE ASK FOR DETAILED BROCHURE ON EACH SERIES

 **JAI PRESS INC.**
P.O. Box 1678
165 West Putnam Avenue
Greenwich, Connecticut 06830
(203) 661-7602   Cable Address: JAIPUBL

Research in Marketing

A Research Annual

Series Editor: **Jagdish N. Sheth, Department of Business Administration, University of Illinois.**

Volume 1. Published 1978 Cloth   333 pages   Institutions: $ 28.50
ISBN 0-89232-041-9   Individuals: $ 14.50

CONTENTS: **Research in Productivity Measurement for Marketing Decisions,** Louis P. Bucklin, University of California - Berkeley. **Simulation of Risk Attitudes in Joint Decision Making by Marketing Firms in Competitive Markets,** Ralph L. Day, Indiana University and Jehoshua Eliashberg, University of Missouri. **Interpretative Versus Descriptive Research,** Ernest Dichter, Ernest Dichter Associates International, Ltd. **The Household as a Production Unit,** Michael Etgar, State University of New York - Buffalo. **Some New Types of Fractional Factorial Designs for Marketing Experiements,** Paul E. Green, University of Pennsylvania, J. Douglas Carroll, Bell Laboratories and Frank J. Carmone, Drexel University. **Optimizing Research Budgets: A Theoretical Approach,** Flemming Hansen, A.I.M., Copenhagen. **Choosing the Best Advertising Appropriation When Appropriations Interact Over Time,** Haim Levy, The Hebrew University and Julian L. Simon, University of Illinois, **Advertising and Socialization,** John G. Myers, University of California - Berkeley. **Multi-Product Growth Models,** Robert A. Peterson, University of Texas - Austin and Vijay Mahajan, Ohio State University. **Advocacy Advertising: Corporate External Communications and Public Policy,** S. Prakash Sethi, University of Texas - Dallas. **An Empirical-Simulation Approach to Competition,** Randall L. Schultz, Purdue University and Joe A. Dodson, Jr., Northwestern University. **Field Theory Applied to Consumer Behavior,** Arch G. Woodside, University of South Carolina and William O. Bearden, University of Alabama.

Volume 2. Published 1979 Cloth   440 pages   Institutions: $ 32.50
ISBN 0-89232-059-1   Individuals: $ 16.50

CONTENTS: **Canadian and American National Character as a Basis for Market Segmentation,** Stephen J. Arnould, Queen's University and James G. Barnes, Memorial University of Newfoundland. **The Products' Needs Matrix as a Methodology for Promoting Anti-Consuming,** Michael A. Blech, San Diego State University and Robert Perloff, University of Pittsburgh. **The Cereal Antitrust Case: An Analysis of Selected Issues,** Paul N. Bloom, University of Maryland. **Gift Giving Behavior,** Russell W. Belk, University of Illinois. **A Process Model of Interorganizational Relations in Marketing Channels,** Ernest R. Cadotte, University of Tennessee and Louis W. Stern, Northwestern University. **The Product Audit System as a Tool of Marketing Planning,** C. Merle Crawford, University of Michigan. **Rudiments of Numeracy,** A.S.C. Ehrenberg, London Business School. **Evaluating the Competitive Environment in Retailing Using Multilicative Competitive Interactive Model,** Arum K. Jain, State University of New York - Buffalo and Vijaya Mahajan, Ohio State University. **The Parametric Marginal Desirability Model,** John F. McElwee, Jr., General Dynamics and Leonard J. Parsons, Georgia Insititute of Technology. **Carry-Over Effects in Advertising Communication,** Alan Sawyer, Ohio State University and Scott Ward, Harvard University and Marketing Science Institute. **Redlining in Mortgage Markets: Research Perspectives in Marketing and Public Policy,** Thaddeus H. Spratlen, University of Washington. **Psychological Geography,** William D. Wells, Needham, Harper & Steers Advertising, Inc. and Fred D. Reynolds, University of Georgia.

Please see reverse side for Volume 3.

Research in Marketing

A Research Annual

Volume 3.	December 1979	Cloth	Institutions: $ 32.50
ISBN 0-89232-060-5		425 pages	Individuals: $ 16.50

INSTITUTIONAL STANDING ORDERS *will be granted a 10% discount and be filled automatically upon publication. Please indicate initial volume of standing order*
INDIVIDUAL ORDERS *must be prepaid by personal check or credit card. Please include $1.50 per volume for postage and handling.*
Please encourage your library to subscribe to this series.

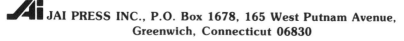 **JAI PRESS INC., P.O. Box 1678, 165 West Putnam Avenue, Greenwich, Connecticut 06830**

Telephone: 203-661-7602   Cable Address: JAIPUBL

JOURNAL of
ECONOMIC ISSUES

Published by the Association for
Evolutionary Economics and
Michigan State University

Recent contributions:

Melville J. Ulmer, "Old and New Fashions in Employment and Inflation Theory"; Gunnar Myrdal, "Institutional Economics"; Jon D. Wisman, "Toward a Humanist Reconstruction of Economic Science"; Howard J. Sherman, " 'Technology vis-à-vis Institutions': A Marxist Commentary"; E. K. Hunt, "The Importance of Thorstein Veblen for Contemporary Marxism"; Ivan C. Johnson, "A Revised Perspective of Keynes's *General Theory*"; Robert Solo, "The Neo-Marxist Theory of the State"; Robert E. Lane, "Markets and the Satisfaction of Human Wants"; Alexander Field, "On the Explanation of Rules Using Rational Choice Models"; Emile Grunberg, " 'Complexity' and 'Open Systems' in Economic Discourse"; and Romney Robinson, "The Theory of Imperfect Markets Reconsidered."

Annual membership dues are: $6.00 per year for three years, student;
$15.00, individual; and $20.00, library. Add $2.50 per year for sub-
scriptions outside North America. Inquiries to: AFEE/JEI Fiscal Office,
Department of Economics, University of Nebraska, Lincoln, NE 68588.